TO SAVE A CHILD

THINGS YOU CAN DO TO PROTECT, NURTURE & TEACH OUR CHILDREN

AUDREY E. TALKINGTON
BARBARA ALBERS HILL

AVERY PUBLISHING GROUP INC.
Garden City Park, New York

Front cover photo supply house: The Image Bank
Front cover photographers: Nancy Brown and Elyse Lewin
Cover designers: Rudy Shur, Janine Eisner-Wall, and Ann Vestal
Original text art: Shea MacKenzie
In-house editor: Joanne Abrams
Typesetter: Bonnie Freid
Printer: Paragon Press, Honesdale, PA

ATTENTION: SCHOOLS AND ORGANIZATIONS

Avery books are available at special quantity discounts for bulk
purchases when used for educational purposes or as fundraisers.
Special books or book excerpts can also be created
to fit specific needs. For information please write to
Marketing Director, AVERY PUBLISHING GROUP,
120 Old Broadway, Garden City Park, NY 11040.

Library of Congress Cataloging-in-Publication Data

Talkington, Audrey E.
    To save a child : things you can do to protect, nurture & teach
our children / Audrey E. Talkington, Barbara Albers Hill.
        p. cm.
    Includes bibliographical references and index.
    ISBN 0-89529-533-4
    1. Safety education. 2. Children's accidents—Prevention.
3. Child rearing. I. Hill, Barbara Albers. II. Title.
HQ770.7.T35 1993
649'.1dc20   93-10473
                                                       CIP

Printed in the United States of America

10 9 8 7 6 5 4 3 2 1

CONTENTS

To the children,
so that they may reach their full potential.
To their parents,
to help them pave the way
with a legacy of love and caring.
And to my sons, Benjamin and
Michael, with love.

Acknowledgments

Writing this book was a labor of love and a community effort. Since 1988, I have come into contact with literally thousands of people from families, cities, towns, and organizations all across North America who touched this work through their commitment to children and family issues. Many people foster-parented this book. In fact, it took each one of us, each with a special gift, to bring this work forward. I thank all of you for your dedication and caring.

Susan Pye Brokaw was the first person to mention that such a book could help so many people. And Janet Oliver was instrumental in creating the original self-published version, and was the primary visionary of the Empathy Wheel concept.

Special thanks to Rudy Shur at Avery Publishing Group for saying "Yes" to this project, designing the powerful cover, and guiding it into the form you now hold in your hands. And thanks to Joanne Abrams who gave her own expertise during the many edits.

Special thanks also to Barbara Albers Hill who brought my extensive research to life through her warm writing style. And thanks to her husband, Kevin, and their three children for sharing Barbara with me during this project.

Mark Riley from the Child Welfare League of America gave generously of his energy, contacts, encouragement, and enthusiasm during the last four and a half years. And special thanks to David Liederman for lending his thoughts in the foreword.

Many thanks to Mary Frances Tucker, Claire Whitman, and Janice McCann for caring for my children so I could meet my deadlines.

Special thanks go to my research assistants Kris Dittman, Chris McCullough, and Claire Whitman, who pored over volumes of information and never tired of cross-checking countless details for accuracy. And thanks to Judith Jakab who tracked down the Canadian resources.

Thanks also to Ed and Mary Averett and to John Quinnhurst for lending me an office space to work in during the crucial times.

For emotional support during the many hours of this project, I honor my friends Mary Frances Tucker, Katia and Eugene Thompson, Pamela and Johan Lindstrom, Janet Oliver, Carolyn Morrison, Susan Cairy, Joyce Horton, Rebecca Powers, Jane Fritz, Kathleen Leskis, and Teresa Evans, who provided many positive comments and much encouragement during the most difficult and frustrating phases of this project. And to my very good friend, kindred spirit, and business partner Bonita Zahara, I offer many thanks.

And finally, special gratitude goes to my children, Benjamin and Michael, who lived and breathed this book with me from start to finish.

For the possibilities that this book holds, I am grateful to each and every one of you.

—A.T.

FOREWORD

Children and families today face seemingly endless obstacles in the pursuit of healthy, stable, gratifying lives. There is the tremendous problem of abuse of alcohol and illegal drugs—a blight on youngsters and adults alike. Our educational system too often fails children. Families are separated due to lack of housing and because of unemployment or underemployment.

Far too many disagreements are settled by violent methods, with the result that more teenagers die from guns than from anything else except automobile accidents. Teenage pregnancy results in children raising children. Reports of child abuse and neglect have reached an all-time high. Day care is costly and often inaccessible, and adequate medical care is beyond the reach of most poor families.

Given these appalling realities, it might seem preposterous to visualize a hopeful future for children and families. But the truth is, I am optimistic and encouraged because people such as Audrey Talkington and Barbara Hill refuse to give up on America's future.

Starting with the thought that each person can make a difference, Audrey and Barbara provide real solutions to the real problems that confront children, teenagers, and their families in cities and towns all across our country. You will come away from this book knowing that each one of us can make a difference in the life of a child, and that together, we can save the children. What a wonderful thought to hold on to!

As we focus on the ways we can best achieve our goal of making life better for children, let us remember that there are issues and activities enough for each of us to carve out an area in which we can be most effective. The particular focus is not as important as our dedication to the idea that all children deserve to grow up in safe, loving environments that prepare them to become healthy and productive adults. With that in mind, let each of us work *to save a child.*

David S. Liederman
Executive Director
Child Welfare League of America

PREFACE

Several years ago, during a chat with a family therapist, it occurred to me that while there are many resources designed to educate and advise professionals about issues that touch the lives of today's children, there are none of this type for *parents*. Long committed to children's causes, I found myself yearning for the chance to place in parents' hands the same facts about health, safety, educational, and family problems that enable child-development specialists to help their clients and patients. After all, most parents already act as advocates for at least one youngster—their own—in the course of everyday parenting. Just imagine what we as an *informed* group could do to enact change on a broader level! The reasons for saving our children were certainly clear enough, I thought. Perhaps all that was needed were some specific objectives, as well as the support and guidance necessary to reach those objectives.

Thus began a five-year journey that put me in touch with hundreds of caring people and organizations all across North America—a journey that culminated in this book, *To Save a Child*. In its pages, you'll find the most current information available on a host of topics—topics of tremendous importance to today's children and their families. You'll also find hundreds of ideas to help you minimize, eliminate, or protect your youngster from these childhood stumbling blocks, whether by becoming more knowledgeable, altering some of your parenting techniques, or working with a group for larger-scale change. And many of these suggestions will not only help you avoid pitfalls, but will also help you provide the *best* for your child—the best health, the best educational environment, the best chance to be a happy, well-adjusted human being.

Each of *To Save a Child's* sixty entries examines a specific aspect of one or more of the following key issues: pre- and postnatal care, parenting, communication, nutrition, general health, mental health, education, safety, addiction, and social action. Here and there, you'll find insets that present greater detail about a particularly important facet of an entry. At the end of most entries is a resource list that provides the names, addresses, and phone numbers of organizations that offer additional information, literature, emotional support, or referrals, depending on your circumstances and goals. When appropriate, a list of related books has also been included—books that can easily be obtained in bookstores or, in the case of some older, out-of-print titles, through your local library system. While it's impossible to cover all child-related issues within the limits of a single book, I've done my best to address today's most widespread concerns and problems.

Certainly, beliefs and purposes can differ widely from one group to the next. Therefore, I have included a variety of organizations whenever possible so that you can select the group whose convictions are closest to your own. Please bear in mind that although I have been in touch with representatives from every organization listed in *To Save a Child*, addresses and phone numbers *do* change. If you find that a particular number is no longer in service, you can call Directory Assistance or contact another group from the same resource list for help in locating the desired organization.

While *To Save a Child* may have started as a resource book for concerned parents, it has evolved into a vehicle—a lifeline—with which to approach problems that can leave their mark on a child. In my case, the resources and suggestions have helped me to achieve my goal of becoming a better parent to my sons. If after leafing through the entries and learning more about those issues that matter most to you, you feel motivated to take action—any action—on behalf of a child, then this book has met its original purpose.

Read this book, by all means. Mark it up. Use it as you see fit, and when you're through, share it with others. For together we can give our children—and *all* children—the gift of a brighter future. I thank you for joining me in the quest *To Save a Child*.

Audrey Talkington
Spokane, Washington

A Word About Gender

Your child is certainly as likely to be a boy as a girl; however, our language does not provide us with a genderless pronoun. To avoid using the awkward "he/she" or the impersonal "it" when referring to your child, while still giving equal time to both sexes, the feminine pronouns "she," "her," and "hers" have been used in odd-numbered entries, while the male "he," "him," and "his" appear in all the rest. This decision was made in the interest of simplicity and clarity.

"Children are our most valuable natural resource."

—Herbert Hoover

INTRODUCTION

This is a book of both shame and hope. The shame lies in the fact that the family, health, and social problems discussed in this book exist at all. The hope lies in the fact that so many people are trying to reverse the trends and overcome the obstacles that stand between our children and the health and happiness they deserve. Surely, many other people would help if they only know how.

Since this book captured your attention, you may already feel some concern about children's issues. With luck, the information contained in the pages of *To Save a Child* will help you decide what you can do on our youngsters' behalf. You see, each entry focuses on a specific childhood risk factor. For instance, some entries look at health issues such as immunizations, substance abuse, and secondhand smoke. Other entries address parenting topics like nutrition, discipline, and child care. And still others examine social problems such as homelessness and child molestation, as well as concerns regarding education, safety, and mental health.

Will you find the contents of this book somewhat jarring? In many cases, the answer is sure to be "Yes." It has been no easy task to sift through the sobering facts and statistics that I've encountered during my research. Many of you may find this information a bitter pill to swallow, and rightfully so. Some topics are quite unpleasant. But, however frightening the initial impact may be, it is my hope that *To Save a Child* will bring important issues to light and act as a catalyst for change. In the end, your reading this book may result in saving the life of a child.

How is this possible? Knowing a little about the book's format will help you understand. Each of the sixty entries begins by providing important background information and some eye-opening figures about a problem that poses a threat to the well-being of our children. The balance of the entry examines the different actions that you can take to improve or eliminate the situation. In some cases, becoming more knowledgeable about an issue may spur you to make simple changes in your parenting habits. For instance, you may begin to look for new ways to improve your child's self-image. Reading about other problems may move you to take safety precautions, such as purchasing a bicycle helmet for your child, or testing your home for the presence of lead. Or you may decide that joining a group on a local or national level is the best way to enact change. If so, you can be sure that the organization you select will welcome your participation.

Whatever your objectives, you'll find the tools you need within the pages of this book. Included are specific guidelines, helpful hints, hotline numbers, and the names of related books. Also listed are organizations through which you can become involved in child-advocacy issues, as well as groups that can provide you with information, counseling, referrals, or educational materials. Since the action you decide to take may involve discussing a frightening issue with your child, suggestions are offered throughout the book on how to address such topics as AIDS, abduction, and the handling of emergency situations. These suggestions, together with your own beliefs and your unique knowledge of your child's personality and level of maturity, can guide you in determining how much information it may be appropriate to share.

Once you've begun to absorb the facts and figures presented throughout this book, I think you'll agree that *To Save a Child* is much more than a parenting guide. In truth, it is an attitude that upholds the worth of children and respects their right to good health, safety, and happiness. It is an appeal to parents and others who care about children to recognize and respond to the risk factors in our midst. And, most important, it is a tool with which you can effect change at home, in your community, or even on a nationwide scale. Please read on, and, in doing so, be filled with a sense of hope for our greatest resource—our children.

1

KNOW WHERE YOUR CHILD IS, WHAT SHE'S DOING, AND WHO HER FRIENDS ARE

"It's ten p.m.," cautions a well-known television public service message. "Do you know where your children are?" Answering this question is an easy task for the millions of parents whose small children are safely tucked in their beds at that hour. In fact, you can ask those parents the same question at any time of day and expect an equally certain response. After all, it's a fairly simple matter to account for children who are too young to wander from beneath the watchful gaze of a parent or care giver. This vigilance shouldn't slacken during your child's growing-up years, however. You see, even as your child matures, becomes independent, and spends increasingly longer periods of time apart from you, she remains vulnerable, impressionable, and—quite often—naive. To offer your child the best guidance, support, and protection, it's important to know where she is, what she is doing, and whom she is with at all times.

The potential for trouble exists whenever your child is unsupervised. Alone, she may be frightened, bored, resentful, or innocent enough to exercise poor judgment or disregard your rules. In the company of friends, it's even easier to go astray, for your child may be subjected to all sorts of potentially harmful activities: drinking, smoking, dangerous—and possibly illegal—horseplay . . . the list goes on and on. Therefore, it's wise to ensure that your child will be chaperoned, accompanied by friends whom you know and trust, or involved in a safe activity whenever she is not with you.

There are many ways in which you can keep track of your child's whereabouts and keep her out of harm's way. Many elementary schools offer before- and after-school child-care programs that your youngster can enjoy for a nominal fee. A neighbor or friend's parents can provide the same service when your older child is alone during weekends or vacations or after school. It is a good idea to establish rules concerning the invitation of schoolmates to your home when you are not present, and the visiting of friends' homes in the absence of their parents. Obviously, you know your child best, so let past experience and your intuition guide you in determining how much freedom she can safely handle.

One of the best moves you can make is to welcome your child's friends into your home. This serves three purposes: it allows you to become acquainted with whomever your child chooses to spend time with, it helps you to earn the respect of your child's young guests, and it enables you to keep tabs on the group's doings and whereabouts. Another way to get to know your child's friends is to frequently offer your services as a driver. There is much that can be learned from back-seat conversations and from your young passengers' behavior in your presence. And, if your child plans to spend a lot of time with a friend who is unknown to you, try to arrange a brief meeting beforehand.

Consider asking your child for a rough itinerary whenever she goes out for an afternoon or evening. If she is unsure of her friends' plans, ask her to call from her destination to let you know what she'll be doing. It's wise to encourage *specific* plans whenever possible, for you'll then be reassured that your child is busy at an appropriate activity. Establishing a phone check-in habit is a good idea for teen-agers, who are often gone for hours at a stretch. Remember to let your child know that you appreciate her calling to keep you posted about her plans.

When setting limits, be very clear about the consequences of breaking rules, and work at matching the form of discipline with the infraction. For example, if your child comes home an hour late, loss of an hour of play time would be a more appropriate punishment than loss of television privileges. It's also beneficial to enforce whatever rules are necessary with consistency, and to explain them in a calm, non-vengeful tone. (See Entry 11 on page 49 for more discipline suggestions.)

Naturally, you don't wish your child to feel that she has no privacy, nor do you want your concern to imply a lack of trust. For this reason, make it a point to remind your child often that your rules regarding her free time, your interest in her friends, and your desire to know what she's up to exist to ensure her safety. Above all, and whenever you can, tell your child that you have faith in her decision-making ability and that you enjoy the people she chooses as friends. By creating an atmosphere of respect—while still insisting that your child comply with the rules and limits that you've set—you'll help keep her free from harm while preserving your own peace of mind.

Resources

You can learn more about keeping abreast of your child's social life and after-school activities from the sources listed below.

ORGANIZATION

Center for Early Adolescence
University of North Carolina
  at Chapel Hill
Carr Mill Mall, Suite 211
Carrboro, NC 27510
(919) 966–1148

This organization provides training and educational materials for parents of latchkey children.

Center for the Study of Parent
  Involvement
John F. Kennedy University
370 Camino Pablo
Orinda, CA 94563
(415) 254–0110

This group provides consultation, information, and workshops to bring parents together as decision makers and advocates for their children.

BOOKS

Kaye, Kenneth. *Family Rules.* New York: Walker and Co., 1984.

Kyte, Kathy. *In Charge: A Complete Handbook for Kids With Working Parents.* New York: Alfred A. Knopf, 1983.

Long, Lynnette. *On My Own: The Kids' Self Care Book.* Washington, DC: Acropolis Books, 1984.

Samenow, Stanton E. *Before It's Too Late: Why Some Kids Get Into Trouble—And What Parents Can Do About It.* New York: Times Books, 1992.

Swan, Helen L., and Victoria Houston. *Alone After School: A Self-Care Guide for Latchkey Children and Their Parents.* Englewood Cliffs, NJ: Prentice Hall, 1985.

2

BE A HEALTHY ROLE MODEL FOR YOUR CHILD

Have you ever been horrified to hear a four-letter word of your own on your child's lips? Have you ever been frustrated by your child's teasing, aggression, or cattiness—only to realize that he learned this behavior from you? If you're like most parents, you find it more than a little unpleasant to claim responsibility for your child's less-than-appropriate actions or language. Certainly, your child's behavior may reflect the influence of a number of other people—friends, relatives, and teachers—as well as the influence of TV and other factors. Ultimately, though, your child's conduct reflects the guidance he receives from you—guidance that goes way beyond the *verbal* setting of limits. You see, when you become a parent, you automatically become a lifelong role model for your child. So it pays to meet this challenge by making yourself the best person you can be.

If you've ever doubted that your child learns as much from your actions as from your words, consider the following. If you are physically demonstrative, your child is probably just as free with hugs and high-fives—to his friends, his relatives, and even his stuffed animals. If you work visibly at expressing your anger in a positive fashion, your child most likely handles frustration in the same way. And if you are consistent and respectful in matters of discipline, your child probably views the setting of limits as a loving act, and has begun to gently point out your mistakes. It's important to remember that a young child has no inner system to help him weed out unacceptable behavior. Good or bad, you can safely expect your youngster to mirror both your words and your deeds as he learns about life.

When you insist upon certain behaviors from your child, do you demand the same of yourself? If not, you are probably sending your child mixed signals. You'll be a much stronger role model—and a better parent—if you take a personal inventory before you set standards for your child. Admittedly, this experience can be unsettling. But it can also result in self-betterment and, from your child's standpoint, the setting of the best possible example.

How can you use a personal inventory to make yourself a better role model? First, ask yourself if there is anything you do that you do not want your child to emulate. Do you smoke? Swear? Constantly misplace things? Lose your temper and lash out at those around you? Make a list of whatever it is that you'd like to change about yourself. For example, your list might read something like the following:

- I want to quit smoking.
- I'd like to become better organized.
- I need to be more assertive.
- I want to break the gossip habit.

Once you've identified one or more ways in which you can improve yourself and have resolved to make these changes, think about how you can reach your goals. Since support is often a vital factor during times of transition, you may want to contact a specific organization, or to simply widen your circle of friends to include those who can offer assistance and understanding. Also consider sharing your good intentions with your child. You may find that comradeship and new-found respect are unexpected results.

Say, for example, that giving up smoking is your top priority. You might begin by listing activities that will help fill the gap left by your habit. You can plan a special purchase for yourself with the money normally spent on cigarettes. Or you may choose to take up crafts, needlework, or another hobby that will occupy your hands and your mind. It might be helpful to contact your local Lung Association or health club—any group, actually, that will involve you in a smoke-free lifestyle. Also consider a trip to the bookstore. A good book can provide numerous suggestions, including information about helpful programs and products. Other tactics may be worth a try, too. You might use the power of visualization to "see" yourself as a nonsmoker. Or you can write notes of encouragement to yourself and carry them in your purse or wallet to help you resist momentary cravings. Positive affirmations like, "I am a nonsmoker," and, "I am stronger than my need for nicotine," can serve the same purpose. You might also arrange for occasional "crisis calls" to a friend who has successfully kicked the habit. And, if necessary, you can seek guidance from a therapist.

No doubt, you will think of other ways to reach the nonsmoking goal, and other goals, as well. But, whatever your circumstances, a self-evaluation will help you identify those areas that you need to work on—one problem at a time. And the fact that you've made self-betterment a priority will not be lost on your child as, step by step, you become the parent you want to be—a role model who teaches through deeds as well as words.

Resources

The following resources can help you in your quest to become the best possible role model for your child.

ORGANIZATIONS

Active Parenting
Suite B
810 Franklin Court
Marietta, GA 30067
(800) 825–0060

This organization offers parenting support materials and sponsors nationwide support groups.

National Association for
  Family-Based Services
PO Box 005
Riverdale, IL 60627
(319) 396–4829

This family-focused service program strives to improve family relations and support the family unit.

BOOKS

Anderson, Joan Wester. *Teen Is a Four-Letter Word: A Survival Kit for Parents*. Whitehall, VA: Betterway Publications, 1990.

Atlas, Stephen L. *Single Parenting: A Practical Resource Guide*. New York: Prentice Hall, 1981.

Dobson, James C. *Parenting Isn't for Cowards*. Irving, TX: Word Books, 1992.

York, Phyllis. *Toughlove Solutions*. New York: Doubleday, 1984.

3

NURTURE THE QUALITIES THAT EXIST IN HEALTHY FAMILIES

Regardless of different parenting styles and personal values, most parents share a common goal: the creation of a healthy, happy, loving family. Unfortunately, the news about parent-child relationships isn't always good, and this fact makes it all too easy to focus on what's *wrong* with today's families, rather than what's *right*. Perhaps a better way to strengthen family connections is to take a positive approach—to identify and nurture within your own home the qualities that exist in healthy families.

During the writing of *Traits of a Healthy Family*, author Dolores Curran conducted a survey among 551 teachers, doctors, counselors, youth leaders, and other professionals who have extensive contact with families. Each respondent was asked to identify the most important characteristics of a healthy family life, based on his or her observations. As you might expect, certain characteristics appeared on nearly every list. The frequency with which particular traits were cited underscored the positive effect each can have on familial relationships.

Curran's list of desirable characteristics is quite comprehensive. As you read about and consider the qualities described below, keep in mind that, in total, they represent the *ideal*. A family can exhibit only a handful of these traits and still offer its members a firm foundation for personal growth.

What follows is a list of fifteen specific traits that Curran's professionals repeatedly cited as contributing to family strength. According to the survey, healthy families:

1. *Communicate and listen.* Communication may well be the most important ingredient in the making of a healthy family. The highest levels of understanding and respect exist within families who freely express thoughts, convey emotions, seek guidance, and relate experiences to one another. Counselors and therapists the world over are joined by such self-help groups as Parents Anonymous, Marriage Encounter, and Effectiveness Training in endorsing positive communication as a fundamental family need. Naturally, some families have an easier time listening and sharing than others. Positive communication is a skill that often requires careful attention and practice.

2. *Affirm and support their members.* Members of healthy families offer one another ongoing support and admiration, freely acting and speaking with affection. The parents have strong self-esteem, which they work hard to pass on to their children, and the entire family maintains a positive outlook on life—even in the face of adversity.

3. *Show respect for others.* Respect within a family is an attribute to be prized. However, respect is not acquired automatically, but is modeled and learned. Within the ideal family, people respect one another's property, decisions, opinions, and unique qualities. In addition, they extend similar consideration to people outside the family unit.

4. *Develop a sense of trust.* Trust is also important to family solidarity. In healthy families, the husband and wife trust each other implicitly, and even very young children are given opportunities to earn trust in daily life. In these families, parents and children act in an honorable manner toward one another, and work at mending any trust that has been broken.

5. *Have a sense of play and humor.* Healthy families keep work and play in reasonable perspective. Parents and children spend time having fun together and enjoying one another's company through recreation. Healthy families have a good sense of humor and laugh together often.

6. *Exhibit a sense of shared responsibility.* Sharing responsibility

within the family is a vital part of raising self-sufficient adults. You see, children learn to be responsible only when they are trained to do so and when parents demonstrate—by word and example—how tasks can be divided.

7. *Teach a sense of right and wrong.* Healthy families hold values and morals in high regard. They set clear-cut boundaries between right and wrong, and hold both children and parents accountable for their behavior. Adults are keenly aware of their position as role models for the youngsters in the household. Frustrations are dealt with in a positive fashion, and wrongdoings are considered with a clear head. When judging actions that require discipline, explanations are heard, motive is taken into account, and decisions regarding punishment are made accordingly.

8. *Have a strong sense of family in which rituals and traditions abound.* Traditions, special practices, and family stories combine to form an important part of everyday life in the healthy family. Rituals provide a sense of continuity, and tales from the past help build a history, which, because it is unique to each household, acts as a "glue" that maintains family unity and strength.

9. *Have a balance of interaction among members.* In healthy families, time together is carefully protected from interference by work or other activities. Parenting is shared, with both father and mother actively nurturing the children. In addition, the family discourages coalitions and cliques from forming among its members.

10. *Have a shared religious core.* A shared religious center tends to strengthen the family and serve as one of its support systems. For many healthy families, faith is one of the building blocks of daily life, and is accompanied by a rich history and a sense of morality that is passed on from parents to children in a positive manner.

11. *Respect the privacy of all members.* Even as its members interact within the family unit, a healthy family also recognizes the importance of privacy, and shows respect for personal possessions and solo pursuits. This regard for privacy extends

to the acceptance of passing fads, friends, confidences, personal space, and the desire to be alone.

12. *Value service to others.* Strong families make service to others a priority. Parents foster an awareness of those who are less fortunate, and act on this empathy by helping out within the community. Healthy families are generous, hospitable, and aware of the lessons to be learned from volunteering side by side. Yet, parents are careful to maintain a balance between community service and other aspects of family life.

13. *Foster mealtime conversation.* The family table has always been a place for a special closeness made possible by the elimination of distractions. In healthy families, the preparation and sharing of at least one meal a day helps to unite members by providing a chance for laughter, relaxation, and conversation.

14. *Share leisure time.* Strong families give play a place in their daily agendas because they recognize the importance of time spent together pursuing leisure activities. Family members support and actively share in one another's interests.

15. *Admit to and seek help with problems.* Healthy families have many of the same problems as dysfunctional families, but strive to see the positive side of circumstances and to face difficulties together. Members discuss and agree upon problem-solving techniques and enlist the aid of a counselor or therapist if matters cannot be resolved within the family.

If you feel that there is room for improvement in your family life, you're in good company. Remember, though, that the characteristics cited as most desirable by Curran's polled professionals describe an optimal, not an average, family. What's important is your desire to improve family relations—not a point-by-point comparison of your family with an ideal one. Curran's list of traits can serve as a basis for discussion; help you and your children pinpoint areas in which change may be needed; and guide you in finding concrete ways to improve day-to-day life.

The above discussion was adapted from Dolores Curran's *Traits of a Healthy Family*, published by HarperSanFrancisco. This adaptation was printed with permission of the author.

Resources

If you would like additional information on healthy family relations, help can be obtained from the following sources.

ORGANIZATIONS

Effectiveness Training, Inc.
531 Stevens Avenue
Solana Beach, CA 92075
(619) 481–8121

This organization offers instructor training, parenting seminars, and referrals to local parent effectiveness training courses.

Family Research Council
Suite 901
601 Pennsylvania Avenue
Washington, DC 20004
(202) 393–2100

This organization provides expertise and information on family issues to government agencies, policy makers, the media, and the public.

Family Resource Coalition
Room 1625
230 North Michigan Avenue
Chicago, IL 60601
(312) 726–4750

This organization of community-based family support groups is concerned with parenting, child development, and family issues.

Family Service America
11700 West Lake Park Drive
Milwaukee, WI 53224
(414) 359–1040

This federation of local service agencies provides family counseling, family life education, and family advocacy services.

In the Company of Kids
Suites 108–109
80 West Center Street
Akron, OH 44308–1033
(216) 762–3700

This organization addresses the needs and concerns of families by creating partnerships with health, business, educational, community, and religious leadership to increase parental awareness and provide support for families.

Institute for American Values
250 West 57th Street, Suite 2415
New York, NY 10107
(212) 246–3942

This research organization focuses on issues affecting American families, and publishes a newsletter dealing with the promotion of healthy family values.

BOOKS

Anderson, Hal W. *Mom and Dad Are Divorced, But I'm Not: Parenting After Divorce.* Chicago: Nelson-Hall, 1981.

Bird, Joseph. *To Live as a Family.* New York: Doubleday, 1982.

Bradshaw, John. *Bradshaw On: The Family.* Deerfield Beach, FL: Health Communications, 1988.

Cline, Ruth K.J. *Focus on Families: A Reference Handbook.* Santa Barbara, CA: ABC Clio, 1990.

Covey, Stephen R. *The Seven Habits of Highly Effective People: Powerful Lessons in Personal Change.* New York: Simon and Schuster, 1990.

Curran, Dolores. *Traits of a Healthy Family.* New York: Ballantine Books, 1983.

Dinkmeyer, Don C., and Gary D. McKay. *Parenting Teenagers: Systematic Training for Effective Parenting of Teens.* Circle Plains, MN: American Guidance Service, 1990.

Fossum, Merle A., and Marilyn J. Mason. *Facing Shame: Families in Recovery.* New York: W.W. Norton and Co., 1989.

Ginott, Haim G. *Between Parent and Teenager.* New York: Avon Books, 1969.

Gordon, Thomas. *P.E.T. in Action.* New York: Bantam Books, 1976.

Guarendi, Ray. *Back to the Family.* New York: Villard Books, 1990.

Hill, Gerald A. *Divorced Father: Coping with Problems, Creating Solutions.* White Hall, VA: Betterway Publications, 1989.

McGinnis, Kathleen, and James B. McGinnis. *Parenting for Peace and Justice: Ten Years Later.* Maryknoll, NY: Orbis Books, 1990.

Meier, Paul D. *Family Foundations.* Grand Rapids, MI: Baker Book House, 1981.

Schuller, Robert Harold. *Power Ideas for a Happy Family.* Tarrytown, NY: F.H. Revell, 1972.

Stinnett, Nick. *Secrets of Strong Families.* Boston: Little, Brown and Co., 1985.

Swindoll, Charles R. *The Strong Family.* Portland, OR: Multnomah Press, 1991.

Weiner-Davis, Michele. *Divorce Busting: A Revolutionary and Rapid Program for Staying Together.* New York: Summit Books, 1991.

4

MAKE A WILL

Most parents take the responsibility for their child's upbringing quite seriously—and rightfully so. Rearing a child is a huge task that goes far beyond physical care. For as long as your child is under your roof, there are lessons to be taught, examples to be set, and affection and support to be provided in large doses. In addition, you're likely to devote much time and emotional energy to thinking, planning, and worrying about your child's future. However, many parents ignore one responsibility that has a potentially far-reaching effect upon their child's upbringing: the making of a will. A will is the only way to ensure the care you want for your child in the event that you are not able to raise him.

For many, it is so difficult to contemplate leaving a job as important as parenting unfinished that the possibility of an early death is not even considered. Yet, there are important choices to be made about the future of your child in the event that he is left without parents—decisions that are best made by you.

HOW A WILL CAN PROTECT YOUR CHILD

A will helps ensure your child's well-being in many ways. First, this document enables you to designate legal guardians—people who will raise your child in the event of your death. It's vital to carefully weigh all the factors that might influence your decision—the potential guardian's age, geographic location, religion, education, and interests, for instance—before deciding which friend or family member to entrust with your child's care and upbringing. Many parents search for someone who would view guardianship as an honor rather than a burden, and whose values, judgment, and goals are similar to their own. Naturally, you should discuss the matter with your child's prospective guardians before naming them in your will.

Of course, there is a practical side to child rearing: namely, the expense involved. Even if you are denied the chance to nurture your child to adulthood, a will enables you to designate someone to look after your youngster's financial interests. However you choose to provide for your child's daily living expenses in the event of your death—through life insurance, say, or through liquidation of assets—there will be bills to pay, expenses to cover, and investments to oversee until your child comes of legal age and assumes the management of his own finances. In most cases, the property and money inherited by a child is placed in trust, and a trustee is appointed to look after the child's financial interests. You may choose to assign this responsibility to your child's designated guardian, or you may choose a different individual as trustee. Whatever the case, a will gives you the means to state your intentions regarding your child's financial security.

A will also requires that you name an executor to carry out the wishes expressed in the document. This appointment, too, has some bearing on your child's future, through the responsible handling of your assets and the timely payment of taxes and satisfaction of debts. As with the management of your child's finances, you may choose someone other than the appointed guardian to serve as executor. Or you may wish a single individual to act as executor, guardian, and trustee.

Another legal consideration that can affect your child's future is a living will. This is a statement of your wishes regarding life-extending medical measures—measures that could financially drain your estate. Another document, Durable Power of Attorney, enables you to designate someone who would temporarily handle your financial affairs if you became incapacitated. An attorney can tell you if these documents might be appropriate in your circumstances.

HOW YOU CAN PREPARE A WILL

Some people choose to draw up their own document without legal assistance. However, you should know that if an error exists anywhere in your will—say, if the number of witnesses is incorrect, or if the signing procedures were not followed as required by law—the entire document can be declared invalid. Therefore, it's wise to secure the services of an attorney. You may wish to select someone who specializes in will preparation, or you may prefer to choose a lawyer with whom you have had other dealings. Don't hesitate to ask friends and family members for their recommendations, to contact your local bar association for a listing of attorneys in your area, or to seek out law school students who can provide this service.

The cost of setting up a will ranges from $50 to $2,500, depending on the document's complexity and the part of the country in which you live. In most cases, you can expect to pay a few hundred dollars for a routine will.

While preparing a will can be a sobering process, it is not a difficult one. If you die before your child reaches adulthood, a will becomes your only means of control over the important issues of your child's custody and financial security. Yet, almost 60 percent of adults die without having left this document. In these cases, extended family must resolve the delicate issue of custody, and the responsibility for finances and property falls to the state. And when this happens, there are no guarantees that the child and the parents' assets will go to those people whom the parents would have chosen. Therefore, if you do not have a will, or if your older will has not recently been updated, it's vital to consult an attorney and take the necessary legal steps. Your child's future—and your own peace of mind—is at stake.

Resources

Listed below are sources of additional information about making a will.

BOOKS

Esperti, Robert A., and Renno L. Peterson. *Loving Trust: The Right Way to Provide for Yourself and Guarantee the Future of Your Loved Ones.* New York: Viking Penguin, 1988.

Lehman, Albert M. *Complete Book of Wills and Trusts*. Englewood Cliffs, NJ: Institute for Business Planning, 1978.

Silver, Don. *A Parent's Guide to Wills and Trusts*. Los Angeles: Adams-Hall Publishing, 1992.

Write a Letter to Your Child

A parent's death is terribly painful to a child, perhaps even more so when circumstances rob the family of the chance to exchange loving good-byes. You can guard against this possibility by composing a special letter to your child, to be given to him in the event of your death. You can preserve this message in an actual written letter or on audio- or videotape, and store it with other personal papers that will come into your executor's hands after your death. It's a good idea to mention this special letter in your will so that your executor—and your child—will know of its existence and whereabouts. You might also wish to update your letter from time to time.

What sort of message might you leave your child? You might simply choose to leave a warm and loving farewell. You might use your letter to give your child a bit of the encouragement and support you'll be unable to provide later on. Or, you could offer specific advice about circumstances that you suspect your child will one day face. If you wish, you can use a letter to share some of your favorite memories as a parent or to describe your own childhood experiences. Certainly, each parent-child relationship is unique, and your instinct and special knowledge of your child will help you put your thoughts and feelings into words. Remember that although your letter might mean little to your young child, its meaning—and its value—will increase dramatically as time passes.

Whatever your child's age, a heartfelt message may ease some of the pain of your passing. The very fact that you've chosen this special way to say good-bye will show the depth of your concern for his happiness and well-being. And through your letter, your child will continue to receive your love and support throughout his life.

5

NEVER SHAKE OR THROW YOUR CHILD

Do you ever toss your child into the air, just to hear her squeals of delight when you catch her? Do you tackle or wrestle her—sometimes roughly—for the same reason? Do you ever take her by the shoulders and give her a shake to stop her crying, get her attention, or vent a bit of frustration? If so, or if you've ever been tempted, it's vital that you recognize how dangerous a vigorous shake, toss, or tumble can be to a child. While it's certainly possible to play roughly without causing injury, these practices have been known to cause whiplash, spinal-cord injury, brain damage, hearing impairment, blindness, seizures, cerebral palsy, paralysis, and even death in babies and small children. Knowing the facts about child-shaking or -tossing—the frightening results of which are often called Shaken Baby Syndrome, or SBS—can help you make sure that your own child never becomes a victim.

The first case of SBS was reported in 1928. And since that time, SBS has been identified as the cause of many thousands of serious injuries to children. The majority of victims are under two years of age, and—although SBS is, unarguably, a form of child abuse—most of the parents and care givers responsible for the injuries are unaware of the potential for harm.

You see, even the hardiest-looking toddler must be handled with care. Young necks simply cannot withstand the stress of shaking or jerking. Just as new parents are warned to support their infant's head when lifting or carrying her, you should understand that until around the age of four, a child's neck remains surprisingly fragile, and her head disproportionately large and heavy.

How can a jolt to a child's neck cause the kinds of damage mentioned earlier? Babies and small children lack a fatty substance called myelin—a substance that protects the brain stem of older children and adults. For this reason, a small child's brain is more susceptible to damage from movement within the child's skull. Jolts or jerks to the neck can burst blood vessels within the child's head, causing undetected inner bleeding, or can result in damage in and around the cervical spine. So, as you see, an angry yank to a child's arm or shoulder, an innocent game of "catch the baby," or even a rollicking romp on the living room rug can have terrible, permanent consequences for the infant or toddler.

Fortunately, there are ways to prevent SBS from harming your child. First, never assume that relatives or care givers are aware of the damage they can cause by shaking, tossing, or jerking your child. It's important to alert everyone who spends time with your child to the dangers of SBS, and to insist that others avoid actions and activities that might be harmful. If you are unsure of a relative's or care giver's ability to cope with such baby-related frustrations as colic, tantrums, mess-making, or stubbornness, do not leave your child in that person's care. Similarly, you should improve your own coping skills by learning to recognize and react to the signals of mounting frustration or rage. (See Entry 6 on page 22.) When you feel yourself losing control, make it a practice to first place your baby in his crib or playpen and then count to ten, call a friend, leave the room, splash your face with cold water—whatever it takes for you to calm down. After all, a momentary loss of composure can have a lifelong effect on your child. And, naturally, you should be as mindful of the hazards of rough horseplay as you expect your child's care givers to be.

Few would deny that child care can sometimes be an exercise in utter frustration. And most parents also agree that romping, rolling, and other physical play can offer a needed outlet for excess toddler energy, as well as a welcome change of pace for the adult in charge. It is all too evident, however, that this kind of rough handling can have tragic, if unintentional, consequences for the infant or small child. But by becoming knowledgeable about SBS, respecting your child's fragility, and insisting on careful handling by those who watch him, you will be doing a great deal to protect your child from accidental injury and to make his play times safe as well as fun.

Resources

Your local children's hospital, mental health center, or crisis nursery can provide you with additional information about SBS. You may also find the following sources helpful.

ORGANIZATIONS

Childhelp USA
6463 Independence Avenue
Woodland Hills, CA 91367
(800) 4–A–CHILD *National Hotline*

This hotline offers immediate support for families in crisis, as well as counseling and referrals to local services.

National Exchange Club
  Foundation for the Prevention
  of Child Abuse
3050 Central Avenue
Toledo, OH 43606–1700
(419) 535–3232

This organization runs a "parent-aide" assistance program that offers one-to-one support to families.

BOOKS

Shukat, Evelyn. *Why Is My Baby Crying? A Practical Guide to What Bothers Babies and Worries Parents During the First Six Months of Life.* New York: Villard Books, 1986.

Vasi, Dianne. *It Shouldn't Hurt to Be a Child.* Washington, DC: Review and Herald, 1986.

6

LEARN TO MANAGE PARENTAL FRUSTRATIONS

When your child begins to "get your goat," whether by accident or design, how do you react? Do you ever silently grit your teeth and seethe, thinking thoughts so unmentionable that you shock even yourself? Do you explode in foot-stamping, fist-banging rage at whatever inanimate object lies in your path, then heave a sigh and wordlessly go on as before? Do you lash out verbally, hurling accusations and bringing up past wrongs that are unrelated, or out of proportion, to the problem at hand? Or do you let your hands express your fury by shaking your child's shoulder or administering a smack to his bottom?

The fact that all of the above responses are inappropriate—and worse, damaging to your child's self-esteem—may not surprise you at all. Yet, if you're honest with yourself, you'll probably have to admit that, like the majority of parents, you've been known to react one or all of these ways at various times. To be sure, there are few endeavors as rewarding as child rearing. But, as you're well aware, it takes tremendous self-control to remain even-tempered through the ups and downs of a day of parenting.

Let's consider the importance of coping with the anger you sometimes feel toward your child. First, since you are your child's primary role model, he no doubt mimics much of your behavior. So if you habitually take out your frustrations on others, your child is also likely to engage in this destructive practice. Then, too, you should consider the effect that angry outbursts have on your child's emotional well-being. If you've ever seen someone else's child cowering in the path of a parent's raised hand or bellowing rage, you were probably quite sickened by the sight. And it is well established that children brought up in volatile households are often excessively fearful and insecure as youngsters, and become increasingly aggressive and uncommunicative as they move through childhood. You see, a child who lives in the shadow of an extremely stressed parent undergoes a daily battering of his self-esteem. It is also important to realize that the inappropriate venting of fury can become a habit—and that, like any other habit, it can grow until it threatens to control you. In some cases, poorly managed parental frustration can even lead to child abuse.

How can you cope with the impatience and anger that so often go hand-in-hand with parenting? It's a good idea to begin by assessing your current stress-avoidance techniques. Here are a few questions you might ask yourself.

- Are you satisfied with your usual behavior when under stress, or do you often lash out and feel guilty afterwards?
- Do you work at improving your parenting skills so that stressful situations can be avoided?
- Do you make communicating with your child a priority?
- Are your household rules and your expectations of your child realistic?
- Are you consistent in your handling of discipline problems and misbehavior?

If your answer to any of these questions is "No," you will do your child a favor by improving your coping skills.

You can better manage parental frustrations in several ways. First, learn to recognize the physical symptoms of increasing tension. Clenched teeth, stiffened limbs, rapid breathing, frenzied activity, and tightness in the chest are all common signs of frustration and anger, and can serve as warnings that you are in danger of losing control. Then, try to diffuse your anger before you have a chance to take it out on your child. You might consider taking a shower, going for a brisk walk, or just leaving the room for a "time out" of your own after explaining to your child that you need to calm down and will address the problem later. Other possibilities include counting aloud, turning your attention to a hobby or distracting chore, practicing deep breathing, and chanting a soothing phrase. Naturally, you should use your child's age and state of mind as guides to the advisability of leaving him unattended. A small child should certainly remain within earshot, while a baby should be safely confined to his crib or playpen.

Taking a little time each day for yourself is another good way to avoid erupting over child-rearing frustrations. Your days are undoubtedly hectic; however, work, chores, and the needs of your child shouldn't be your only priorities. It's wise to appreciate the dividends paid by a brief change of focus, and then vow to reenergize yourself daily through a half hour spent reading, jogging, doing aerobics, watching a favorite TV show, working on a hobby, or just soaking in a hot tub. After all, a relaxed parent is likely to be a more patient, more controlled parent.

Finally, you and your child will probably get along better than ever if you make yourself aware of those situations that seem to trigger his whining, obstinacy, or tantrums—and your own mounting tension. Once you recognize potential trouble spots, you can take steps to avoid them, whether it means moving up your child's mealtime, putting a temporary halt to child-accompanied errands, or altering your usual routine in favor of additional time spent with your youngster. Your interactions with your child will, no doubt, improve in the bargain.

Will these techniques always prevent you from losing your temper or yelling at your child? Probably not. But a realization of the damage that your loss of composure can do to your child, as well as a resolution to practice effective parenting techniques, can go a long way toward keeping both you and your child from becoming victims of parental frustrations.

Resources

If you sense that you may be in need of immediate help with your parenting practices, you can get advice and support by calling a local crisis nursery or parenting hotline, or by contacting Childhelp USA, listed on page 25. If you do not need immediate help, but would like assistance in dealing with the normal ups and downs of child rearing, the other organizations in the following list can provide the information you need.

ORGANIZATIONS

Active Parenting
Suite B
810 Franklin Court
Marietta, GA 30067
(800) 825–0060

This organization educates, motivates, and supports parents through a series of audio- and videotaped programs designed to improve parenting skills.

Childhelp USA
6463 Independence Avenue
Woodland Hills, CA 91367
(800) 4–A–CHILD *National Hotline*

This service offers on-the-spot assistance for families in crisis, as well as counseling, mediation, and referrals to local family-service organizations.

National Exchange Club
  Foundation for the Prevention
  of Child Abuse
3050 Central Avenue
Toledo, OH 43606–1700
(419) 535–3232

This parent-aide assistance program offers one-to-one support to families in need of advice, information, and referrals to local services.

National Parent Aide
  Association
Suite 950
332 S. Michigan Avenue
Chicago, IL 60604–4357
(312) 663–3520

This program offers one-to-one assistance and ongoing parenting support to families in crisis.

Nurturing Parenting Programs
c/o Family Development
  Resources, Inc.
3160 Pinebrook Road
Park City, UT 84060
(800) 688–5822

This organization provides a mail-order catalog of helpful parenting materials.

Parents Anonymous
Suite 316
520 South Lafayette Park Place
Los Angeles, CA 90057
(800) 421–0353

This network of parent-organized self-help groups is geared toward strengthening parenting skills and improving family relationships.

Positive Pregnancies and Parenting
  Fitness
c/o Be Healthy, Inc.
51 Salt Rock Road
Baltic, CT 06330
(203) 822–8573
(800) 433–5523

This organization offers parenting support materials.

Toughlove, International
100 Mechanic Street
PO Box 1069
Doylestown, PA 18901
(215) 348–7090
(800) 333–1069

This self-help program teaches mediation as a solution to family crisis situations.

BOOKS

Barrish, Harriet H. *Managing and Understanding Parental Anger.* Kansas City, MO: Westport Publishers, 1989.

Bluestein, Jane, and Lynn Collins. *Parents in a Pressure Cooker: A Guide to Responsible and Loving Parent/Child Relationships.* Albuquerque, NM: I.S.S. Publications, 1983.

Dobson, James. *Parenting Isn't for Cowards.* Waco, TX: Word Books, 1987.

Dorn, Lois. *Peace in the Family: A Workshop of Ideas and Actions.* New York: Pantheon Books, 1983.

"Our children are not treated with sufficient respect as human beings, and yet from the moment they are born they have this right to respect."

—Pearl S. Buck

7

Nurture your child's self-esteem

Thumb through almost any of today's parenting and self-help publications and you're likely to come across articles on self-esteem—understanding it, protecting it, and, perhaps most important, carefully nurturing its development in your child. As a parent, you see, you hold the key to your child's self-esteem. To understand this is to understand how crucial your love, your respect, and your appreciation of your child's special qualities are to her happiness.

What exactly is self-esteem? It is a fundamental belief in yourself—an assurance than you have great personal value and potential. A child whose self-esteem is high understands that she can succeed personally, academically, and socially simply because of who she is, and that she is deserving of respect. On the other hand, a child with low self-esteem often has little faith in her ability to succeed at even the smallest task, and has serious doubts about her worth. Obviously, high self-esteem is an important ingredient in a child's overall makeup.

To nurture your child's self-esteem, you should see yourself as the gardener of your child's character. Clearly, self-esteem is related to the way a child is treated by those around her. What is more, self-esteem is developed over time—not all at once. Therefore, you would do well to watch for opportunities to praise your child every day. Notice her efforts, and commend her for trying. Commiserate with her failures, and help her try again by discussing what might be done differently. Take the time to help your child understand life's lessons.

Will you face times of disappointment with your child? Almost certainly. But by masking whatever dissatisfaction you feel and by managing your frustration appropriately (see Entry 6 on page 22), you will give your child's developing self-esteem the kid-glove treatment it needs. Rather than voicing such discouraging thoughts as "We've been over this a hundred times! What does it take for you to understand?" it's far better to be positive. "I know how hard this is for you. But you're making progress and I'm so proud of your effort," conveys your support for and belief in your child.

Physical displays of affection—hugs, kisses, back-pats, high-fives, or whatever seems natural to you—will also tell your child that she is loved. And you can do even more for your child's self-esteem by reminding her each day how important she is to you. It's sometimes difficult to tell whether you're getting through to your child, so ask her periodically whether she *feels* loved. Remind her that your love is unconditional—that you will love her no matter what she says or does. You might also wish to make some of the following questions and phrases part of your every-day interactions with your child.

- I like how you handled that.
- I see that you've been making a real effort to be kinder to your brother.
- I understand that you're upset and angry with me, and I love you anyway.
- I appreciate how difficult this is for you.
- Let's talk about this.
- How do you think we should handle this?
- What are your ideas about this?
- Tell me about your creation/game/project/work.
- Tell me what happened.

A healthy self-image is one of the greatest gifts you can give to your child. A carefully nurtured belief in her own worth will carry her through the many challenges she will face while growing up, and stay with her throughout her adult life. And when your child becomes a parent, she will know how to give the same gift of self-esteem to her own child. What a loving legacy!

Resources

The books listed below can provide additional information on the nurturing of your child's self-esteem.

BOOKS

Albert, Linda, and Michael Popkin. *Quality Parenting: How to Transform the Everyday Moments We Spend With Our Children Into Special, Meaningful Time.* New York: Ballantine Books, 1989.

Baldwin, Rahima. *You Are Your Child's First Teacher.* Berkeley, CA: Celestial Arts, 1989.

Bateman, C. Fred. *Empowering Your Child: How to Help Your Child Succeed in School and in Life.* Norfolk, VA: Hampton Roads, 1990.

Ketterman, Grace H. *A Circle of Love: How You Can Nurture Creative, Caring, and Close-Knit Parent-Child Relationships.* Tarrytown, NY: F.H. Revell, 1987.

Lockerbie, Bruce D. *Fatherlove: Learning to Give the Best You've Got.* New York: Doubleday, 1981.

Price, Alvin H. *How to Boost Your Child's Self-Esteem: 101 Ways to Raise a Happy, Confident Child.* New York: Golden Press, 1984.

Rolfe, Randy. *You Can Postpone Anything But Love.* New York: Warner Books, 1990.

White, Joe. *What Kids Wish Parents Knew About Parenting.* Sisters, OR: Questar, 1988.

Ziglar, Zig. *Raising Positive Kids in a Negative World.* Nashville, TN: Oliver-Nelson Books, 1985.

8

PROVIDE HEALTHY, NONVIOLENT ENTERTAINMENT

Have you ever wondered about the ways in which different children play? Why the wooden blocks that one child uses to construct an elaborate building become guided missiles in the hands of another? Or why one child seems to have a never-ending supply of creative play ideas, while his playmate insists upon game after game of superheroes? Certainly, personality and social skills have much to do with the way your child acts and interacts. But there are other influencing factors, as well—factors over which you, his parent, have a strong measure of control. In fact, you can do a lot to shape your child's interests and behavior simply by monitoring and staying involved in his choices of entertainment.

What do your child's leisure activities have to do with his attitude and behavior? Quite a lot, actually. The fact that values, or attitudes about right and wrong behavior, are formed primarily during childhood makes your youngster particularly vulnerable to what he sees and hears during the course of his day. Study after study has shown that exposing a child to glamorized violence—through television, movies, reading material, musical lyrics, or toys and games that promote aggression—causes a measurable increase in hostile, rebellious, and combative behavior. However, you can see that your child receives healthy, positive messages from his free-time pursuits by suggesting quality movies and TV programs, introducing different kinds of music, and providing intriguing books and informative playthings.

Of course, it's rarely a simple matter to hold the line against inappropriate entertainment. Even during the preschool years, when your child largely accepts any restrictions placed upon household recreation, he is still subject to the influence of TV commercials, print advertisements, and the playthings he discovers at friends' homes. And his exposure to questionable toys, games, and viewing material is likely to increase as he grows older and spends more time among his peers. No matter what your child's age, however, it's important to realize that he still needs your guidance and input into his recreational pursuits.

The following list of ideas can help you monitor your child's entertainment and present alternatives to television, movies, toys, games, and music that you feel are unacceptable or inappropriate.

☐ Subscribe to *Parent's Choice* (see page 35) for a quarterly review of children's books, videos, toys, audiocassettes, computer programs, television shows, games, movies, and music. Also refer to other periodicals that review children's media. This information can help you decide what your child may watch, rent, or purchase.

☐ Check your newsstand for the November and December issues of magazines like *Parenting, Parents,* and *Sesame Street Parents' Guide,* which annually present such lists as "The Year's Top Twenty Toys" and "Best-Bet Videos for Holiday Giving." Clip and save these columns for use throughout the year. The children's magazine *Zillions* offers similar reviews on a monthly basis.

☐ Set clear-cut limits on the amount of time your child is allowed to spend watching TV. Be equally clear about which programs and stations he is permitted to view and, if necessary, use a parental control box, available through many cable companies, to lock out those channels whose programming is inappropriate for your child.

☐ Make it a point to occasionally watch television with your child. Use this opportunity to suggest educational programs, share quality movies, and introduce service channels that regularly feature local sporting events, the fine arts, consumer advice, and interesting news about weather conditions, agriculture, science, and the business world. Your child may be surprised by TV's many options.

☐ Consider previewing new television shows or movies. This

practice will enable you to make informed decisions about each program's suitability for your child.

☐ Cultivate your child's taste for movie classics by occasionally surprising him with the video version of a beloved film from your childhood.

☐ Ask a children's librarian for lists of award-winning children's books. The Caldecott medal and Newberry award are just two of the annual prizes given for top-quality children's literature. Borrow several books from these lists for your child.

☐ Browse through the children's magazines on display at your library, and borrow—or subscribe to—one or two that you think would appeal to your child.

☐ Ask to look at any tapes or compact discs your child purchases or borrows. The cover photograph and song titles often furnish clues to the music's content. If what you see or read strikes you as inappropriate, you may wish to listen to the lyrics before discarding the register receipt. Few music stores will refuse a refund to an unhappy parent.

☐ Introduce your child to different kinds of music by playing jazz, classical, country, and "oldies" compositions.

☐ Carefully read the description on the video-game box before buying the game for your child. Also consider renting a copy from a video store prior to your purchase and discovering the exact nature of the game by reading the accompanying instruction booklet.

☐ To find out what sort of creative, non-mainstream toys are available, visit a toy library or an educational toy store. These establishments often serve as showcases for novel, high-quality playthings. You can get additional toy ideas from the catalog companies listed at the end of this entry.

☐ If you strongly object to certain toys and playthings, let friends and relatives who buy gifts for your child know of your feelings, and be ready to suggest a few acceptable alternatives. If an item that you dislike comes into your home anyway, explain the problem firmly and clearly to your child and then return the toy to the store or throw it away.

☐ If you find a game or toy particularly offensive, express your views in a strong letter to the manufacturer, the management of the television station that carries related commercials, and the producers of the show during which the commercial appears. Take a similar stand against inappropriate or violent music, movies, and TV programs by targeting the advertisers, producers, distributors, and theater management.

☐ Make it a point to also express *positive* sentiments to producers and manufacturers. A strong show of public appreciation increases a product's value, and can help keep creative, entertaining, and educational material on television, in the movies, and on the market.

☐ Research, organize, and supply alternative entertainment for your child. Depending on your child's age and tastes, you can spark his interest in reading (see Entry 49 on page 257), form a play group, enroll him in a sport or club, seek out or teach your own crafts class, or get him started on a new and exciting hobby.

☐ Raise the topic of nonviolent children's entertainment at meetings of civic, church or temple, parents', and school groups. Inform the members of the 1990 Children's Television Act, which states that TV stations must offer full-length programming geared toward the cognitive, social, emotional, and educational needs of children in order to retain their licenses. Enlist the support and suggestions of other local parents.

It's important to explain to your child that your dislike of certain forms of entertainment stems not from a desire to wield control, but from the knowledge that children learn a great deal—both good and bad—from the forms of recreation they pursue. Try to spell out the subtle difference between parental guidance and censorship. Involving your child in entertainment selection from an early age can be helpful, as can showing your child that you apply the same high standards when making your own entertainment choices. Above all, let your child know of your loving concern, as well as your intention of remaining firm in your rules about how he spends his free time. And as your child grows older, encourage him to exercise similar control when selecting entertainment for himself. Time spent enjoying interesting, informative, and nonviolent pastimes can serve to broaden your child's interests, instill good values, and spark his imagination—all in the name of fun!

Resources

The organizations listed below welcome comments about children's programming, toys, and games, as well as advertising aimed at the youth market. This list also includes good sources of information and ideas about worthwhile entertainment for children.

ORGANIZATIONS

Action for Children's Television
20 University Road
Cambridge, MA 02138
(617) 876–6620

This group seeks to improve the content and quality of television programs for children through stronger regulations and increased public awareness.

Americans for Responsible Television
PO Box 627
Bloomfield Hills, MI 48303
(313) 646–4248

This nonprofit organization encourages the responsible use of public airwaves through work with advertisers, networks, media executives, legislators, and educational and health professionals.

Federal Communications
Commission (FCC)
Media Services Bureau
1919 M Street NW
Washington, DC 20554
(202) 632–7000
(202) 632–6999 *For the Hearing Impaired*

This organization regulates interstate and foreign communications by radio, television, wire, satellite, and cable to protect public interests.

National Advertising Review
Board
845 Third Avenue
New York, NY 10022
(212) 832–1320

This organization strives to maintain standards in national advertising through self-regulation and constructive responses to public complaints.

Parents Music Resource Center
1500 Arlington Boulevard
Arlington, VA 22209
(703) 527–9466

This organization supports the use of warning labels on audiocassettes and compact discs as a means of protecting young consumers from musical lyrics that may be offensive or inappropriate.

Toy Manufacturers of America
200 Fifth Avenue, Suite 740
New York, NY 10010
(212) 675–1141
(800) 851–9955

This alliance of toy manufacturers strives to improve the quality and safety of children's playthings by monitoring consumer complaints and raising standards throughout the industry.

MAIL-ORDER COMPANIES

Childcraft
PO Box 29149
Mission, KS 66201–9149
(800) 631–5657

The Childcraft catalog features age-appropriate, entertaining toys that build skills in different learning areas.

Constructive Playthings
1227 East 119th Street
Grandview, MO 64030
(800) 832–0572
(816) 661–5900 *In Kansas City*

Through its catalog and showrooms, this company offers child-safe educational toys and games both to schools and the general public.

Toys to Grow On
2695 E. Dominguez Street
PO Box 17
Long Beach, CA 90801
(800) 542–8338
(310) 603–8890 *In Los Angeles*

This catalog company features high-quality books and playthings designed to spark creativity and to appeal to the imagination of children of all ages.

BOOKS

Kelly, Michael R. *A Parent's Guide to Television: Making the Most of It.* New York: John Wiley and Sons, 1982.

Miedzian, Myriam. *Boys Will Be Boys: Breaking the Link Between Masculinity and Violence.* New York: Doubleday, 1991.

Minton, Lynn. *Movie Guide for Puzzled Parents.* New York: Delacorte Press, 1984.

Palmer, Edward L. *Television and America's Children: A Crisis of Neglect.* New York: Oxford University Press, 1988.

Tuchscherer, Pamela. *TV Interactive Toys: The New High Tech Threat to Children.* Bend, OR: Pinnaroo Publishing, 1988.

Winn, Marie. *The Plug-In Drug.* New York: Viking, 1985.

PERIODICALS

Consumers Union of U.S. *Zillions: Consumer Reports for Kids.* Yonkers, NY: Consumers Union of U.S.

Parents' Choice Foundation. *Parents' Choice.* Newton, MA: Parents' Choice Foundation.

9

TEACH HEALTHY VALUES AND UNIVERSAL MORALS

During childhood, appropriate behavior occurs more by design than by accident. It is important for your child to learn to recognize the difference between right and wrong, and to understand that her behavior will often affect many other people. Imparting this knowledge to your child is a labor of love—a job that should not be left to schools or religious institutions and, in fact, builds strong family bonds and can help to keep lines of communication open.

What exactly is moral behavior? Perhaps it is easiest to define this term by looking at its root: empathy. Empathy—sometimes described as "walking a mile in another person's shoes"—enables a person to understand another's feelings and situation, and therefore makes it more likely that she will treat that person with compassion. From empathy springs all other tools of character: justice, cooperation, self-respect, respect for others, tolerance, gratitude, honesty, wisdom, courage, forgiveness, and responsibility. These traits are illustrated in the Empathy Wheel on page 37.

Instilling healthy values and universal morals in your child requires some creativity. However, you can teach these values by pointing out instances of moral behavior in everyday life, by setting examples, and, at times, by *inventing* opportunities for the learning and practice of empathy. The following suggestions may be helpful.

☐ Encourage your child to give a possession that she values to someone who needs it more. Or help her use her own money to buy something special for someone else. Let her experience the joy of giving.

☐ Set examples of generosity. Let your child see you helping others, making and giving gifts, paying compliments, and sharing

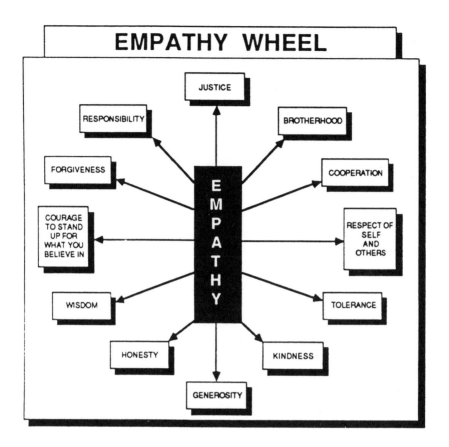

EMPATHY WHEEL

JUSTICE

RESPONSIBILITY

BROTHERHOOD

FORGIVENESS

COOPERATION

COURAGE TO STAND UP FOR WHAT YOU BELIEVE IN

EMPATHY

RESPECT OF SELF AND OTHERS

WISDOM

TOLERANCE

HONESTY

KINDNESS

GENEROSITY

your time with others. Make it a family tradition to donate time or money to charity.

☐ Practice feeling and *expressing* a sense of gratitude. By counting your blessings from time to time, you'll make your youngster aware that she is more fortunate than many.

☐ Teach your child the helping habit. Encourage her involvement with younger siblings, neighbors, the physically challenged, the elderly, and the poor. Also consider giving your child the responsibility of caring for a pet.

☐ Give your child someone to look up to. Make her aware of the admirable character of a relative, teacher, famous citizen, professional athlete, or television hero. Let your child know who your own role models are, and why. Talk about the qualities possessed by the person you admire, as well as what he or she gives to others through example.

☐ Make worship a part of your daily routine, and involve your family in church or temple activities such as fundraising and service projects. This can help to promote and reinforce a commitment to moral values that may become a lifetime habit for your youngster.

☐ Encourage your child to join a youth organization—4-H or Girl Scouts, for instance—that promotes moral behavior and fosters involvement in community service. There is much your youngster can learn from working with her peers for the good of others.

☐ Be selective about letting your child watch television and movies that glorify undesirable characters. Explain any story elements that might be misinterpreted, and talk about the harmful effects certain actions could have on others. (See Entry 8 on page 30 for more information on choosing entertainment.)

☐ Share books, TV shows, and movies about people of courage, compassion, and principle. You might wish to start with tales of people who left their mark on history, like Martin Luther King or Eleanor Roosevelt. Classics that send a positive message, like *Huckleberry Finn* or *Little House on the Prairie,* can also be helpful. (Try *The Last Leaf* or *Twelve Angry Men* for your older child.) A children's librarian should be able to suggest some other titles well suited to your child's age and interests.

☐ Hold your child accountable for her actions. Help her to understand the cause-and-effect relationship between what she says and does and the feelings of others.

☐ Encourage the development of your child's self-esteem based on doing right, instead of feeling good. Praise her for kindness.

☐ Acknowledge that sticking to your values may prove difficult and can sometimes lead to feeling shut out or doing without something you want. Teach your child to minimize any social consequences by avoiding tattletale or self-righteous behavior.

A young child is often motivated to do good deeds simply to win the favor of the adults around her. An older child's actions, however, are often based on her own ideas of right and wrong, accountability and consequences. The work of developing your youngster's values and morals will take place throughout her childhood through your teaching, your examples, and the ideals and principles by which your family lives. Sometimes, your task may seem difficult, but its rewards will be plentiful as you watch your child grow into a caring and compassionate human being.

Resources

The following are excellent sources of information on instilling healthy values in your child.

ORGANIZATIONS

American Institute for Character
  Education
Dimension 11 Building, Suite 220
8918 Tesoro Drive
San Antonio, TX 78217
(512) 829–1727

This organization provides materials designed to help teachers build character and cultivate self-esteem and self-determination of goals and values in students.

B'nai B'rith Youth Organization
1640 Rhode Island Avenue NW
Washington, DC 20036
(202) 857–6633

This organization promotes the education and civic involvement of Jewish youth; sponsors committees on leadership training, education, recreation, and community service; maintains a library; and offers youth-oriented publications.

Boy Scouts of America
1325 Walnut Hill Lane
PO Box 152079
Irving, TX 75015
(214) 580–2000

This organization operates educational programs and local groups designed to build character, teach the value of com-

munity service, and promote civic involvement.

Boys Club of America
771 First Avenue
New York, NY 10017
(212) 351–5900

This group of urban clubs promotes activities that foster social, educational, vocational, and character development in boys.

Campfire, Inc.
4601 Madison Avenue
Kansas City, MO 64112
(816) 756–1950

This group, which provides educational opportunities for boys and girls up to twenty-one years of age, focuses on building positive self-image and encouraging responsibility and creative thinking.

Century III Foundation
PO Box 3762
Oak Brook, IL 60522
(312) 852–7255

This educational foundation offers a variety of teaching materials about morals, values, and public policy.

Girl Scouts of America
830 Third Avenue at 51st Street
New York, NY 10022
(212) 940–7500

*This organization is designed to pro-
mote character development and to encourage and teach girls to become self-
sufficient and to serve the communities
in which they live.*

National Association of Girls'
  Clubs
5808 16th Street NW
Washington, DC 20011
(202) 726–2044

*This association, designed to serve the
needs of African American girls between
the ages of six and eighteen, promotes
moral, mental, and social development.*

National 4-H Council
7100 Connecticut Avenue
Chevy Chase, MD 20815
(301) 961–2800

*This organization, which provides edu-
cational materials concerning citizen-
ship and leadership training for young
people, has branches in most cities.*

Society of Christian Ethics
Department of Religious Studies
University of Tennessee
Knoxville, TN 37996
(615) 974–2466

*This organization promotes Christian
social ethics and conducts discussions*

*and debates concerning the importance
of ethics in society.*

YMCA (Young Men's Christian
  Association)
101 North Wacker Drive
Chicago, IL 60606–7386
(312) 269–1126
(800) 872–9622

*This organization puts moral princi-
ples into action through programs that
aim to develop healthy bodies, healthy
minds, and healthy spirits in all members.*

YM/YWHA (Young Men's/Young
  Women's Hebrew Association)
1395 Lexington Avenue
New York, NY 10128
(212) 427–6000

*This association offers a wide variety of
programs designed to promote physical
and emotional fitness and to encourage
the growth of interfaith friendships
within the community.*

YWCA (Young Women's Christian
  Association)
726 Broadway
New York, NY 10003
(212) 614–2700

*This association, composed of women
and girls of diverse cultures and beliefs,
promotes leadership and service to improve the quality of life within communities.*

BOOKS

Batten, Joe D. *Tough-Minded Parenting.* Nashville: Broadman Press, 1991.

Carroll, David. *Spiritual Parenting.* New York: Paragon House Publishers, 1990.

Eyre, Linda, and Richard Eyre. *Teaching Children Responsibility.* New York: Ballantine Books, 1986.

Eyre, Linda, and Richard Eyre. *Teaching Children Sensitivity.* New York: Ballantine Books, 1987.

Lickona, Thomas. *Raising Good Children.* New York: Bantam Books, 1983.

Popkin, Michael. *Active Parenting: Teaching Cooperation, Courage, and Responsibility.* San Francisco: Harper and Row, 1987.

Schulman, Michael. *Bringing Up a Moral Child: A New Approach for Teaching Your Child.* Reading, MA: Addison-Wesley Publishing, 1985.

Become a Youth Leader

Peer friendships can bring many positive elements to the life of a child—opportunities to practice social skills, employ the imagination, exercise the body, and learn to evaluate character. But another type of friend can also make a difference in a child's attitudes, interests, and behavior: an adult friend, or a youth leader.

It's important for a child to have adult friends. Such relationships enable a child to view adults as something other than authority figures, thus promoting trust and encouraging her to share emotional burdens that may be too difficult to shoulder alone, but too embarrassing to share with friends. As a youth leader, you can act as a positive role model, offer emotional support when needed, and teach by example about the responsibilities and give-and-take of friendship. In addition, you can use your leadership status to impart whatever special gift you possess, be it your love of basketball, your artistic ability, your interest in nature, or just a big heart and an understanding ear.

When hearing the phrase "youth leader," you may at first envision an inner-city program that aims to keep underprivileged children from going astray. But the truth is that youth leadership is sorely needed by many children from all walks of life—particularly in today's society, where heroes and parental free time are often in short supply. Children from single-parent families or troubled home lives, for example, have much to gain from contact with another caring adult.

What of your relationship with your own child when you volunteer a block of time to leading others? Surprisingly, it may improve. Chances are, your child will enjoy your participation in her scout troop, say, for it will allow for extra time spent together in enjoyable activities. No doubt, you'll be pleased by the opportunity to learn more about your child's social skills, as well as her interests and her friends. You'll also gain insight into the fads and trends among your child's age-mates, which may help you better understand your youngster's attitudes and behavior. Finally, your child will almost certainly appreciate the unique social benefits that come from having a parent who is held in high esteem by those whose opinions matter a great deal—other children.

Resources

Listed below are several organizations that offer opportunities to serve today's children as a youth leader. The list on pages 39–40 includes other groups that serve children and welcome parent participation.

ORGANIZATIONS

American Youth Foundation
1315 Ann Avenue
St. Louis, MO 63104
(314) 772–8626

This organization seeks to help children achieve their personal best, live balanced lives, and serve others. The foundation also conducts research on leadership development in youth.

Big Brothers/Big Sisters of America
230 North 43rd Street
Philadelphia, PA 19107
(215) 567–7000

This organization provides children with a volunteer adult friend who offers encouragement, guidance, understanding, and acceptance.

Special Olympics International
Suite 500
1350 New York Avenue NW
Washington, DC 20005
(202) 625–3630

This group provides opportunities for the physical, social, and psychological development of disabled children and adults through participation in sporting events.

10

PROTECT YOUR CHILD FROM PARENTAL ABDUCTION

It might seem strange or cruel for a mother or father to deny a child access to his other parent. Yet thousands of the more than 350,000 children reported missing every year have been taken or concealed by a parent or by someone acting on that parent's behalf. And although love or desperation may be the abducting parent's primary motive, the child still pays dearly for this experience. Fortunately, there is a great deal you can do to reduce the possibility of your child ever becoming a parental-kidnapping victim, and to bring him home quickly and safely if, by chance, he is abducted.

What would drive a parent to kidnap his or her own child? All too often, a desire for revenge against a former spouse figures largely in the plans of an abducting parent. Long-term hostility, a sense of betrayal, or a particularly bitter divorce can certainly take its toll on a parent's resolve to be civil and fair, and cause him or her to act rashly or out of spite. Sometimes, too, child protection is the motivating factor in an abduction. A noncustodial parent may believe that a child is being abused, ignored, or otherwise harmed in his current environment. A custodial parent may be similarly suspicious of a child's well-being during visitations with the noncustodial parent. Sometimes, a parent may react with outrage to the custodial parent's noncompliance with visitation rights, and feel that abduction is the only way to regain control of the situation. And, finally, a parent may simply be so distraught over having to surrender a precious child to a former spouse, and feel so certain that he or she is the better parent, that a desperate act like kidnapping seems like the only option.

Regardless of a person's motives, and despite the fact that many children cooperate willingly—even happily—with abduction plans, parental kidnapping can inflict emotional scars that last a lifetime. The consequences to a child of losing his home, his possessions, and, quite often, his identity; of living life "on the run"; and of coming to terms with the reason for the abduction can be devastating. And it is for this reason that law enforcement authorities, the legal community, and child-rearing experts alike urge parents *not* to take the law into their own hands in this manner.

IF YOU ARE CONSIDERING PARENTAL ABDUCTION

If you have ever considered abducting your child, even for the sake of his safety and well-being, it's important to realize that most states consider this act a felony—regardless of the circumstances. More important, think about the trauma that abduction would cause your child. In many cases, the long-term effects of parental kidnapping are just as damaging as a child's initial environment. Instead of fleeing, put your energy into researching and investigating every possible legal means of eliminating your problem. The support organizations listed on page 48 can furnish you with eye-opening literature, as well as valuable advice and assistance. You might consider a mediation program, such as the one sponsored by Child Find of America, Inc., as a way of resolving disputes with your former spouse. And, finally, you can arrange for counseling—for yourself and for all willing family members—as a means of coping with your fear, frustration, anger, or pain.

IF YOU FEAR PARENTAL ABDUCTION

But what if you have reason to worry that, at some point, your former spouse might turn to kidnapping? Fortunately, there are a number of steps you can take to prevent parental abduction.

☐ Try to obtain temporary or permanent legal custody of your child. At the very least, this will minimize the amount of time your child will be alone with his other parent.

☐ Give a certified copy of your custody order to the administrators of your child's school, and be sure to inform all personnel exactly who is to be allowed to escort your child from the building.

☐ Keep on hand vital information about your former partner and his or her family, such as bank records, social security numbers, driver's license numbers, and credit card information. This data can help track the abducting parent and can offer clues as to whether another family member is helping to hide your child.

☐ Avoid interfering with your former spouse's visitation rights or alienating your former in-laws. A civil relationship decreases the chances of kidnapping and, in the case of in-laws, might help you secure valuable information concerning your child's whereabouts in the event that he is ever taken from you.

☐ Make certain that your local police department has copies of any restraining orders that are in effect.

☐ If parental abduction has been threatened or attempted in the past, be certain that another party is present during all of your child's visits with his other parent. An attorney can help you make the necessary arrangements.

☐ Keep on hand your child's fingerprints (many schools and law enforcement agencies provide this service), as well as several recent photographs. Inform the Passport Office in writing that your child may not be taken out of the country without your written permission.

☐ Most important, discuss the kidnapping issue with your child. His age will help you decide how much information is appropriate, of course, but even a preschooler can be warned to disbelieve stories of your sudden death or abandonment, and can learn to dial 911—or even your own number, including the area code—for help.

IF YOUR CHILD IS ABDUCTED

What if the worst comes to pass? Sometimes, in spite of a parent's best efforts, a child is kidnapped by the other parent. Luckily, there is much you can do to see that your child is returned safely to your side. The following steps will help.

☐ Request a felony warrant for the abductor. To accomplish this, ask your local police or your state's missing children's clearinghouse what documentation is needed. (The police can tell you if a clearinghouse exists in your area.) Take these documents to your local police station and file a missing persons report, noting the name, badge number, and telephone number of the desk officer. Secure a copy of the report for yourself.

☐ Ask the desk officer to enter the necessary data in the National Crime Information Center (NCIC) Missing Persons File. Wait twenty-four hours, and check to see whether this has been done by asking your police department for either a copy of the print-out or the NIC number assigned to your child's case by the NCIC. If information on your child has not been entered, contact a missing children's organization (see page 48) or your local FBI office for assistance. After another twenty-four hours have passed, check again.

☐ If you suspect that your child has been taken to another state, register your custody order, any restraining orders, and your child's photograph and fingerprint records with the police in that state. If you have evidence that your child is living in another state—through reported sightings, bank or credit card transaction records, or phone or mail contact with your former spouse—get in touch with your local FBI office and request issuance of an Unlawful Flight to Avoid Prosecution (UFAP) warrant.

☐ Contact your child's school and have your child's health and academic records flagged. This way, school personnel will know to contact the police if they receive a request to transfer your child's school records.

☐ If you suspect that someone you know has been in contact with the abductor, request that the police issue search warrants for phone records, as well as a mail cover, which will enable the post office to report on correspondence sent to that individual.

☐ If the abducting parent was or is in the military, contact the appropriate Worldwide Locator Service listed below for help in finding the parent.

United States Army
Army Worldwide Locator Service
Fort Benjamin Harrison, IN
  46249–5301
(317) 542–4211

United States Air Force
Headquarters, AFMPC/BPMD 003
Attn: Worldwide Locator Service
Randolph AFB, TX 78150–6601
(512) 652–5774

United States Navy
Naval Military Personnel
  Command 036CC
Navy Locator Service
Washington, DC 20370
(202) 694–3155

United States Coast Guard
Commandant, U.S. Coast Guard
Coast Guard Locator Service
2100 2nd Street SW
Washington, DC 20593
(202) 267–1615 *Regarding Enlisted*
  Personnel
(202) 267–1667 *Regarding Officers*

United States Marine Corps
Commandant of the Marine Corps
Headquarters, Marine Corps
Code MMRB-10
Attn: Worldwide Locator Services
Washington, DC 20380–0001
(202) 694–1624
(202) 694–1861
(202) 694–1610
(202) 694–1913
(202) 694–2380

☐ Contact the Federal Parent Locator Service (FPLS), a computerized national location network operated by the Office of Child Support Enforcement in the U.S. Department of Health and Human Services. The law does not permit parents to initiate FPLS inquiries on their own behalf. However, the FBI, the police, a state judge, or your attorney can help you use this service.

Parental kidnapping has grave legal consequences for the abducting parent, and exacts an even greater toll on the child and on the parent from whom he was taken. If you are thinking of fleeing with your child, try all legal means to remedy your situation. If it is your child's other parent who poses the threat of abduction, become as knowledgeable as you can about your personal rights and about the agencies that exist to help you protect or recover your youngster. Regardless of the circumstances, you'll serve your child best by offering him as much stability as possible, and by making his happiness and safety your number-one goal.

Resources

The following organizations can provide information and support to help you avoid a parental abduction or to locate a child who has been kidnapped by a parent.

ORGANIZATIONS

Child Find of America, Inc.
PO Box 277
New Paltz, NY 12561–9277
(800) A–WAY–OUT *For Mediation*
(800) I–AM–LOST *National Hotline*

This organization locates missing children in fifty states and seven foreign countries, helping parents who have exhausted the resources of law enforcement agencies.

Find the Children
11811 West Olympic Boulevard
Los Angeles, CA 90064
(213) 477–6721

This agency acts to prevent child abduction and facilitate the recovery of missing children. It also offers long-term therapy for recovered children.

The National Center for Missing
   and Exploited Children
2101 Wilson Boulevard, Suite 550
Arlington, VA 22201
(703) 235–3900 *National Hotline*
(800) 826–7653 *For the Hearing
   Impaired*

This missing children's clearinghouse is the largest in the United States and works directly with the Justice Department. Services include information and referrals to local organizations.

Roberta Jo Society, Inc.
329 E. Main Street
PO Box 916
Circleville, OH 43113
(614) 474–5020

This organization educates the public about the plight of missing children and works to prevent kidnappings.

Vanished Children's Alliance
1407 Parkmoor Avenue, Suite 200
San Jose, CA 95126
(408) 971–4822
(800) VANISHED *National Sighting
   Line*

This group works to prevent kidnappings and recover missing children.

In Canada:

Canadian Centre for Missing
   Children and Victims of Violence
Provincial Court House, Third Floor
1-A Sir Winston Churchill Square
Edmonton, AB T5J 0R2
(403) 422–4698

This organization works to locate missing children, and acts as a referral and information service.

BOOKS

Jance, Judith A. *Dial Zero for Help*. Edmonds, WA: Charles Franklin Press, 1985.

National Association for Missing Children, Inc. *My Child Is Not Missing: A Parent's Guide Book*. Plantation, FL: Child Safe Products, 1984.

11

BE CONSISTENT WITH DISCIPLINE

There is a world of difference between disciplining and punishing your child. Whereas punishment is "pay-back" for a wrongdoing, discipline involves setting well-defined limits and consistently shaping behavior so that your child will one day be able to discipline herself. In order to develop self-discipline, your child must be taught the difference between right and wrong, and learn to measure her behavior against generally accepted standards. The journey from parental discipline to self-discipline is often a difficult one, but you can make your child's trip smoother by being clear and consistent about what you expect from her, and by explaining that as she becomes better able to discipline herself, a world of new rights and privileges will be opened to her.

Of course, there are different schools of thought on the form that discipline should take. Some parents favor a firm spanking when a rule is broken; others believe in a hands-off approach to misdeeds. Some parents tend to indulge their child's willful side; others permit no deviation from rules and routines. And, of course, children themselves differ greatly in their need to please, their acceptance of limitations, and their desire to mimic their peers. Ultimately, the mode of discipline you use in your home becomes an extension of your personal parenting philosophy and your child's personality. Help is widely available if you are unsure about what behaviors are consistent with your child's age group, or if you need information on effective discipline techniques. The discipline issue is addressed in many of the books found in the child-care section of your library or local bookstore. Parenting magazines also feature helpful articles on discipline. And additional behavior-management ideas, as well as reassuring feedback from other parents, are available from parenting support groups. (See Entry 12 on page 53.)

Perhaps the most important question is this: Are your current disciplinary tactics consistent enough to enable your young child to anticipate the consequences of unacceptable behavior? Or, if your child is older, is she beginning to make proper choices even without your instruction or supervision? If so, your child is well on her way toward self-discipline. If not, it may be time for some changes.

How can you become more consistent about discipline? Perhaps the most important step you can take is to manage your anger and frustration appropriately. (See Entry 6 on page 22.) Responding to your child's infractions in a controlled, predictable manner will teach her far more than, say, lashing out today for a wrongdoing that you ignored—and, thus, seemed to accept—yesterday. In the same vein, it's important not to change your rules for your own convenience. For instance, if your child is not permitted to watch a popular television show, this rule should be enforced even when a project demands your undivided attention or guests are present. It's also important for the consequences of your child's misdeeds to be immediate and in some way related to the infraction. For example, banning your child from a Saturday outing because of Monday's wrongdoing will seem terribly unjust by the time the weekend rolls around. Your method of discipline may well prove most effective when you show respect for your child's opinions on the subject—no matter how offbeat or comical—while still making it clear that she must abide by house rules. If your child is old enough to understand, it's a good idea to include her in the formulation of rules and the setting of consequences at regular family meetings. Doing so can improve your child's awareness of the need for restrictions, clarify the connection between misdeeds and lost privileges, and help her assume responsibility for her actions.

When your child is able to anticipate your response to inappropriate behavior, she will be more likely to consider your adult perspective on right and wrong. Certainly, your child will go out into the world among peers, teachers, and, eventually, coworkers and bosses whose values vary greatly. But you can help her develop a conscience, a healthy work ethic, and an appreciation of appropriate behavior by setting consistent limits in a calm, predictable manner throughout her childhood. Becoming a more effective disciplinarian may also have hidden benefits: less tension, deeper understanding, and better communication between you and your child.

Resources

If you think that you need immediate assistance in the area of discipline, a family therapist, a parenting support group, or your local mental health center can help you find ongoing support. For additional information on the importance of consistent discipline, you can refer to the following sources.

ORGANIZATIONS

Center for the Study of Parent Involvement
John F. Kennedy University
370 Camino Pablo
Orinda, CA 94563
(415) 254–0110

This group provides consultation and information to bring parents together as decision makers and advocates for their children.

Nurturing Parenting Programs
c/o Family Development Resources, Inc.
3160 Pinebrook Road
Park City, UT 84060
(800) 688–5822

This organization provides a mail-order catalog of helpful parenting materials.

Parents Anonymous
Suite 316
520 South Lafayette Park Place
Los Angeles, CA 90057
(800) 421–0353

This network of parent-organized self-help groups is geared toward strengthening parenting skills and improving family relationships.

Toughlove, International
PO Box 1069
Doylestown, PA 18901
(215) 348–7090
(800) 333–1069

This parenting support organization assists families who are working through parent-child crises.

BOOKS

Adams, Daniel J. *The Child Influencers: Restoring the Lost Art of Parenting.* Cuyahoga Falls, OH: Home Team Press, 1990.

Canter, Lee. *Lee Canter's Assertive Discipline for Parents*. New York: Canter and Associates (distributed by Harper and Row), 1982.

Christophersen, Edward R. *Beyond Discipline: Parenting That Lasts a Lifetime*. Kansas City, MO: Westport Publishers, 1990.

Dobson, James. *Dare to Discipline*. Wheaton, IL: Tyndale House Publishers, 1970.

Dobson, James. *The Strong-Willed Child*. Wheaton, IL: Tyndale House Publishers, 1978.

Dreikurs, Rudolf. *Children: The Challenge*. New York: E.P. Dutton, 1987.

Evoy, John J. *Parents on Successful Parenting*. Kansas City, MO: Sheed and Ward, 1987.

Gordon, Thomas. *Discipline That Works*. New York: Plume, 1991.

Kersey, Katherine. *Don't Take It Out on Your Kids*. Reston, VA: Acropolis Books, 1991.

Moore, Dorothy, and Raymond S. Moore. *Home Built Discipline*. Nashville: Thomas Nelson, 1990.

Peters, Ruth A. *Who's in Charge? A Positive Parenting Approach to Disciplining Children*. Clearwater, FL: Lindsay Press, 1990.

Samalin, Nancy. *Love and Anger*. New York: Viking, 1991.

Schaefer, Charles. *Teach Your Child to Behave*. New York: Plume, 1991.

Singer, Elizabeth, and Yvette Zgonc. *Discipline*. Syracuse, NY: New Readers Press, 1990.

Varni, James. *Time-Out for Toddlers*. New York: Berkley Publishing Group, 1991.

Wyckoff, Jerry. *How to Discipline Your Six-to-Twelve-Year-Old—Without Losing Your Mind*. New York: Doubleday, 1991.

12

JOIN A PARENTING SUPPORT GROUP

If you sometimes feel that rearing your child is a seat-of-the-pants effort, you're probably right! After all, parenting skills are usually a potpourri of approaches taken from books, magazines, our own parents, and siblings and friends whom we've watched in action with their own children. And just as you adapt and practice some child-rearing techniques, you no doubt reject many others, sensing that they are somehow wrong for you and your child. In the end, even the best prepared, most motivated parents wind up doing most of their learning on the job. And, as you're well aware, this experience is frightening, challenging, frustrating, bewildering—*and* intensely rewarding—by turns. Fortunately, you can make a positive move toward removing the guesswork and isolation from your twenty-four-hour-a-day job by joining a parenting support group.

Support services for parents in crisis have existed for many years, but it was only during the last decade that the need for support of a more social nature was recognized. This is not to say that child-rearing problems are something new, of course. However, the previous generation of parents tended to downplay their own needs in favor of child-rearing duties, and were often able to seek advice from any number of nearby relatives. In contrast, many of today's parents make their careers and interests a high priority and are much harder pressed to find a willing, sympathetic ear into which they can voice confusion or pose questions. It is precisely this need for support and information that has caused parenting support groups to take hold and blossom.

Today's parenting support groups vary greatly in origin, focus, and size. But whether a group is church-sponsored, hospital-run, affiliated with a social agency, or initiated by a group of neighborhood parents, you will find it to be a gathering of mothers and fathers who wish to share experiences, gather ideas, vent frustrations, and discuss the issues that color their everyday lives with their children. Participants join out of a sense of loneliness, boredom, inadequacy, or stress, or simply because they want to hear new ideas or meet others like themselves.

Can an occasional support-group meeting really make you a better parent? Absolutely! First, you—and your child, if youngsters are invited—will be exposed to new people with whom you have a great deal in common. You're likely to come away from meetings with tried-and-true ideas on the handling of child-rearing problems. If you've felt isolated or overwhelmed by parenthood, you'll probably find that sharing your stories with parents in similar circumstances helps to eliminate these feelings and—even more important—diffuse much of the stress that may currently plague your family life. You may even be treated to guest speakers whose experience and advice will help you tackle some of the troublesome issues facing today's parents. Finally, participation in a support group is likely to win you renewed patience and a rekindled sense of purpose about your job as a parent.

If you feel the need for more immediate assistance with parenting problems, crisis nurseries and child-help hotlines can be contacted for support and advice. Remember that a call for help to one of these organizations is *not* an admission of failure, but a sign of strength. Their agents and volunteers are on the job to assist rather than judge you, and—barring an imminent threat to a child's safety—will not interfere in family life.

As you know, child rearing is never an easy task, and financial woes, marital or family problems, or unfamiliarity with effective parenting methods can sometimes make life seem particularly bleak. By joining a parenting support group and, when necessary, enlisting the help of other family services, you can take an important step towards meeting the ongoing challenges of parenthood. And with new skills and a fresh perspective, you're sure to find life with your child easier and far more rewarding.

Resources

To find out about parenting support groups in your area, you can contact your community mental-health center, library, church, hospital, school system, or local Parents Without Partners chapter. The following sources may also be helpful.

ORGANIZATIONS

Active Parenting
810 Franklin Court, Suite B
Marietta, GA 30067
(800) 825–0060

This organization offers parenting support materials and sponsors support groups nationwide.

Boys Town
Father Flanagan's Boys' Home
Boys Town, NE 68010
(402) 498–3200
(800) 448–3000 *National Hotline*
(800) 448–1833 *National Hotline for the Hearing Impaired*

This support program includes in-home crisis counseling and sponsors Boys Town communities nationwide with a focus on increasing family communication.

Childhelp USA
6463 Independence Avenue
Woodland Hills, CA 91367
(800) 4–A–CHILD *National Hotline*

This child-abuse-prevention agency offers treatment, referrals, family services, research data, public education, and a national toll-free child-abuse-prevention hotline number.

Homebuilders
Behavioral Sciences Institute
34004 9th Avenue South, Suite 8
Federal Way, WA 98003–6737
(206) 874–3630

This private nonprofit organization uses therapy and education to prevent family breakups.

National Association for Family-Based Services
PO Box 005
Riverdale, IL 60627
(319) 396–4829

This family-focused social-services program strives to preserve and support the family unit.

National Council on Family Relations
3989 Central Avenue NE, Suite 550
Minneapolis, MN 55421
(612) 781–9331

This nonprofit organization offers family education, social-services referrals, and information on family-related legislation being introduced at state and federal levels.

National Parent Aide Association
332 S. Michigan Avenue, Suite 950
Chicago, IL 60604–4357
(312) 663–3520

This agency offers assistance to those who wish to start parenting support groups.

Nurturing Parenting Programs
c/o Family Development
  Resources, Inc.
3160 Pinebrook Road
Park City, UT 84060
(800) 688–5822

This organization offers parenting support materials and programs aimed at stopping child-abuse trends and promoting a solid family structure.

Parents Anonymous
Suite 316
520 South Lafayette Park Place
Los Angeles, CA 90057
(800) 421–0353

This professionally organized parent-led self-help organization offers support groups and services to families in the community.

Parents United International
232 East Gish Road, First Floor
San Jose, CA 95112
(408) 453–7611

This agency offers a newsletter with topics of interest to parents, birth mothers, adoptees, and abuse survivors.

Toughlove, International
100 Mechanic Street
PO Box 1069
Doylestown, PA 18901
(215) 348–7090
(800) 333–1069

This parenting support organization promotes mediation as a solution to family crisis situations.

In Canada:

Parents Without Partners Inc.,
  Canada
PO Box 1218, Station A
Oshawa, ON L1J 5Z1

This organization serves as a support network for single parents and offers self-help assistance, speakers, discussion groups, and social activities.

BOOKS

Anderson, Joan Wester. *Teen Is a Four-Letter Word: A Survival Kit for Parents*. White Hall, VA: Betterway Publications, 1990.

Atlas, Stephen L. *Single Parenting: A Practical Resource Guide*. New York: Prentice Hall, 1981.

Dobson, James C. *Parenting Isn't for Cowards*. Irving, TX: Word Books, 1992.

York, Phyllis. *Toughlove Solutions*. New York: Doubleday, 1984.

13

KNOW THE SIGNS OF CHILD ABUSE

To most parents, the very term "child abuse" conjures up terrible images of beatings or sexual overtures inflicted upon a defenseless youngster. The jarring truth is that such behavior *does* take place. And there are other forms of abuse that are just as damaging and more easily hidden. In fact, child abuse as a whole is much more prevalent than most people realize. More than 2 million incidents of child abuse were reported in the United States during 1991 alone, and experts feel that many more cases go unreported. Because child-abuse laws vary from state to state, the type of protection available to children varies greatly. But by knowing the signs of child abuse, you, too, can play a role in protecting your child and other children from harm.

Child abuse is a far-reaching issue that can be broken down into four distinct categories: physical abuse, neglect, psychological maltreatment, and sexual abuse. The causes of child abuse are as varied as the methods used to inflict harm. A parent, teacher, or other authority figure may have little control over her temper, for example, and, therefore, habitually lash or strike out at children in her care. Or an adult might get perverse enjoyment or a sense of control from witnessing a child's mental anguish. Child abuse can also have roots in poverty, ignorance, self-absorption, emotional instability, or feelings of inferiority. But perhaps the most common contributing factor is the abuser's own childhood history of maltreatment. Overwhelmingly, adults who suffered pain at the hands of their own parents are in danger of displaying similarly abusive behavior toward the next generation of children. To help you become more knowledgeable about child abuse, each form of abuse is defined and explained below. Also listed are symptoms you should watch for in your child—symptoms that could signal that she has become a victim of some form of abuse.

PHYSICAL ABUSE

Physical abuse is any act of punishment that inflicts injury upon a child. This type of abuse can include slapping, hair-pulling, pinching, and shoving, as well as more violent behavior. Interestingly, rough horseplay can also be a form of abuse, since throwing or shaking a young child may cause permanent injury. (See Entry 5 on page 19.) A child who has been physically abused may show one or more of the following symptoms.

- Distinctively shaped cuts, bruises, or scars, suggesting that an object was used to inflict the injury.
- Bruises caused by pressure from the fingers, suggesting that the child was grabbed, choked, or shaken.
- Bite marks, burns, or injuries that are unlikely to have resulted from a fall—bruises on the genitals, say, or the back of the legs.
- Black eyes, swollen lips, or broken teeth.
- Repeated fractures or broken bones.
- Rope burns on the wrists or ankles.
- Swelling or bruises on the abdomen, which could be a sign of internal bleeding.

NEGLECT

A parent or guardian is guilty of neglect when he or she fails to meet a child's need for appropriate food, clothing, or shelter. The denial of a healthy, nurturing home environment is a less visible, but equally damaging, form of neglect. A child who is the victim of neglect may show the following signs.

- The "failure to thrive" syndrome, which can stem from the withholding of attention and affection. "Failure to thrive" babies often have their physical needs met, but, due to emotional deprivation, fail to develop according to schedule.

- Chronic hunger or malnourishment.
- Persistent fatigue or listlessness.
- Dental problems or chronic infections that go untreated.
- Dirty clothing and poor hygiene.

PSYCHOLOGICAL MALTREATMENT

This form of abuse encompasses any emotional harm inflicted upon a child. Psychological maltreatment can be a result of physical abuse, or can be deliberately inflicted by means of endless teasing, hurtful remarks, shaming, blaming, profanity, and other forms of verbal cruelty. The following behaviors are childhood signs of psychological maltreatment.

- Long bouts of unexplained, uncontrollable crying.
- A dull, deadened facial expression.
- Low self-esteem, characterized by an unwillingness to participate in an activity or frequent self-criticism—"I'm a dummy," or "I'm a bad girl."
- Excessive fearfulness.
- Repetition of abusive statements, such as, "Daddy wishes I'd never been born."
- Frequent bed wetting.
- Aggressive behavior toward oneself or others.
- Involvement with a gang as a way to feel powerful and "belong."

SEXUAL ABUSE

This form of abuse includes any act between an adult and a child that involves touching or other contact with the penis, anus, buttocks, breast, or vulva. Exhibitionism, lewd or suggestive behavior, and exploitation through sexually explicit performances, videos, or photographs are forms of sexual abuse, as well. A child who has been sexually abused may begin to ask an unusual number of questions about sexual behavior, initiate age-inappropriate sexual play, or act in a self-destructive, aggressive, or extremely childish manner. In addition, childhood sexual abuse may result in telltale physical evidence, such as the symptoms listed below.

- Swelling, bleeding, or infection in the vaginal or anal area.
- An inflamed, infected, or swollen penis or scrotum.
- Bite marks or scars in the genital area.
- Chronic genital itching, cystitis (bladder infection), abnormal vaginal or penile discharge, or a sexually transmitted disease.
- A sudden onset of bed wetting.
- Loss of appetite or other eating problems, including gagging.

WHAT YOU CAN DO

Can you help protect your youngster from child abuse? Certainly. To begin with, it is vital to know and recognize the symptoms of abuse described in this entry and to act on any suspicions you may have. It is also important to understand the danger of inappropriately handled parental frustration, which can easily escalate into physical or psychological abuse. (See Entry 6 on page 22 for further information.) If you or a family member sometimes acts inappropriately toward your child and you worry that the situation might worsen, family counseling or a support group may be helpful. And, naturally, you should never leave your child alone with someone whom you do not trust completely.

Despite your best efforts to protect your child, you may still suspect that she is in immediate danger of abuse, whether by your own hand or by that of a spouse, relative, teacher, baby-sitter, or friend. If so, you should sound a cry for help at once. It's reassuring to know that help is available to spare your youngster, or any youngster, from the physical and psychological effects of child abuse.

Resources

Your local police department, community mental health center, crisis nursery, or family physician can be an excellent source of information about child abuse. You may also wish to talk to the principal of your child's school or to someone at the Department of Health and Human Services or Child Protective Services, both of which are listed in the state government section of your telephone directory. If the situation seems like an emergency, do not hesitate to call the Childhelp USA hotline number provided below. Also listed are other organizations that can provide information on and assistance with child-abuse issues.

ORGANIZATIONS

American Association for
  Protecting Children
c/o The American Humane
  Association
63 Inverness Drive East
Englewood, CO 80112–5117
(303) 792–9900
(800) ZASK–AHA

This organization offers assistance, research and information, and educational programs to protective service agencies and the public.

C. Henry Kempe National Center
  for the Prevention and Treatment
  of Child Abuse and Neglect
1205 Oneida Street
Denver, CO 80220
(303) 321–3963

This agency provides training, research, and child-abuse treatment and prevention services on a clinical level.

Child Welfare League of America
440 First Street NW, Suite 310
Washington, DC 20001–2085
(202) 638–2952

This agency is dedicated to protecting children, and advocates and lobbies to improve child-abuse laws.

Childhelp USA
6463 Independence Avenue
Woodland Hills, CA 91367
(800) 4–A–CHILD *National Hotline*

This child-abuse-prevention organization offers treatment, referrals, family services, research data, public education, and a national toll-free hotline number.

Clearinghouse on Child Abuse
  and Neglect Information
PO Box 1182
Washington, DC 20013
(703) 821–2086
(800) FYI–3366

This national information center funds and leads various programs for the prevention of child abuse.

National Child Abuse Coalition
733 15th Street, NW
Washington, DC 20005
(202) 347–3666

This association includes volunteer and professional groups that lobby for children's rights on a federal level.

National Committee for
  Prevention of Child Abuse
Suite 1600
332 South Michigan Avenue
Chicago, IL 60604–4357
(312) 663–3520

This volunteer organization is dedicated to ending child abuse through the promotion of public awareness, education, research, and advocacy on a national level.

National Council on Child Abuse
  and Family Violence
Suite 300
1155 Connecticut Avenue, NW
Washington, DC 20036
(202) 429–6695
(800) 222–2000 *National Hotline*

This agency supports community-based prevention and treatment programs that provide assistance to children, women, the elderly, and families who are victims of abuse and violence. The council also collaborates with similar organizations to form an information network.

National Exchange Club Foundation
  for the Prevention of Child
  Abuse
3050 Central Avenue
Toledo, OH 43606–1700
(419) 535–3232

This parent-aide assistance program seeks to eliminate circumstances in which child abuse is possible by offering one-to-one support to troubled families.

National Victims Resource Center
c/o Office for Victims of Crime
PO Box 6000
Rockville, MD 20850
(301) 251–5500
(800) 627–6872

This organization serves as a national data base for information on crime victims.

In Canada:

Canadian Child Welfare
  Association
Suite 401
2211 Promenade Riverside Drive
Ottawa, ON K1H 7X5
(613) 738–0697

This organization publishes a national newsletter on child welfare issues.

Canadian Children's Foundation
Kids' Help Phone
60 Bloor Street West
Toronto, ON M4W 1A1
(416) 920–5437
(800) 668–6868

This organization provides a twenty-four-hour telephone counseling service for abused, neglected, or troubled children and youth.

Canadian Institute of Child Health
55 Parkdale Avenue
Ottawa, ON K1Y 1E5
(613) 238–8425

This organization provides child-abuse-prevention services for Canadian children and families.

Child Abuse and Education
  Productions Association
Suite 101
10070 King George Highway
Box 183
Surrey, BC V3T 4W8
(604) 581–5116

This group offers educational materials, and works to prevent child abuse in Canada.

Child Welfare League of America
  (Canadian Office)
33 Charles Street East
Toronto, ON M4Y 1R9
(416) 324–2180

This agency works to change Canadian laws that affect children and families, and offers a referral service to other Canadian children's organizations.

BOOKS

Ackerman, Robert J., and Susan E. Pickering. *Abused No More: Recovery for Women From Abusive or Co-Dependent Relationships.* Blue Ridge Summit, PA: TAB Books, 1989.

Berger, Gilda. *Violence and the Family.* New York: Franklin Watts, 1990.

Farmer, Steven. *Adult Children of Abusive Parents: A Healing Program for Those Who Have Been Physically, Sexually, or Emotionally Abused.* New York: Ballantine Books, 1990.

Friel, John C., and Linda D. *Adult Children: The Secrets of Dysfunctional Families.* Pompano Beach, FL: Health Communications, 1988.

Kellogg, Terry. *Broken Toys, Broken Dreams: Understanding and Healing Boundaries, Codependence, Compulsive Behaviors and Family Relationships.* Amherst, MA: BRAT Publications, 1990.

14

TALK TO YOUR CHILD ABOUT SEX

Many of today's parents grew up in homes where evasion about such things as bodily maturation and reproduction made sex seem a mysterious, embarrassing topic. Adolescent discomforts die hard, so it's altogether common to feel a lingering sense of unease or shame when discussing sex with your own child. Nevertheless, it is your responsibility to give your child accurate information about sex, while also promoting a healthy body image and respect for the opposite gender. Addressing the subjects of reproduction and sexuality in a manner appropriate to your child's ability to understand is the key to accomplishing these goals.

Why is it so important to talk to your child about sex? First, raising the topic will give you the opportunity to present your child with positive, factual information before he is exposed by friends or the media to a distorted version of the truth. A child who learns to view sex between committed partners as a normal, pleasurable, consensual activity may be far less susceptible than other children to the effects of suggestive advertising and erotic or pornographic magazines, as well as to the irresponsible or violent messages often conveyed by movies and TV shows. Discussing sexuality will also enable you to reinforce religious and family values regarding premarital and extramarital sex, the connection between sex and love, and the use of birth control. Early matter-of-fact discussions about sex will prepare your child for the onset of puberty, and can make bodily changes, self-exploration, menstruation, and nocturnal emissions more easily understood. And just as talking about sex can help your child feel comfortable about his maturing body, it will also provide you with ongoing opportunities to teach him about the need to respect others. Finally, on a practical note, accurate information about sex will help to protect your child against AIDS and other sexually transmitted diseases (STDs), unwanted pregnancy, and sexual exploitation through physical or emotional abuse and pornography. (For specific information on talking with your child about AIDS and protecting him from molestation, see Entry 23 on page 118 and Entry 32 on page 167.)

Many parents do not realize that sex education takes place in the home whether or not the topic is addressed. Your child absorbs a great deal about human sexuality just by watching and being cared for by you, and the message you send is determined as much by your behavior as by your words. For instance, a baby who receives lots of hugging, patting, and stroking also receives the idea that his body is good. The young child who is spared harsh reactions to his genital curiosity and who receives honest answers to every question is less likely to feel bodily shame and will communicate more freely about his emerging sexuality. And the adolescent whose maturation is treated with respect rather than teasing and who is well-versed in such subjects as hormones, sexual urges, homosexuality, pregnancy, and STDs is better prepared to greet life with a healthy body image and equally healthy, realistic information about sex.

Certainly, despite the best of intentions, many parents make mistakes where their child's sex education is concerned. Some parents avoid the subject or hedge on particular topics, either from embarrassment or from a misguided fear of sparking an unhealthy curiosity in their child. Other parents forego physical displays of affection between spouses for the same reason. But such actions do little but imply that sexual behavior is secret, dirty, or dangerous. Another common mistake is to minimize or avoid discussions about the less pleasant aspects of sex—the threat of AIDS, teen pregnancy, and molestation, for example—because of a desire to shelter a child from reality for as long as possible. However, such ignorance can prove dangerous to an unsuspecting child or a sexually active teen. Beware of going overboard, however, in an attempt to arm your young child against lewd behavior. Whereas it is wise to teach that immoral and criminal sexual behaviors exist and can be avoided, shifting all of the responsibility for your child's protection to his shoulders can arouse lifelong guilt if he ever experiences or witnesses something inappropriate or frightening. Treat the subject with balance, and stay personally vigilant where your child's well-being is concerned.

Parents sometimes make other mistakes, as well. Particularly hesitant parents may leave sex education in the hands of the church or school, in many cases denying their child all but the most basic and clinical information. Others grit their teeth and plow stiffly through a prepared speech, setting the stage for the child's own unease about human sexuality. In the end, it's much better to acknowledge your discomfort, explain its cause, and ask your child's indulgence as you investigate together the topics of reproduction and human sexual behavior.

As you can see, talking to your child about sex is an important, but often difficult, undertaking. Child psychologists agree that the single, momentous parent-child "talk" that was so common a generation ago should be replaced with ongoing age-appropriate information. Of course, children vary widely as far as their interest in and ability to absorb information about sex, but you need not worry about telling your child more than he can handle. You see, it's been shown that children tend to listen hard for specific answers to their questions about sex, and then shrug off further details. Nor should you be concerned if your child expresses little or no curiosity about sex. Quite often, you can still determine what he is ready to hear by watching his everyday behavior for stirrings of interest—his pointed stare at an expectant mother, perhaps, or his solemn study of a kissing scene on TV. By all means, take these opportunities to raise the subject of sex. Whether your child's reaction is one of fascination, boredom, or disbelief, you'll be conveying the idea that the topic is always open for discussion.

Of course, it's important for your child to have a fundamental understanding of human reproduction and physical maturation by the time he reaches puberty. It's also vital for your child to know enough about sexuality at any point during childhood to protect himself from molestation. Even a toddler can be taught that bodies are to be respected. The following suggestions can help you do and say the right things in your quest to give your child timely, accurate information about sex.

☐ Educate yourself about the processes of physical development and reproduction, and provide your child with illustrated books that he can read in private. (See the inset on page 68.)

☐ Use the correct terms for body parts. Renaming breasts and genitalia while calling other body parts by their proper names conveys an air of secrecy and embarrassment.

☐ Do not tease a child of any age about his body, and discourage him from teasing others. Make sure your child understands that different children mature at different rates, but that an outwardly maturing body does not change the person within.

☐ Do not shame your child for nudity or masturbation. Ignore such events in the very young, and calmly suggest that your school-aged child avoid self-exploration in front of others.

☐ Avoid emphasizing physical appearance. Consider your child's playthings, books, and media entertainment carefully to avoid sending the message that facial beauty or particular physical characteristics determine a person's worth. Instead, voice admiration for your child's inner qualities and gifts. (See Entry 7 on page 27 for details.)

☐ Avoid embarrassed reactions if your child sees you undressed or comments and asks questions about your mature body. Answer your child's questions matter-of-factly.

☐ Let your child witness plenty of nonsexual touching between the caring adults in his life.

☐ Promote same-sex friendships in your preadolescent child. Interacting with peers helps to prepare a youngster for the male-female relationships that are part of the teen-aged years.

☐ Prepare your child to deal with peer pressure to have sex. Strong self-esteem, involvement in group activities, appreciation of the complexity of intimate relationships, and some practiced responses can help your child avoid becoming sexually active before he's ready.

☐ Foster positive communication with your child. Raise sensitive topics like sex, ask open-ended questions, and let your child know that he should feel free to express uncertainty and anxiety about any subject.

☐ Counterbalance information about such harsh realities as STDs

Children's Books and Videos About Sex and Reproduction

Before discussing the different aspects of sexuality with their children, many parents find it helpful to refer to books such as those listed on page 70. There are also a number of children's books—and videos, as well—that address many of the questions commonly asked by today's youngsters through the use of simple explanations, drawings, diagrams, and charts. You might wish to review a book or video of this nature with your child, or to simply present it to your older child to study in private. In either case, he's likely to learn a great deal. Several helpful titles are listed below. For additional suggestions, you may wish to consult a children's librarian or your child's health teacher.

Books for Children

Blank, Joani. *A Kid's First Book About Sex.* Burlingame, CA: Yes Press, 1983.

Gardner-Loulan, JoAnn, Bonnie Lopez, and Marcia Quackenbush. *Period.* Volcano, CA: Volcano Press, 1991.

Mayle, Peter. *What's Happening to Me?* Secaucus, NJ: Carol Publishing Group, 1989.

Mayle, Peter. *Where Did I Come From?* Secaucus, NJ: Carol Publishing Group, 1990.

Miller, Jonathan. *The Facts of Life.* New York: Viking, 1984.

Pomeroy, Wardell B. *Boys and Sex.* New York: Laurel-Leaf Books, 1991.

Videos for Children

Am I Normal? New Day Films, 1979.

Sex, Drugs, and AIDS. O.D.N. Productions, 1987.

What Kids Want to Know About Sex and Growing Up. Pacific Heights, undated.

Where Did I Come From? LCA/Consolidated, 1986.

with interesting facts about heredity, multiple births, and advancements in the field of infertility.

☐ If your child poses a question that you cannot answer, admit your ignorance, and offer to track down the information or to research the subject with him.

☐ Address anything your child might witness that is related to sexuality. You'll be better able to satisfy his curiosity about sex if you acknowledge such things as a friend's opposite-sex infant or a pair of kissing teen-agers.

☐ Promote respect for the opposite sex by voicing your feelings about exploitative magazines, wolf-whistles, and the like.

☐ Educate your child about birth control. Stress the concept that responsibility must go hand in hand with sexual activity.

☐ Present abstinence and celibacy as viable options to adolescent sexual activity. Remind your child that 50 percent of teens are *not* sexually active, and that the currently widespread acceptance of casual sex isn't necessarily a positive or healthy trend.

☐ If you cannot overcome your discomfort about discussing sex with your child, make sure he has a teacher, adult friend, or counselor in whom he can confide and from whom he will receive accurate answers to his questions. You might also consider family counseling to open up the lines of communication.

On the average, today's children reach puberty a full year and a half earlier than did the children of a century ago. The 10 percent of sexually active fifteen-year-olds identified in the 1960s has grown to 50 percent, and "dating" in one form or another is now commonplace among grade schoolers. In light of this information, your child needs the best possible defense against sexually transmitted diseases, sexual exploitation, and unwanted pregnancy. You can steer him in the right direction by providing accurate, age-appropriate information about sex, and by creating an atmosphere in which he feels free to ask questions, voice concerns, and seek guidance as needed.

Resources

You can get additional information about discussing sex with your child from your family doctor, your house of worship, your community mental health center, and the books listed below.

BOOKS

Acker, Loren E. *AIDS-Proofing Your Kids: A Step-by-Step Guide.* Hillsboro, OR: Beyond Words Publishing, 1992.

Benson, Michael D. *Coping With Birth Control.* New York: Rosen Publishing Group, 1988.

Bernards, Neal, and Lynn Hall. *Teenage Sexuality: Opposing Viewpoints.* St. Paul, MN: Greenhaven Press, 1988.

Brown, Gabrielle. *The New Celibacy: A Journey to Love, Intimacy, and Good Health in a New Age.* New York: McGraw Hill, 1989.

Cassell, Carol. *Straight From the Heart: How to Talk to Your Teenagers About Love and Sex.* New York: Simon and Schuster, 1987.

Cobb, John B. *Matters of Life and Death.* Louisville, KY: Westminster/John Knox Press, 1991.

De Parrie, Paul. *Romanced to Death: The Sexual Seduction of American Culture.* Brentwood, TN: Wolgemuth and Hyatt Publishers, 1990.

Gordon, Sol, and Judith Gordon. *Raising a Child Conservatively in a Sexually Permissive World.* New York: Simon and Schuster, 1989.

Hughes, Tracy. *Everything You Need to Know About Teen Pregnancy.* New York: Rosen Publishing Group, 1988.

Johnson, Eric W. *Love and Sex and Growing Up.* New York: Bantam Books, 1990.

Nieder, John. *What You Need to Tell Your Child About Sex.* Nashville: Thomas Nelson, 1991.

Rosenberg, Ellen. *Ellen Rosenberg's Growing Up Feeling Good.* New York: Puffin Books, 1987.

Tengbom, Mildred. *Talking Together About Love and Sexuality.* Minneapolis: Bethany House Publishers, 1985.

15

RECOGNIZE THE SIGNS
OF AN EATING DISORDER

It may be hard for you to think of food as anything other than a source of nourishment. For the millions of young people who suffer from eating disorders, however, the issue of eating—or not eating—is stressful and emotion-charged. Adolescent and twenty- to thirty-year-old females are particularly at risk of developing an eating disorder, though males can be affected, as well.

In the past, it was quite common for a teen or young adult to spend years battling an eating disorder before getting help. Today, however, information about these conditions is widely available. This fact, combined with the willingness of high-profile sufferers to share their experiences, has made the general public more knowledgeable about and more understanding of eating disorders. In the best of circumstances, you, as a parent, will foster a healthy attitude toward food in your child right from the start. But it's also important to educate yourself about the dynamics, symptoms, and treatment of eating disorders, in case your child develops a problem with food. You see, with your encouragement—and professional assistance, when needed—most eating disorders can be successfully overcome.

Just what might cause an eating disorder to develop? In many instances, the affected child or young adult has a history of underlying emotional struggles, such as an intense need for approval or a lifetime habit of repressing anger and frustration. Family strife or experience with any form of abuse can also be a contributing factor. Or a strong preoccupation with fashion and appearance, on the part of either a child's family or her friends, can instill a poor or distorted body image, as can social and media-based pressures to be thin. A child's resulting desire to improve her looks can become an obsession and a source of tremendous stress and confusion. Depending on the circumstances, you see, food can easily become an enemy or a source of comfort, and a child's eating behavior may reflect this distorted view of food. The following sections provide a closer look at the nature and symptoms of three all-too-common eating disorders.

A LOOK AT COMMON EATING DISORDERS

Anorexia Nervosa

This disorder, which most often affects female adolescents, is characterized by self-starvation and excessive weight loss. Often, an anorexic exhibits perfectionist tendencies, and suffers damage to her self-esteem each time she cannot live up to her own very high standards. Victims of anorexia nervosa also have an unrealistic body image that tends to become more distorted over time. In fact, they often envision themselves as "fat" even after dramatic weight loss. A child's prolonged refusal of food can lead to damage to or breakdown of her various body systems. As a parent, you have cause for concern if your child insists on keeping her weight below a healthy level, and begins to turn toward excessive exercise and away from food as a means of doing so. Full-blown anorexia nervosa is a strong possibility if your child exhibits some of these symptoms:

- Erratic and inexplicable mood swings.
- An overwhelming fear of gaining weight.
- A loss of 15 percent of her body weight.
- The skipping of three consecutive menstrual periods.

Bulimia Nervosa

This condition, most commonly found in twenty- to thirty-year-old women, is characterized by a secret cycle of overeating followed by purging or fasting to rid the body of consumed calories. Unlike the anorexic child, a bulimic turns *toward* food as a way of coping with low self-esteem, anxiety, anger, or depression; yet, she feels out of control during each food binge and remains obsessed with her weight and physical appearance. Naturally, not every child who diets or exercises is in danger of becoming bulimic. However, if your child seems to be consumed by these activities, or if she is overly anxious and depressed or involved with drugs or alcohol, she may eventually fall victim to this eating disorder. Already-existing bulimia nervosa can cause a child to exhibit some of the following symptoms:

- Suicidal feelings.
- Signs of dehydration, such as headaches, infrequent urination, mouth dryness, or sleepiness.
- Habitual eating binges.
- Forced vomiting, fasting, or the use of laxatives, diet pills, or diuretics after eating.
- A deterioration of the tooth enamel and scarring of the fingers due to stomach acids from forced vomiting.

Compulsive Overeating

This disorder is far more common than either anorexia or bulimia, and affects people of all ages. Typically, a compulsive overeater either eats almost constantly during her waking hours or gorges sporadically, alternating overeating episodes with fad diets or fasting. Food and eating are sources of comfort to the compulsive overeater; nevertheless, her poor body image and disgust at what she perceives to be a lack of self-control often lead to low self-esteem, fatigue, apathy, and irritability. Your child may be in danger of becoming a compulsive overeater if she is unhappy with her weight and shape, starts and abandons diets frequently, or feels that her interpersonal relationships are negatively affected by her size. The child who is already a compulsive overeater may exhibit some of the following symptoms:

- Nearly constant snacking that is unrelated to physical hunger.
- Frequent episodes of significant weight loss, followed by weight gain.
- Mood swings that correlate with episodes of overeating and dieting.
- Self-disgust or suicidal feelings.
- Social isolation through purposeful distancing from friends and family.

WHAT YOU CAN DO

You can eliminate much of the risk of your child's becoming anorexic, bulimic, or a compulsive overeater by treating food as a staple of life, rather than a reward or a source of pleasure. After all, "eating to live" is very different from "living to eat." If you instill in your child a healthy attitude toward food, she is unlikely to be overly concerned with its consumption or avoidance. From the very beginning, avoid overfeeding your child or pressuring her to eat. Encourage your child to recognize hunger signals so that she seeks food for nourishment rather than entertainment. Teach her to eat slowly and to stop eating when full, rather than when her plate is empty. And try to keep mealtimes pleasant as another means of placing food and eating in a positive light. (See Entry 16 on page 77 for additional information on the development of good eating habits.)

Your child's relationship with food notwithstanding, you should always bear in mind that eating disorders have an emotional component. It helps to be aware of—and to avoid—the family and social factors that can tip the scales in favor of an eating disorder. Naturally, you should teach your child that abuse of any sort—physical, emotional, or verbal—is not to be practiced or tolerated from others. Encouraging your child to freely express her feelings is also wise, as is making a family commitment to resolve conflicts in a healthy and timely way. And it pays not to overemphasize your child's appearance and achievements. You see, while her attributes and accomplishments are important, it's best to avoid giving your child the impression that attractiveness, good grades, or special abilities will increase her personal worth. Convince her that it's the inner self that is to be valued, instead. And, finally, it's important to tolerate growth and change among family members by keeping your expectations and rules flexible and open to discussion.

But how can a parent help a child who already shows signs of an eating disorder? Happily, there are several things you can do to help your child regain control of her life if her eating habits have become a problem. Knowing—and watching out for—the symptoms discussed earlier in this section is important, as is expressing your concern, support, and desire to help your child. It's also vital to consult your family physician, who will be able to tell you a great deal about the disorder's progression by examining your child. Naturally, a second opinion may be in order if your suspicion of an eating disorder's existence goes unconfirmed. A physician will also be able to provide medical and dietary guidance and refer you to a therapist who specializes in eating disorders. You see, it's vital that your child sort out and find healthier ways to cope with the underlying conflicts that brought about the problem in the first place. Often, it's the family system that needs a closer look. Naturally, you should avoid nagging, blaming, or shaming your child about eating or dieting since, at present, she has little control over her condition. Negative comments will only do more damage to her self-esteem.

It's no wonder why so many children, teen-agers, and young women become consumed with their appearance. After all, Barbie dolls, television, movies, magazine advertisements, and the fashion industry all glorify the slender figure. However, by helping your child develop a healthy attitude toward food, by unconditionally appreciating her special qualities, and by knowing the signs of eating disorders, you can minimize the risk of your child becoming a victim and help her to successfully overcome any eating disorders she may already have.

Resources

If you would like additional information about eating disorders, the following sources may be helpful.

ORGANIZATIONS

Child and Adolescent Services
Golden Valley Health Center
4101 Gold Valley Road
Golden Valley, MN 55422
(612) 588–2771
(800) 321–2273

This medically-based facility treats children who suffer from eating disorders. Intervention programs are also available for adults.

National Association of
   Anorexia Nervosa and
   Associated Disorders
Box 7
Highland Park, IL 60035
(708) 831–3438

This organization provides support materials for people with eating disorders and their families.

Overeaters Anonymous
(800) 743–8703 *National Hotline*

This national group offers education and support to people who are recovering from eating disorders.

The Rader Institute
Third Floor
1663 Sawtelle Boulevard
Los Angeles, CA 90025
(800) 255–1818

This center offers adolescent inpatient and outpatient services specifically designed for recovery from eating disorders.

BOOKS

Byrne, Katherine. *A Parent's Guide to Anorexia and Bulimia: Understanding and Helping Self-Starvers and Binge/Purgers.* New York: Schocken Books, 1987.

Kranz, Rachel, and Michael Maloney. *Straight Talk About Eating Disorders.* New York: Facts on File, 1991.

Minirth, Frank, et al. *Love Hunger.* Nashville: Thomas Nelson, 1990.

Mitchell, James E. *Anorexia Nervosa and Bulimia: Diagnosis and Treatment.* St. Paul, MN: University of Minnesota Press, 1985.

Squire, Susan. *The Slender Balance: Causes and Cures for Bulimia, Anorexia, and the Weight-Loss Weight-Gain Seesaw.* New York: Putnam, 1983.

---

*"If a child lives with approval,
he learns to live with himself."*

—Dorothy Law Nolte

16

TEACH YOUR CHILD HEALTHY EATING HABITS

"Come on, just three more bites." "No dessert till you've eaten everything on your plate." How many parents haven't occasionally been guilty of such mealtime begging or bullying? While these pleas—when successful—may result in increased calorie consumption, they do little to encourage healthy eating habits or to teach your child anything about nutrition. And, needless to say, a great deal of conflict is avoided when the family table ceases to be a battleground and instead becomes a place of peaceful communication and sharing. You can do a lot to ensure good eating habits and better health in your child by focusing on nutrition and exercise, rather than dwelling on food consumption.

Good eating habits may be more important to your child than you think. The right foods in the right quantities can reduce the frequency of such chronic complaints as indigestion and diarrhea, and can help your child avoid obesity, a condition that plays a part in many physical disorders. Proper diet can even prevent serious health problems—heart disease, diabetes, and cancer, for instance—in later life. Good nutrition can have emotional and social benefits, as well. First, the practice of eating for health can spur the development of a child's self-control. Second, a healthy eater is likely to feel fit, energetic, and focused, rather than sluggish, passive, and unable to focus on the task at hand. In fact, there is growing evidence that undiagnosed food allergies and reactions to certain food additives may have strong psychological and behavioral effects on some children. (See the inset on page 86 for more information on food allergies.) Chronic malnutrition in children has been linked to impaired learning abilities and slower acquisition of social and verbal skills.

To be sure, parents have reason to work at improving their

child's eating habits. But altering mealtime routines and making nutritional changes are rarely easy tasks, particularly when willful toddlers or junk-food lovers are concerned. The suggestions listed below can help you gradually shift the responsibility for good nutrition to your child, sparking healthier eating habits and reducing mealtime stress in the bargain.

☐ Feed your infant on demand from the start. As solids are introduced, offer a variety of foods. Reintroduce any dishes that are refused, but accept the fact that even babies have their likes and dislikes.

☐ Invite your baby to join the family at the table. At first, feed him beforehand and let him amuse himself with toys or a snack while you eat and chat. Gradually offer him samples of your meal until he is ready to make the switch to table food, at which point he will already have learned a great deal about mealtime behavior just from watching you.

☐ Keep the mealtime atmosphere pleasant. Play soft, peaceful music. Set an attractive table, perhaps with a centerpiece made by your child. Discourage tantrums by giving your child plenty of attention. Make up your mind to avoid clashing over food consumption. When your child appears to be finished eating, remove his plate and allow him to leave the table.

☐ Allow your child a flexible eating schedule. Some nutritionists believe that small children need to eat every three hours, so allow snacking. If your child is hungry right before a meal, serve him part of the meal ahead of time, if possible.

☐ Make sure that your child's snacks are nutritious. This is best accomplished by limiting the purchase of salty, sugary, and fatty foods, and giving your child choices of fruits, vegetable sticks, whole-grain crackers, and low-fat cheeses, instead. (Be aware, though, that bites of hard foods—cookie chunks and apple pieces, for instance—as well as "round" foods—grapes and frankfurters— have been known to cause choking in children under age five. Never leave your baby or small child alone while he is eating.)

☐ Resist the temptation to limit your child's food intake. What he views as food deprivation may lead to an unhealthy obsession with snacking and, ultimately, overeating. (See Entry 15 on page 71 for information about eating disorders.)

☐ On the flip side, avoid worrying about your finicky eater. Erratic eating habits, "food jags," and lack of interest in mealtimes are all quite normal for children—and, most often, are outgrown. Offer a variety of nutritious foods at each meal, but let your child choose what, and how much, he wishes to eat.

☐ Learn all you can about nutrition. For instance, did you know that according to current recommendations, the largest portion of your diet should be comprised of whole grains? After doing your research, put your new-found information to work by preparing nutritionally balanced meals. (See the inset on page 83 for more nutritional guidelines.)

☐ Share your knowledge of healthful eating with your child by explaining the need for the various foods served at each meal, and involving him in menu-planning, food shopping, and label-reading.

☐ Involve your child in food preparation. He may be more tempted to sample snacks and dishes that he has helped to concoct and serve. Even toddlers can wash carrots or tear lettuce.

☐ Encourage physical activity. Exercise burns calories, increases fitness, and improves a growing child's appetite. (See page 80.)

☐ Teach your child to pay attention to how certain foods make him feel. Energized? Sluggish? Overly full? Chances are, healthy foods are the ones that make him feel good.

During your child's early years, the responsibility for providing varied, wholesome foods and discouraging nutritionally worthless snacks is yours. Of course, there's nothing wrong with an occasional indulgence. In fact, too much rigidity where your child's diet is concerned may cause him to go on a forbidden-food spree when you aren't there to watch him. It's important to remember that your child's long-term diet is what's most important. And by giving your child a choice of nourishing foods as well as plenty of solid information about nutrition, you'll be handing him the key to a lifetime of good health.

Resources

For additional information about encouraging good eating habits in your child, see your family doctor or a registered dietician. The following resources may also be helpful.

BOOKS

Conners, C. Keith. *Feeding the Brain: How Foods Affect Children*. New York: Plenum Publishing, 1989.

Franz, Marion J., Betsy Kerr Hedding, and Gayle Leitch. *Opening the Door to Good Nutrition*. Minneapolis: International Diabetes Center, 1985.

McEntire, Patricia. *Mommy, I'm Hungry: How to Feed Your Child Nutritiously*. Sacramento: Cougar Books, 1982.

Smith, Lendon. *Feed Your Kids Right: Dr. Smith's Program for Your Child's Total Health*. New York: Delta Books, 1979.

Promote Family Fitness

When many of today's parents were growing up, a fat baby was considered a healthy baby. But nowadays the medical community stresses a healthy diet and recommends regular exercise from toddlerhood on. And not only has fitness come into vogue with many of today's adults, but it is known to signal good health and lead to exercise habits that last a lifetime. Passing the desire for fitness down to your child can be a challenge, however, especially if your youngster is among the 30 percent of school-age boys who cannot run a mile in under ten minutes, or the 56 percent of girls who cannot do even one pull-up. The knowledge that heart-disease risk factors—high blood pressure, high cholesterol, and obesity—exist in some 40 percent of today's five- to eight-year-olds further highlights the need to promote fitness in your family.

What can regular exercise do for your child? Physical activity that is sustained for just twenty minutes will give your child's heart and lungs a workout, build muscles, and keep his ligaments and joints limber. The more your child moves his body, the better his levels of cardiovascular and muscular endurance will be. In addition, a strong, flexible child is less likely to suffer such minor injuries as muscle pulls and sprains, and more likely to succeed at the games he chooses. Clearly, it pays to introduce your child to fitness at an early age, to provide enough novel activities to keep him moving, and—above all—to make exercising fun. Here are some suggestions that can help.

☐ Be a good role model by making physical fitness part of your everyday life. Your child will then be more likely to value exercise and want to join in.

☐ Work family fitness time into your weekends. Go hiking or swimming; ride your bikes together; or take a brisk walk—even if it's just through a local shopping mall.

☐ Assign active chores. Enlist your child's help with car-washing, leaf-raking, and vacuuming.

☐ Be supportive of your child's physical pursuits. Attend dance recitals, be willing to drive him to and from practices, and cheer from the sidelines during games.

☐ To ensure your child's success at the games he chooses, provide age-appropriate equipment—oversized bats, undersized racquets and riding toys, properly fitting protective gear, and the like. (See Entry 35 on page 184 for more information about protective sports gear.)

☐ Attend sporting events with your child. As a spectator, your child can learn a great deal about team sports and such individual pursuits as tennis or marathon-running.

☐ Buy or rent a children's exercise video and work out with your child.

☐ Promote indoor fitness by having on hand a small trampoline, an exercise bicycle, or a tumbling mat. If space and conditions permit, allow your child to roller skate or use a scooter in your basement. (Naturally, these activities require adult supervision.)

☐ Build exercise into your family's reward system and gift buying. Present your child with a day at the shore or a new soccer ball, rather than a trip to the movies or a CD.

☐ Look into community recreation programs that offer families and children a medal, certificate, or other concrete reward for participation.

☐ Sign your family up for a walk-a-thon, bike-a-thon, fun run, or similar activity. Schools, religious institutions, and charitable organizations often sponsor these events to raise funds for charities.

☐ Do not press your child into team sports if he finds them boring or frustrating. Instead, suggest dance, yoga, aerobics, running, cycling, horseback riding, or golf.

☐ Make your child aware that exercise can feel good. If you're playing badminton together, mention that running makes you feel exhilarated. If you're tossing a ball back and forth in the yard, comment on the warm sun or the cool breeze.

☐ Urge your local school board to expand intramural sports programs and to teach physical education at all grade levels.

☐ Tailor the pace of family activity to your child's attention span. Be flexible about switching to another form of exercise midstream.

☐ Schedule your child's homework in the evening whenever possible, so that it replaces television rather than after-school play.

☐ When time and weather permit, walk to school and errands with your child.

Twenty minutes of sustained exercise three times a week is all that's needed for minimum cardiovascular fitness. It's important to check with your child's doctor before introducing any activities that are particularly strenuous. In addition, be sure to provide plenty of water when your child is playing hard, and be aware that he may not notice when outdoor temperatures reach extremes. And, finally, avoid encouraging competitive activities if your child is under eight years of age. Young children are often upset or discouraged by competition.

When considering forms of exercise to pursue with your child, remember that the keys to promoting fitness are movement, variety, competence, and fun. Exercising with your child should be healthy and relaxing, not exhausting or discouraging. Perhaps most important of all, the pursuit of family fitness should enable you to spend time together laughing, talking, and playing at an activity you all enjoy.

Your Child's Nutritional Needs

Most of today's parents grew up believing that there were four main food groups—(1) meat, poultry, and fish; (2) dairy and eggs; (3) fruits and vegetables; and (4) breads and cereals—and that meat should form the largest part of nearly every meal. Today, however, it is recommended that you plan your family's meals around the new four-level USDA Food Guide Pyramid (see page 84), which shows both the foods necessary for a healthful diet and the relative proportions in which these foods should be eaten.

The pyramid is built on a broad base of carbohydrate- and fiber-rich breads, rice, cereals, and pasta. These are the foods that should be eaten in greatest abundance. There is also strong emphasis on fruits and vegetables—the two groups that make up the next level of the pyramid. The narrower third level includes another two food groups: milk, yogurt, and cheese; and meat, poultry, fish, dry beans, eggs, and nuts. The uppermost level contains fats, oils, and sweets, which are to be eaten only sparingly. The pyramid shows exactly how many servings should be eaten from each group.

Choosing the Best Foods at Each Level

There are several guidelines that can help you apply the USDA pyramid to the planning of your child's meals and snacks. First, it's best to offer the maximum number of daily servings whenever possible so that your child will have the greatest variety of foods from which to choose. Breads, cereals, rice, and pasta are healthiest when served in their whole-grain forms. Some excellent choices are brown rice, buckwheat, barley, and oats. Try some of the more unusual grains—couscous and bulghur, for instance—to keep meals interesting.

Serve fruits fresh and unsweetened. Good choices include cantaloupe, citrus fruits, bananas, honeydew melon, mango, kiwi, and berries, as these are high in vitamins and minerals. Vegetables should be served raw, lightly steamed, or quickly stir-fried to preserve minerals and vitamins. Offer a large variety—broccoli, cauliflower, cabbage, and leafy greens are among the best—to make sure your child gets all the nutrients he needs.

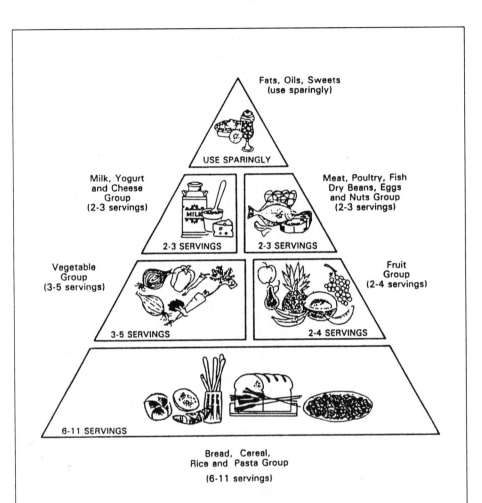

Fats, Oils, Sweets
(use sparingly)

USE SPARINGLY

Milk, Yogurt
and Cheese
Group
(2-3 servings)

2-3 SERVINGS

Meat, Poultry, Fish
Dry Beans, Eggs
and Nuts Group
(2-3 servings)

2-3 SERVINGS

Vegetable
Group
(3-5 servings)

3-5 SERVINGS

Fruit
Group
(2-4 servings)

2-4 SERVINGS

6-11 SERVINGS

Bread, Cereal,
Rice and Pasta Group
(6-11 servings)

The USDA Food Guide Pyramid

Milk fat is important to children under two years of age. After that, it's better to serve low-fat or skim milk. For those youngsters with allergies to dairy products, soy products and sea vegetables like nori can provide daily calcium requirements. It's also wise to serve low-fat yogurts and cheeses whenever possible.

To further reduce your child's fat intake, buy only lean red meat and remove the skin from poultry before cooking. Also bear in mind that eggs, while a good source of iron, are high in cholesterol, and should be limited to two to four per week. Dried beans, on the other hand, are high in protein, fiber, and many other nutrients, while being low in fat. And with all the different types available—chickpeas, kidney beans, lentils, black beans, and pinto beans, to name just a few—there should be no problem in making tempting low-fat high-protein dishes.

Determining Serving Size

When reviewing dietary guidelines, many people are uncertain as to what constitutes a "serving." Listed below are typical serving sizes for teen-agers and adults.

- Bread, cereal, rice, and pasta: 1 slice whole-grain bread; $1/2$ whole-grain bun or muffin; $1/2$ cup cooked brown rice, whole-grain pasta, or whole-grain cereal; 1 ounce dry cereal.
- Fruits: $1/2$ cup diced fruit; $3/4$ cup juice; 1 medium apple, orange, or banana.
- Vegetables: 1 cup raw leafy greens; $1/2$ cup other vegetables; $3/4$ cup vegetable juice.
- Milk, yogurt, and cheese: 1 cup milk or low-fat yogurt; $1^1/2$ ounces low-fat cheese.
- Meat, poultry, fish, dry beans, eggs, and nuts: 2 to 3 ounces.

When modifying adult dietary guidelines for your young child, it's best to cut down on portion size—except in the case of the calcium-rich milk group—rather than the number of daily servings. As a rule, preschoolers need approximately half of an adult-sized serving, with food amounts gradually increasing as your child's appetite grows. By the time your child reaches her teen years, her portion sizes should be about the same as yours. Of course, every child is different, and you may wish to discuss your child's needs with her doctor.

Finally, if your child is a picky eater, you may find it helpful to serve "fun"—but nutritious—foods when possible. Corn on the cob, cherry tomatoes, vegetable sticks served with low-fat yogurt dip, and whole-grain-bread sandwiches cut into amusing shapes are just some ideas that can keep your youngster on the road to good health.

Food Allergies in Children

Can a child be allergic to what he eats? For about one percent of all children, the answer is "Yes." A food allergy occurs when the body's immune system reacts to a food, or to a substance in food, by producing antibodies. These antibodies can cause a variety of symptoms, such as hives, wheezing, eczema, runny nose, headache, or diarrhea—symptoms that can surface immediately after, hours after, or even days after eating the problem food. A food allergy is not to be confused with a food intolerance, in which physical discomfort after eating certain foods is related to digestion. (An inability to break down the lactose contained in milk products, for example, can cause gas, bloating, abdominal cramps, and diarrhea.) Nor is a food allergy the same as a food sensitivity, in which chemical changes can dramatically alter a child's behavior or activity level. (Processed sugar and preservatives, for instance, have been known to cause hyperactivity.) Only food allergies are related to a person's immune system.

Reducing the Likelihood of Food Allergies

Can anything be done to reduce the chances of your child developing a food allergy? The following suggestions may be helpful.

☐ Breastfeed your baby for as long as possible. The later a baby is exposed to food allergens—the substances that trigger allergic reactions—the less likely he'll be to experience a reaction. (See Entry 19 on page 101 for more information on breastfeeding.)

☐ When you start your baby on solid foods, introduce new foods one at a time, and wait four or five days before starting the next food. Then, if your child does develop a food allergy, it will be much easier to pinpoint the cause.

☐ Carefully follow your health-care provider's advice about introducing the most highly allergenic foods—cow's milk, soy products, nuts, egg whites, shellfish, wheat, corn, chocolate, cola, citrus fruits, and tomatoes.

☐ *If you have a family history of food allergies, ask your health-care provider about leaving troublesome foods out of your child's diet completely.*

☐ *Be aware that food coloring and preservatives are potential allergens. As much as possible, choose fresh foods rather than processed foods and beverages, and avoid packaged food products with additives listed on the label. Also avoid giving your child vitamins or medications that appear to contain colorings.*

Detecting Food Allergies

If your child has an immediate-type food allergy, symptoms will appear within seconds after eating the problem food. Itching of the mouth, hives, an asthma-like reaction, and vomiting are all symptoms of this type of allergy—symptoms that, in all but the most extreme cases, disappear within an hour.

Delayed food allergies are much harder to detect. This type of reaction takes place when, during the course of digestion, the body changes food into allergenic by-products. A delayed allergy can also stem from the body's reaction to chemicals formed during the digestion of certain food combinations. The list of possible symptoms from delayed food allergies is a long one, and includes fatigue, muscle aches, depression, weight problems, hoarseness, middle-ear fluid, dizziness, irregular heartbeat, and mouth sores. Not surprisingly, these symptoms can be easily attributed to other disorders, and may be present so much of the time that food allergy is at first overlooked as a source of trouble. However, if your child continues to display symptoms after her doctor has ruled out other health problems, you may want to contact an allergist.

The allergist will review your child's symptoms, and, if warranted, order a skin or blood test to determine whether a common food allergen may be causing the trouble. Current allergy testing isn't foolproof, but a positive test can be supported by the absence of symptoms when a suspect food is removed from your child's diet, and confirmed by the recurrence of symptoms when small quantities of the food are reintroduced two weeks later. It's usually a good idea to note your child's symptoms—and their frequency—for use as a baseline against which to compare your child's health after dietary modifications have been made or treatment has been administered.

If Your Child Has Food Allergies

Despite a parent's precautions, food allergies do sometimes develop. If your child is diagnosed as having a food allergy, it may not be as easy as you think to eliminate the troublesome substance from his diet. Here are some helpful tips.

☐ Read labels carefully. The food your child is allergic to may be used as an ingredient in other foods. For example, many frankfurters contain milk products. And franks also contain nitrates—a substance that is often allergenic.

☐ Be aware that cooking sometimes changes milk and egg proteins to make them more easily tolerated by an allergic child. Ask your health-care provider if your child should try a small amount of the cooked food rather than entirely eliminating the food from her diet.

☐ Make it a point to inform grandparents, teachers, and other care givers of your child's food allergies. Also explain the steps that you routinely take to help your youngster avoid the foods that cause him problems.

☐ Keep oral antihistamines—or injectable medication, if your doctor prescribes it—on hand to treat allergic reactions in case your child accidentally eats a troublesome food.

☐ Since food allergies can fade, have your child retested for allergies every two or three years.

Happily, many children outgrow food allergies by the age of five. You can reduce the chances of your child developing such an allergy, or of your allergic child suffering an uncomfortable reaction to food or food additives, by following your doctor's advice and by watching your child's diet carefully from the start.

17

GET COMPLETE PRENATAL CARE

When you are pregnant, the well-being of your unborn child is greatly dependent upon the state of your health. Certain medical conditions and circumstances are unavoidable, of course. But on the whole, the better care you take of yourself before and during the nine months of pregnancy, the better your chances of having an uncomplicated delivery and a healthy baby.

There are two aspects of prenatal care: the supervision of a medical professional, and a self-care regimen that provides optimal nutrition, sufficient rest, and adequate exercise for the expectant mother. Both of these aspects are discussed below.

OBSTETRICAL OR MIDWIFE CARE

Studies show that the risk of infant mortality and delivery complications is greatly reduced when an expectant mother is seen by a medical professional on a regular basis throughout her pregnancy. In the best of circumstances, even before a woman is pregnant, she consults a doctor or midwife for advice on providing the healthiest possible fetal environment. (See Entry 18 on page 93.) When prepregnancy consultation is not possible, it's advisable to seek medical care as soon as pregnancy is confirmed.

Both an obstetrician—a physician who specializes in obstetrics and gynecology and is hospital-affiliated—and a certified nurse-midwife—a registered nurse with extensive childbirth training who handles at-home, birthing-center, and some in-hospital deliveries—are qualified to identify, monitor, and treat problems during pregnancy and, ultimately, to deliver your baby. As such, the selection of a birth attendant is largely a matter of preference if your pregnancy is uncomplicated, and if provisions can be made for immediate hospital access in the event of an emergency during labor. Some couples prefer the relaxed, natural, family-centered atmosphere of a midwife-assisted delivery, while others feel more at ease knowing that their baby's birth will take place in the high-tech surroundings of a hospital delivery room. Only you can decide which option is best for your family.

Since no two pregnancies are alike, even parents who have already experienced a delivery or two may have a long list of questions about their newest baby-to-be. In addition to monitoring your pregnancy and overseeing the delivery of your baby, your doctor or midwife can provide information and advice on such important topics as fetal development, prenatal testing, prepared-childbirth classes, birth plans, breastfeeding, and the selection of a pediatrician. He or she can also provide reassurance that your pregnancy is progressing normally.

SELF-CARE

Pregnancy, labor, and delivery place great demands on even the healthiest bodies, so it's a good idea to pay close attention to your physical well-being when you are expecting a baby. Examine your living and working environments, your diet, and your level of physical activity. Each of these aspects of your daily life plays a vital role in influencing your health and that of your baby.

Living and Working Environments

Your unborn baby may be susceptible to any toxins that are part of your everyday life. Entry 18 on page 93 explains how you can avoid substances and conditions that may be harmful to your baby. For more information, consult your health-care professional.

Diet

What you eat during pregnancy fuels your unborn baby's steady growth and prepares you for childbirth, the rigors of new parenthood, and breastfeeding. It's important that you select wholesome foods and consume sufficient calories to meet your increased nutritional needs. Your baby's birth weight will be affected by the amount of weight you gain during pregnancy, so it's vital to heed the advice of your birth attendant. He or she should be able to provide you with dietary guidelines. Your doctor or midwife may also recommend herbal tea for morning sickness and other problems of pregnancy, as well as vitamin and mineral supplements that will guarantee your baby sufficient amounts of crucial nutrients. You may also wish to refer to the books listed on page 92 for dietary suggestions to follow during pregnancy.

Rest and Exercise

You may find that you have an increased need for sleep while you're pregnant, particularly during the early months. As your pregnancy advances, you may also find that your sleep is sometimes disturbed by your baby's movements or by such pregnancy-related discomforts as heartburn. At any point during pregnancy, irritability and lethargy are two signs that you may not be getting enough sleep to cope with the physical and emotional changes that accompany your condition. You may simply need to retire for the night at an earlier hour, or you may want to try a number of ten-minute rest periods throughout the day. Also try to heed your body's signals that you are overexerting yourself, and reduce your activity level accordingly. Shortness of breath, backache, leg cramps, dizziness, rapid heartbeat, and profuse sweating are all signs that you should slow down. During pregnancy, regular *moderate* exercise is beneficial to cardiovascular fitness, which can help you meet the demands of carrying and delivering your baby. Generally, any exercise that you were involved in before you became pregnant can be continued during pregnancy. However, it is wise to consult with your health-care professional about the best forms of exercise for your particular circumstances, and about increasing your caloric intake to compensate for calories burned during physical activity.

The surest road to health and fitness during your pregnancy is through complete prenatal care. But there are other dividends, as well. Daily self-care and regular visits to your physician or nurse-midwife will allow you to begin caring for your baby before she is even born, and will help you prepare for her arrival with confidence and peace of mind.

Resources

The following resources can provide additional information on taking care of yourself and your unborn baby during pregnancy.

ORGANIZATIONS

Healthy Mothers, Healthy Babies
  Coalition
409 12th Street SW
Washington, DC 20024–2188
(202) 863–2458
(800) 673–8444

This group offers materials concerning health maintenance and injury prevention during pregnancy, as well as information on breastfeeding, genetics, immunizations, and adolescent pregnancy.

The Specialty Catalogue for
  Expectant and New Parents
c/o Be Healthy, Inc.
51 Saltrock Road
Baltic, CT 06330
(203) 822–8573
(800) 433–5523

This company offers books, tapes, and videos on fitness programs for expectant and new parents, as well as exercise wear and baby products.

BOOKS

Brinkley, Ginny, Linda Goldberg, and Janice Kukar. *Your Child's First Journey.* Garden City Park, NY: Avery Publishing Group, 1988.

Goodman, Richard Merle. *Planning for a Healthy Baby: A Guide to Genetic and Environmental Risks.* New York: Oxford University Press, 1986.

Hegland, Jean. *The Life Within: Celebration of a Pregnancy.* Clifton, NJ: Humana Press, 1991.

Holstein, Barbara A. *The Childbearing Year.* Syracuse, NY: New Readers Press, 1990.

Jimenez, Sherry L.M. *The Pregnant Woman's Comfort Guide.* Garden City Park, NY: Avery Publishing Group, 1991.

Marshall, Connie C. *From Here to Maternity.* Rocklin, CA: Prima Publishing, 1991.

Noble, Elizabeth. *Essential Exercises for the Childbearing Year.* Boston: Houghton Mifflin, 1982.

Olken, Sylvia Klein. *Positive Pregnancy Fitness.* Garden City Park, NY: Avery Publishing Group, 1987.

18

Avoid hazards that can harm your unborn child

Pregnancy is a time of joy and anticipation. It also marks the real beginning of parenthood, because responsibility for your baby's health starts long before birth. In fact, it is recommended that prior to conception, couples avoid substances that might harm the developing fetus. You see, parents' general health at the time of conception is known to directly influence the development of the fetus. Moreover, much of what passes through a pregnant woman's body makes its way to her fragile unborn baby, as well. For these reasons, if you are planning to have a child or are already expecting, it's essential that you evaluate your lifestyle, home, and place of work with an eye toward eliminating chemicals and conditions that can adversely affect fetal development.

Prenatal hazards generally fall into two categories: environmental health risks, which are often unseen and, therefore, unrecognized; and dangerous habits such as smoking, drinking, or using drugs. The information that follows should guide you in making your pregnancy a safer time for both yourself and your baby and, perhaps, help you begin a lifetime of healthier living.

HAZARDS IN YOUR ENVIRONMENT

Since a fetus is most vulnerable during the first three months of pregnancy, it's important to identify environmental hazards as early as possible. The information presented below should serve as a springboard for discussions with your doctor or birth attendant. You may also wish to contact the American Medical Association or the National Institute for Occupational Safety and Health (see pages 98–99) for their recommendations.

Heat

The occurrence of hyperthermia—high body temperature—in the early stages of pregnancy increases a baby's chances of a brain or spinal cord defect. This risk rises with the number of exposures to high temperatures. Therefore, if you are planning to conceive or are in the first months of pregnancy, you should avoid prolonged baths or showers, hot tubs, saunas, and anything associated with very high temperatures. When pregnant, it is also advisable to avoid strenuous physical activities that cause you to perspire heavily, and to contact your doctor for guidance if you have a fever.

Video Display Terminals (VDTs)

Health experts are looking closely at a possible link between proximity to VDTs and an increased risk of miscarriage. Although VDTs are known to have a strong electromagnetic field (EMF), it has not yet been firmly established that their use is dangerous to a pregnant woman. However, you can minimize any potential risk by wearing a radiation-blocking shield when operating your VDT, and by adding an EMF shield to the terminal itself.

X-Rays

Years of study and research have indicated that exposure to under five rads—five units of measure for radiation—causes no harm to an unborn baby. While procedures such as therapeutic radiation for cancer are considered dangerous to a fetus, even several sets of diagnostic x-rays add up to less than one rad, and are therefore believed to be perfectly safe. Nevertheless, it pays to err on the side of caution and inform your doctor or dentist of your pregnancy. If x-rays are indicated, ask whether a different diagnostic test can be used. If not, request that a lead shield be placed over your abdomen, and have your x-rays performed by a certified technician at a regularly inspected facility.

Dangerous Substances in the Air, Water, and Soil

It is known that exposure to radiation, toxins, and certain metals can pose a health risk to you and your unborn baby. When pregnant, therefore, it is wise to avoid fumes, lead (see Entry 46 on page 239) and other heavy metals, radon, solvents, pesticides, and prolonged contact with aerosol cleaners, dry cleaning agents, and the mercury vapors that can linger in dental offices. Be sure to discuss your specific living and working conditions with your health-care provider as early as possible to determine whether there is anything in your daily environment that might interfere with fetal development. You might also wish to contact your local health department for information on testing the air, water, and soil around your home, particularly if you live near an industrial area or busy highway, or in an older dwelling that might contain lead piping or heavily leaded paint. Consider drinking and cooking with distilled water or buying a water purification system for your home.

HAZARDS FROM TOBACCO, CAFFEINE, ALCOHOL, AND DRUGS

If you are considering having a child or are already pregnant, it's important to remember that much of what you take into your body—for better or for worse—is shared with your developing fetus. As a result, many aspects of your baby's health lie in your hands before and during the nine months of gestation. If you smoke or drink alcohol, now is the time to stop. If you use prescription or over-the-counter drugs, you may have to give them up as well—or, at least, to find safer substitutes. It's imperative to ask your doctor for his or her recommendations. (See Entries 2 and 17, on pages 6 and 89, for more information on changing habits and on prenatal care.)

Tobacco

Tobacco smoke contains nearly 4,000 chemicals—carbon monoxide, formaldehyde, and benzene among them. If you smoke while you are pregnant, harmful gases pass from your blood through the placenta into your baby's blood. Smoking also interferes with the amount of oxygen and nutrients that travel through the blood to your baby. This is why a woman who smokes or is exposed to secondhand smoke is more likely to have a small baby or a premature delivery than is a woman who avoids this hazard. The incidence of stillbirth and infant death is also higher in mothers who smoke. On the other hand, a child who grows up in a smoke-free environment—both before birth and after—is less likely to develop such chronic lung problems as pneumonia, respiratory disease, bronchitis, emphysema, and lung cancer than is a child whose parents smoke. The American Lung Association, the American Heart Association, and the American Cancer Society can furnish additional information about creating a smoke-free environment. Check the white pages of your phone book for the chapters nearest you. (See also Entry 20 on page 104.)

Caffeine

Caffeine crosses the placenta readily. And because it is metabolized more slowly during pregnancy, it stays in an expectant woman's system—and, therefore, her baby's system—up to three times longer than it remains in the system of a nonpregnant woman. The effect of caffeine on the fetus is still not clear, but it has been suggested that high consumption can lead to increased incidence of miscarriage, birth defects, and low birth weight. And the effects on the mother—anxiety, irritability, and sleeplessness—are well known. It's wise, therefore, to avoid caffeine when you're pregnant by eliminating caffeinated beverages, cocoa, and chocolate from your diet, and by steering clear of over-the-counter medications containing caffeine.

Alcohol

The damage to a developing fetus from alcohol has been well documented. The most serious consequence of drinking alcohol during pregnancy is Fetal Alcohol Syndrome (FAS). A baby with FAS suffers alcohol poisoning in the womb and is subsequently born addicted to alcohol and with disorders ranging from physical deformity to neurological damage and mental retardation. While FAS is usually the result of regular drinking, the U.S. Surgeon General and the American Medical Association maintain that even a small amount of alcohol can cause damage to a developing brain. Therefore, it is best to abstain completely from alcohol if you are pregnant or hope to become so soon. If you need help in this regard, your local chapter of Alcoholics Anonymous can provide additional information and support. This number can be found in your telephone directory's white pages.

Prescription and Over-the-Counter Drugs

Because of the potential for damage to a developing fetus, it's not advisable for a pregnant woman to use any medication unless directed to do so by her physician. If you suffer from a chronic condition for which medication is necessary—diabetes, hypertension, or epilepsy, for instance—it would be wise to check with your doctor before conceiving to find out whether your medication should be adjusted. For minor ailments, it's a good idea to investigate homeopathic remedies and to use medication only when absolutely necessary. Aspirin, ibuprofen, many cold remedies, cough medicines, tetracycline, and isotretinoin (Accutane) are just a few examples of drugs that should be avoided during pregnancy. If you are pregnant and are considering taking over-the-counter medication, it's important to read the label carefully for warnings against use by expectant mothers. Naturally, you should always stick to recommended dosages of any medication you use. Most important, *always check with your doctor first.*

Illegal Drugs

The chemical components of marijuana, cocaine, crack, heroin, and a long list of other illegal drugs readily cross the placenta and place a fetus at risk of stillbirth, as well as brain hemorrhage, respiratory distress syndrome, central nervous system damage, and other serious medical problems. In addition, use of addictive drugs during pregnancy may sentence a newborn to painful withdrawal symptoms during his first days of life. If you are planning to conceive or are already expecting a child and feel that you need help becoming drug-free, don't hesitate to consult your doctor, a local drug treatment center, or your community mental health center.

As an expectant parent, it is up to you to create the safest possible environment for your unborn child. For someone considering pregnancy, there is time to do even more to ensure that your home, your work place, and, ultimately, your body are all free of health-threatening chemicals and toxins. Remember that your developing fetus shares your exposure to hazardous substances and is particularly vulnerable to their effects. Fortunately, just by paying a little more attention to your activities, diet, and environment before and during pregnancy, you'll be doing a great deal to give your baby the best possible start in life.

Resources

The American Cancer Society, the American Lung Association, the American Heart Association, and Alcoholics Anonymous can all help you eliminate dangerous habits. The organizations and resources listed below can also provide information about ensuring your baby a healthy prenatal environment.

ORGANIZATIONS

Action on Smoking and Health
2013 11 Street, NW
Washington, DC 20006
(202) 659–4310

This group works to bring tobacco-use prevention and education issues to the attention of federal legislators, policy makers, and the general public.

American Medical Association
535 North Dearborn Street
Chicago, IL 60610
(312) 645–4818

This organization dispenses information both to members and to the public on medical and health legislation, operates a library for use by physicians, and organizes committees on various topics, including health-care planning and the principles of medical ethics.

Americans for Nonsmokers'
  Rights
2530 San Pablo Avenue, Suite J
Berkeley, CA 94702
(510) 841–3032

This nonprofit advocacy group was created to develop legislative action that supports the right of nonsmokers to avoid involuntary exposure to secondhand smoke.

Healthy Mothers, Healthy Babies
  Coalition
409 12th Street, SW
Washington, DC 20024–2188
(202) 863–2458
(800) 673–8444

This coalition of national and state organizations is concerned with maternal and child health and serves as a network for sharing ideas and information about prenatal care, nutrition for pregnant women, and infant mortality.

March of Dimes Birth Defects
  Foundation
1275 Mamaroneck Avenue
White Plains, NY 10605
(914) 428–7100

This organization promotes the prevention of birth defects by focusing on maternal and child health issues in educational campaigns, community programs, and research grants.

National Institute for Occupational
  Safety and Health
c/o Dr. Roy E. Albert
University of Cincinnati Institute
  of Environmental Health
3223 Eden Avenue
Cincinnati, OH 45267
(513) 558–5701

This organization of universities offering graduate training and continuing education for occupational health and safety professionals provides a forum for the exchange of information and works to facilitate the operation of training programs.

Office for Substance Abuse
  Prevention
Public Health Service Alcohol,
  Drug Abuse, and Mental Health
  Administration
c/o U.S. Department of Health and
  Human Services
Rockwall II, 5600 Fishers Lane
Rockville, MD 20857
(Prefers mail inquiries.)

This agency seeks to educate the public about the dangers of alcohol and drug addiction, and initiates and supports educational efforts directed toward the prevention of substance abuse.

Office on Smoking and Health
c/o U.S. Public Health Service
5600 Fishers Lane, Room 1-10
Rockville, MD 20857
(Prefers mail inquiries.)

This agency works to bring tobacco-use prevention and education issues to the attention of federal legislators, policy makers, and the public.

In Canada:

Maternal Health Society
Box 46564, Station G
Vancouver, BC V6R 4G8
(604) 465–3150

This organization seeks to educate the general public about issues concerning pre- and postnatal care and maternal and child health.

Pre- and Peri-Natal Psychology
  Association of North America
36 Madison Avenue
Toronto, ON M5R 2S1
(416) 929–5051

This group conducts research and provides information on factors contributing to healthy pregnancy and delivery among Canadian women.

BOOKS

Abel, Ernest. *Fetal Alcohol Syndrome and Fetal Alcohol Effects.* New York: Plenum Publishing, 1984.

Abrams, Richard S. *Will It Hurt the Baby?* Reading, MA: Addison-Wesley Publishing, 1990.

Dorris, Michael. *The Broken Cord.* New York: Harper and Row, 1990.

Fried, Peter A. *Pregnancy and Lifestyle Habits.* New York: Beaufort Books, 1983.

Fried, Peter. *Smoking for Two.* New York: Macmillan, 1980.

Goodman, Richard Merle. *Planning for a Healthy Baby: A Guide to Genetic and Environmental Risks.* New York: Oxford University Press, 1986.

Hawksley, Jane. *Teen Guide to Pregnancy, Drugs, and Smoking.* New York: Franklin Watts, 1989.

McCuen, Gary. *Born Hooked.* Hudson, WI: G.E. McCuren Publications, 1991.

---

*"Into the woman's keeping
is committed the destiny
of generations to come after us."*

—Theodore Roosevelt

19

BREASTFEED YOUR BABY

When parents welcome a baby into the world, they are suddenly faced with a host of crucial decisions. Which pediatrician should be used? How long should one parent remain at home? What sort of child care should be selected? But one of the most important and far-reaching choices of all concerns your baby's nourishment. You see, though bottlefeeding is certainly an acceptable option, child-rearing experts and the medical community overwhelmingly endorse breastfeeding as a means of achieving optimal infant health and growth and the best possible parent-child bond.

Women have been breastfeeding their children since the beginning of time, of course. Indeed, for centuries, breastfeeding was viewed as just another facet of an infant's creation—as much a part of development as the months she spent in the womb! And this positive, healthy attitude persists in many of today's cultures, whether necessitated by poverty or perpetuated by tradition.

In our society, however, a movement began some forty-five years ago that dismissed breastfeeding as an unscientific and outdated alternative to commercially made formulas. And so, at the urgings of their pediatricians, many 1950s mothers chose to bottlefeed their babies. Recently—and to the benefit of American infants—the tide has begun to turn back, and a more knowledgeable population now recognizes the unmatched value of breastfeeding. More and more of today's mothers choose to nurse.

Let's look at what breastfeeding does for your baby. First, breastmilk can reduce or delay the onset of allergies in your baby by postponing the introduction of foods to which she may be sensitive until her system is sufficiently mature to handle them.

Breastmilk can also protect your baby from disease by arming her with your own immunities, lining her digestive tract as protection against certain organisms, and destroying or slowing the growth of bacteria. Formula and cow's milk both lack these unique properties.

Because nature designed the infant mouth and chin to perfectly conform to a mother's breast, nursing your baby promotes healthy oral development. And, through a bottlefed infant can have much of her sucking need met by a latex or silicone nipple, the breastfed infant usually works harder to get her nourishment, and so satisfies her sucking urge more quickly. In addition, she requires fewer interruptions for burping, and can continue to nurse leisurely without ingesting air even after her hunger is satisfied. As a result, a breastfed baby is likely to be relaxed and blissfully content at the end of a feeding. In addition, the medical establishment is becoming increasingly aware of the value of skin-to-skin contact between mother and nursing infant, having discovered that it enhances the nurturing instinct, furthers bonding, strengthens family ties, and promotes a vital sense of security in a baby.

The makeup of breastmilk actually varies over time to suit a baby's changing dietary needs as she grows. In fact, the composition of mother's milk ingested during a single breastfeeding session changes from start to finish, from thinner to thicker and from richer in protein and carbohydrates to higher in fats and calories. Formula, naturally, remains constant in form. And for you, the mother, breastfeeding can have emotional, physical, financial, and time-saving benefits that make it an even more desirable choice.

And the best news of all is that virtually any mother can nurse. Midwives and other birth attendants are quite knowledgeable about breastfeeding, as are the nurses in your hospital's maternity unit, so support is available from the moment of birth. Many hospitals also employ lactation specialists to offer assistance and advice even after you and your baby are discharged. In addition, La Leche League International, a well-known nursing support group, has chapters in many cities. Friends or family members who have breastfed are also good sources of information.

Naturally, like all parents, you want the best for your baby. By breastfeeding your child, you'll be giving her the best possible nutritional start as well as providing a unique closeness that will yield emotional benefits for years to come.

Resources

You can get additional information and assistance from a pediatrician, a lactation consultant, a maternal and child-health nurse, a breastfeeding support group, or the sources listed below.

ORGANIZATIONS

La Leche League International
9616 Minneapolis Avenue
PO Box 1209
Franklin Park, IL 60131
(800) LA–LECHE

This worldwide organization of professionals promotes breastfeeding and its benefits to both mother and child through education, support groups, and one-to-one consultation.

In Canada:

Infant Feeding Action Coalition
10 Trinity Square
Toronto, ON M5G 1B1
(416) 595–9819

This organization works to raise public awareness of the importance of breastfeeding, and to ensure adequate nutrition for all infants.

BOOKS

Brinkley, Ginny, Linda Goldberg, and Janice Kukar. *Your Child's First Journey*. Garden City Park, NY: Avery Publishing Group, 1988.

Eiger, Marvin S., and Sally Wendkos Olds. *The Complete Book of Breastfeeding*. New York: Workman Publishing, 1987.

Huggins, Kathleen. *The Nursing Mother's Companion*. Boston, MA: Harvard Common Press, 1990.

La Leche League International. *The Womanly Art of Breastfeeding*. Franklin Park, IL: La Leche League International, 1981.

Nursing Mothers' Council of the Boston Association for Childbirth Education. *Breastfeeding Your Baby: A Practical Guide for the New Mother*. Garden City Park, NY: Avery Publishing Group, 1989.

Pryor, Karen, and Gale Pryor. *Nursing Your Baby*. New York: Pocket Books, 1991.

Woessner, Candace, Judith Lauwers, and Barbara Bernard. *Breastfeeding Today: A Mother's Companion*. Garden City Park, NY: Avery Publishing Group, 1991.

20

PROTECT YOUR CHILD FROM SECONDHAND SMOKE

Less than ten years ago, the designation of separate lounge and eating areas for nonsmoking adults by schools, restaurants, and offices was viewed as a progressive move. Now, in response to growing numbers of nonsmokers as well as conclusive research on the hazards of so-called "secondhand smoke"—environmental tobacco smoke, or ETS—most public buildings across North America confine *smokers* to a separate area, or prohibit lighting up altogether. There's no question that the air is now clearer in public places. But what about the air your family breathes at home? According to some estimates, half of all infants and children are regularly exposed to ETS—a substance that the Environmental Protection Agency (EPA) has recently reclassified as a Class A carcinogen, on par with asbestos. Certainly, it's vital that the air your child breathes day in and day out be free of this dangerous substance.

THE HAZARDS OF SECONDHAND SMOKE

Because so many of today's parents grew up around smokers—and, in fact, received regular doses of tar, nicotine, and a host of undesirable chemicals even during their nine months in utero—it's easy for them to view their own good health as proof that tobacco smoke can't be all that harmful to babies and children. But research has proven otherwise. In fact, a 1993 EPA report concluded that secondhand smoke annually causes an estimated 3,000 deaths from lung cancer in the United States, and severely affects hundreds of thousands of asthmatics, *many of whom are children.* The sections that follow spell out some of the immediate and long-term effects of exposure to secondhand smoke in utero and during childhood.

Pregnancy and Infancy

A significant percentage of premature deliveries have been linked to smoking during pregnancy. And when compared with babies of nonsmokers, even full-term babies of smokers are born an average of one week earlier and tend to be a half-inch shorter, weigh nearly a half-pound less, and have lungs that are smaller and less developed. (Page 95 of Entry 18 explains why.) There is also an increased incidence of miscarriage and stillbirth among women who smoke, and of Sudden Infant Death Syndrome (SIDS) among babies of smokers. In addition, there is growing evidence that tobacco smoke may affect an infant's behavior and intellectual development. Babies born to smoking mothers tend to be more irritable and more hyperactive than babies of nonsmokers, and also score lower on neurological tests. Perhaps most frightening, the EPA's 1993 report stated that passive smoking annually causes between 150,000 and 300,000 cases of pneumonia, bronchitis, and similar infections in children under eighteen months of age.

Childhood

In one study, the average three-year-old child of smoking parents was a pound lighter and a half-inch shorter than the same-age child of nonsmoking parents, and scored five points lower on intelligence tests, as well. Moreover, children whose parents smoke at home have a higher-than-average incidence of tonsillitis, colds, middle-ear infections, and hospitalizations for respiratory illness. And the combination of smaller lungs at birth and continued inhalation of ETS greatly increases a child's chances of developing asthma and, according to recent studies, worsens the condition of up to one million asthmatic children annually.

Later Life

The long-term consequences of regular exposure to secondhand smoke in childhood are often grave, for ETS increases the likelihood of dying from heart disease by as much as 30 percent. The risk of lymphoma, leukemia, and brain cancer increases by 20 percent among children of smokers, as well. ETS exposure has also been linked to emphysema, chronic bronchitis, and other adult respiratory diseases. And ETS may be responsible for 17 percent of all lung cancer cases in adult nonsmokers.

CREATING A SMOKE-FREE ENVIRONMENT

In light of recent findings, it's clear that you need to protect your child from the many health risks of secondhand smoke. Doing so can prevent impaired lung development both before and after birth, improve your child's resistance to respiratory disease, arm him against heart disease and cancer in adulthood, and set a nonsmoking example for him to follow throughout his formative years.

What can you do? If you smoke, make plans to break the habit at once. You may choose to go "cold turkey," or you might find it easier to quit smoking gradually with lower-tar cigarettes, special filters, and the like. Prescription chewing gum and skin patches, both of which satisfy nicotine cravings, may be helpful. You can also get help becoming smoke-free at a behavior modification program, or through hypnosis, acupuncture, or herbal remedies. The American Cancer Society, the American Lung Association, and the American Heart Association, all of which are listed in the white pages of your phone book, can help you get started. Your family physician is another good source of information about quitting smoking. And, of course, there are a number of excellent books that offer guidance and encouragement.

Naturally, not every quit-smoking method is right for everyone. But whatever means you use to help end your smoking habit, it's important to enlist the support of your family—particularly your child, who stands to learn an important lesson from your efforts to fight the attraction of nicotine. And, finally, it's vital to stop others from smoking around your child. It's perfectly acceptable to ask friends and relatives who visit your home to step outdoors before lighting up, and to hire only nonsmoking babysitters. You might also wish to exercise care when choosing a restaurant table, airline seat, or railroad car, taking pains to stay far away from the often-ineffective boundaries set up between smokers and nonsmokers. Both you and your child are sure to be healthier for your efforts.

Resources

The resources listed below can furnish pamphlets, books, and additional information about the dangers of environmental tobacco smoke and breaking the smoking habit.

ORGANIZATIONS

American Academy of Pediatrics
Committee on Environmental
  Hazards
141 Northwest Point Boulevard
PO Box 927
Elk Grove Village, IL 60009
(708) 228–5005
(800) 433–9016

This professional organization strives for ongoing improvements in the field of pediatrics, and maintains some forty committees to address different aspects of child health.

National Cancer Institute
Room 10A24
Building 31
9000 Rockville Pike
Bethesda, MD 20892
(301) 496–8664

This agency conducts research, compiles statistics, and educates medical professionals and the public about cancer risks and treatments.

BOOKS

Casey, Karen. *If Only I Could Quit: Becoming a Nonsmoker.* New York: HarperCollins, 1987.

Henningfield, Jack E. *Nicotine: An Old-Fashioned Addiction.* New York: Chelsea House, 1985.

Krumholz, Harlan M., and Robert H. Phillips. *No If's, And's or Butts: The Smoker's Guide to Quitting.* Garden City Park, NY: Avery Publishing Group, 1992.

Rogers, Jacquelyn. *You Can Stop Smoking.* New York: Pocket Books, 1987.

21

PROTECT YOUR CHILD FROM THE SUN

Until recently, many people considered a deep tan not only attractive, but also a sign of health. Some believed that golden- and olive-skinned children—children who tanned easily—had natural protection from the sun. And for the child with fair skin or freckles who burned instead, no precaution seemed necessary beyond a T-shirt and a few dabs of zinc oxide on the already-crimson areas of her face and body.

Today, most people know better. They're aware that the sun's ultraviolet rays can be dangerous, and that no one, regardless of skin color or type, should spend time outdoors without protection. Fortunately, you can significantly reduce your child's risk of sun damage by taking steps to limit her exposure to ultraviolet rays and by teaching her to practice sun sense whenever she plays outdoors.

KNOWING YOUR SUN FACTS

Why has sunlight suddenly been termed dangerous? Research has shown that there are two types of solar rays that can damage skin: ultraviolet A (UVA) rays and ultraviolet B (UVB) rays. UVA rays, long called "tanning rays," penetrate to the dermis—the second layer of the skin—and can cause premature aging and, over time, contribute to the development of skin cancer. UVB rays are even more harmful, and can cause sunburn and skin-cell changes that sometimes develop into one of the deadliest cancers: malignant melanoma.

Until recently, the Earth was protected from dangerous sunlight by a band of atmospheric gas called the ozone layer, which absorbs ultraviolet radiation. However, our ozone layer is rapidly thinning due to the effects of the chlorofluorocarbons and hydro-chlorofluorocarbons—CFCs and HCFCs—that are used in packaging and refrigerants, halons (a compound found in fire extinguishers), carbon tetrachloride and methyl chloroform (cleaning solvents), and methyl bromide (an insecticide). The fact that potentially dangerous UVB rays can now filter through to the Earth's surface has led environmental experts and the medical community to anticipate some 12 million additional cases of skin cancer over the next four decades.

While all of us should protect ourselves from the sun's rays, children are in special need of protection. Research has shown that at least 80 percent of a person's lifetime sun-related skin damage takes place during childhood. It is now known that a single blistered sunburn doubles a child's risk of developing malignant melanoma later in life. And even in small doses, long-term sun exposure has been linked to less-serious basal and squamous cell skin cancers. Regardless of tone or texture, a child's skin is sensitive to sunlight. Young skin is thin and fragile, and its pigment-producing cells—melanocytes—are more vulnerable to sun damage than are these same cells in adults. In addition, it is widely believed that sun-damaged cells take time to pass through a series of stages en route to malignancy. Therefore, the earlier skin damage occurs in a child's life, the more time a malignancy has to develop.

USING SUN SENSE

Short of keeping your youngster indoors, what can you do to protect her from the sun's ultraviolet rays? You and your child may find the following suggestions helpful.

☐ Discourage sunbathing. If a suntan is important to your child for cosmetic reasons, suggest one of the many bronzers or sunless tanning lotions currently available. These products contain ingredients that interact with the skin's surface to produce a tanned look without sun exposure.

☐ Keep your child out of the sun when the rays are strongest—

between ten a.m. and two p.m. (eleven a.m. and three p.m. daylight savings time). The American Academy of Dermatology recommends the "shadow test," which teaches children to avoid the sun whenever their shadows are shorter than they are.

☐ Before your child goes outdoors, cover all exposed areas of her skin with a sunscreen that has a sun protection factor (SPF) of at least 15. Because ultraviolet rays are always present, sunscreen is needed regardless of the weather or time of year. If your child is perspiring or swimming, you should reapply her sunscreen every sixty to ninety minutes. Look for a creamy lotion that contains no alcohol, and consider a sunscreen stick, which doesn't run, for your child's face. Use an ounce or two of sunscreen—at least a palmful—for each application. Do not use sunscreen on an infant under six months of age. Instead, keep your baby completely out of the sun.

☐ Whenever your child is going to be in direct sunlight, cover as much of her skin as possible with opaque clothing. A wide-brimmed hat, long sleeves, and slacks are recommended. (100-percent cotton is a good choice for hot days, as it "breathes," and is therefore more comfortable.) Remember that sheer clothing and light-filtering umbrellas actually provide little protection from solar rays.

☐ Be particularly careful about sun exposure if your child is taking medication, as the combination of certain drugs and sunlight reduces the amount of time needed for skin damage to occur. Antihistamines, tetracycline, and sulfa drugs are among those that can cause sun sensitivity. Check with your child's physician for more information.

☐ Be extra vigilant about sun protection if you live in the South or Southwest. Skin-cancer rates in these areas of the United States are twice as high as they are in other parts of the country.

☐ Bear in mind that fair-skinned people, whose skin burns without tanning or tans less than average, are often particularly sensitive to the sun's rays.

☐ Make sun protection a family habit. Your child is more likely to practice sun sense if she sees that you, too, apply sunscreen and cover up before going outdoors.

There's nothing like a bright, beautiful day to lure your child into the sun for some fresh air and exercise. And as long as you practice good sun sense, time spent outdoors will be not only fun, but also safe and healthy.

Resources

Your family physician can keep you abreast of the latest findings about the Earth's ozone layer, ultraviolet rays, and skin protection. The following organizations are also good sources of information on sun sense.

ORGANIZATIONS

American Academy of
  Dermatology
1567 Maple Avenue
PO Box 3116
Evanston, IL 60201–3116
(708) 869–3954

This association of dermatologists conducts research, compiles statistics, publishes literature, and seeks to educate the public about matters concerning skin care.

American Academy of
  Pediatrics
141 Northwest Point Boulevard
PO Box 927
Elk Grove Village, IL 60009–0927
(708) 228–5005
(800) 433–9016

This professional organization of pediatricians works for advancements in all areas of child health.

BOOKS

Levenstein, Mary Kerney. *Everyday Cancer Risks and How to Avoid Them.* Garden City Park, NY: Avery Publishing Group, 1992.

Novick, Nelson Lee. *Super Skin: A Leading Dermatologist's Guide to the Latest Breakthroughs in Skin Care.* New York: Clarkson N. Potter, 1988.

Siegel, Mary-Ellen. *Safe in the Sun.* New York: Walker and Co., 1990.

22

PROTECT YOUR CHILD FROM LYME DISEASE

It wasn't long ago that wooded areas and grassy fields seemed ideal places for children to romp and play. But that was before reports of Lyme disease, a potentially serious bacterial infection that can be transmitted by the deer tick, began multiplying at an alarming rate. Nowadays, these once-popular childhood haunts—also home to rabbits, mice, and other small animals on which deer ticks feed—have become places to avoid. Lyme disease has been identified in all fifty states and in Canada, as well as in other parts of the world. Fortunately, there are steps you can take to reduce the chances that your child will become infected with this increasingly common disorder.

KNOW THE FACTS ABOUT LYME DISEASE

Lyme disease, so named for the Connecticut town where the infection was identified in 1975, can be transmitted when the pinhead-sized deer tick attaches itself to an animal or human to feed on blood. In the process, the tick sometimes regurgitates a small amount of fluid into its victim, and thus shares any bacteria carried in the tick's body. Not all deer ticks carry the bacteria that cause Lyme disease, but research shows that in high-risk areas such as the northeastern United States, 60 to 70 percent of the ticks are infected. The risk of contracting Lyme disease is greatest from May through August, when ticks and animals are most active and people spend more time outdoors and wear less clothing. While adult ticks usually choose deer or other large mammals as their hosts, young ticks latch onto humans—not to mention cats, dogs, mice, rabbits, birds, and other animals that, in turn, transmit the ticks to humans or carry the threat of Lyme disease to new areas of the country.

Unfortunately, your child may not be aware of a deer-tick bite. The bite itself is not painful, and deer ticks often gravitate toward hard-to-spot areas of the body—the groin, the back of the neck, the armpit, and the back of the knee. In addition, over 25 percent of Lyme victims display none of the disease's early symptoms. And even when present, the symptoms of Lyme disease are easily confused with those of other conditions.

In Stage I of the infection, which can last from several weeks to several months, a victim may suffer from fatigue, headache, fever, chills, stiff neck, and joint and muscle pain. Perhaps the best known and surest early sign of Lyme disease is a distinctive red-rimmed rash at the site of the bite. Stage I Lyme disease is easily treated with antibiotics, but without medical attention, the condition can progress.

Stage II Lyme disease causes inflammation of the membranes around the brain and spinal cord. The resulting damage to the central nervous system can lead to dizziness, jaw pain, and sight or hearing impairment. If Lyme disease is identified in Stage II, treatment with antibiotics brings about a cure—and, with it, the reversal of physical damage—in almost 100 percent of all cases. Without medication, however, the disease may slowly progress to Stage III.

Like the early symptoms of Lyme disease, Stage III symptoms—which can include chronic, debilitating arthritis and such neurological problems as exhaustion, paralysis, and dementia—often mimic other conditions. Compounding the confusion is the fact that Stage III often doesn't develop until years after the initial infection. When identified, Stage III Lyme disease is treated with antibiotics, painkillers, and anti-inflammatory agents. At this point, however, antibiotic therapy has a lesser success rate than it does during earlier stages of Lyme disease.

PROTECT YOUR CHILD FROM TICKS

How can you help your child avoid deer ticks and the potential for infection? Listed below are several steps you can take.

☐ For outdoor play, dress your child in tightly woven clothing that covers as much of his body as possible. Hats and scarves, bound hair, and long sleeves are recommended. Pulling your child's socks over his pants legs, tucking in his shirt, and running a strip of wide masking tape over the edges of each garment can keep ticks from burrowing underneath. Light-colored clothing is best, as it will enable you to easily spot any ticks.

☐ Apply an insect repellent containing no more than 10 percent diethyl toluamide (DEET) to the areas of your child's skin that remain exposed. The inset on page 116 provides additional information on the safest use of insect repellents.

☐ Consider a professional application of insecticide around paths, pool or patio shrubbery, or other areas of your property that see heavy use. (Carbaryl, chlorpyrifos, and cyfluthrin are all effective against ticks.) Be sure to consult with your doctor or local board of health before taking this step, and to advise the company you hire that your children often play in the treated areas.

☐ Keep the grass cut short in areas where your child plays. Deer ticks like dark, damp areas, so teach your child to avoid stone walls, rock piles, tall grass, and thick bushes. Prune shrubs to let in more light, and avoid piling brush anywhere near your home.

☐ Dogs and cats have been known to return from a run through the woods carrying a dozen or more ticks in their fur. As much as possible, keep your pet away from thick brush, tall grass, and shrubbery. Ask your veterinarian for the name of a safe tick repellent, and spray your dog or cat before he goes outside. Brush your pet's fur vigorously and feel his skin for burrowed ticks before allowing him back in the house.

☐ When your child comes in from outdoors, check his entire body carefully for ticks. Pay special attention to skin folds and damp areas, and look for rashes that could signal an earlier bite. You may want to make tick checks a regular part of your child's bed- or bathtime routine.

TREAT TICK BITES PROMPTLY

Despite all the above precautions, your child may still suffer a tick bite. Remember that many such bites are harmless. However, to be on the safe side, you should consider having the tick—and your child—tested for infection.

First, remove the tick carefully by grabbing it with tweezers at the point of contact and pulling it off firmly. Do not twist or squeeze the tick, as this can cause bacteria to be released. A slow, steady pull is recommended.

Place the tick in a sealed container with a blade of grass or a moistened cotton ball. Cleanse the site of the bite with alcohol, and apply an antibiotic ointment. Then, take your child and the tick to the doctor. Blood tests for Lyme disease are available, and your doctor may prescribe a precautionary course of treatment, as well.

Research into Lyme disease is ongoing, for the disease has reached epidemic proportions within the past few years. You can always hope for a vaccine against Lyme disease, a surefire cure for Stage III symptoms, or an environmentally sound way of eliminating deer ticks altogether. In the meantime, however, you can do a great deal to protect your child by being careful about your property, monitoring where your child plays, and dressing him with care whenever he plays outside. These precautions may take a little time, but they're sure to translate into hours of worry-free outdoor enjoyment for your whole family.

Resources

Your pediatrician or family practitioner can tell you about the latest developments in the prevention and treatment of Lyme disease. Other good sources of information are listed below.

ORGANIZATIONS

American Academy of
  Pediatrics
141 Northwest Point Boulevard
PO Box 927
Elk Grove Village, IL 60009–0927
(708) 228–5005
(800) 433–9016

This professional society of pediatricians maintains a reference library, publishes educational literature, and sponsors some forty committees on all aspects of pediatric care.

National Institutes of Health
U.S. Department of Health and
  Human Services
Bethesda, MD 20892
(Prefers mail inquiries.)

This government organization is concerned with all health issues, and works for improved public awareness and research efforts.

BOOKS

Arnosky, Jim. *Crinkleroot's Guide to Walking in Wild Places*. New York: Bradbury Press, 1990.

Landau, Elaine. *Lyme Disease*. New York: Franklin Watts, 1990.

Lifton, Bernice. *Bug Busters: Poison-Free Pest Controls for Your House and Garden*. Garden City Park, NY: Avery Publishing Group, 1991.

Silverstein, Alvin. *Lyme Disease, the Great Imitator: How to Prevent and Cure It*. Lebanon, NJ: AVSTAR Publications, 1990.

The Safest Use of Insect Repellents

The use of insect repellent to protect a child from ticks and other biting or stinging insects is a controversial subject. After all, DEET (diethyl toluamide), a component of some repellents that is particularly effective against ticks, is absorbed through the skin into the bloodstream. It can irritate the skin, and, in large quantities, can lead to liver failure and swelling around the brain. When balancing the risk of Lyme disease against the risks posed by minimal absorption of DEET and the other chemicals in most repellents, many doctors recommend careful, sporadic use of a product containing no more than 10 percent DEET. However, you may prefer to use an organic, nontoxic repellent, which is available at health food stores and many outdoor supply stores. Other suggestions for the safe use of insect repellents are listed below.

☐ *Reduce the amount of repellent needed by covering limbs with clothing and applying the substance only to the skin that remains exposed. Never apply a repellent to skin that will be covered by clothing, or to the clothing itself.*

☐ *Avoid getting the repellent in your child's eyes, nose, or mouth, or on his hands.*

☐ *Never allow your child to apply repellent himself.*

☐ *For use on a child, choose a stick or roll-on repellent, as this will give you more control than you'd have with a spray.*

☐ *Apply repellent to the palm of your hand first. Then rub your hand over your child's skin.*

☐ *Remember that most repellents are effective for four to eight hours. Re-application is not necessary during that time.*

☐ *If your child is prone to allergies, be sure to consult your doctor before using any insect repellent.*

☐ *Do not apply repellent to a child under twelve months of age.*

If carefully applied and used only when needed, insect repellents can provide your child with effective protection from ticks and other unwanted "wildlife." Naturally, common sense should always be exercised. If your child shows any reaction to the repellent—a rash, for instance—use should be discontinued, and a different repellent should be found.

"Each child carries his own blessing into the world."

—Yiddish Proverb

23

TALK WITH YOUR CHILD ABOUT AIDS

Few parents want to consider their children at risk of contracting the HIV (human immunodeficiency virus) organism that leads to AIDS (acquired immune deficiency syndrome). But the facts are that HIV is easily transmitted and that AIDS is alarmingly widespread and, at present, incurable. Because so many of today's teen-agers are sexually active, and since intravenous drug use is a problem at some high schools and colleges, it's important to inform your older child that AIDS knows no age, socioeconomic, racial, or ethnic boundaries. Your younger child, who may share a classroom with an HIV victim, should be taught to keep her distance from the bodily fluids of others, and that biting and scratching are absolutely unacceptable. You see, it *is* possible to help protect your youngster from AIDS by sharing age-appropriate facts about the transmission of HIV, and by discussing the behaviors that have been shown to place people at risk.

There are several things to consider before you broach the topic of AIDS with your child. Since an eight-year-old, for instance, is not as equipped to handle medical details as a fourteen-year-old, your child's age should help you decide what information is appropriate. You should also bear in mind your child's knowledge of sex, and then adopt a realistic attitude toward the subject. This will enable you to present new information, and will prevent your discussion of HIV and AIDS from being viewed as "preaching." And even though the average youngster is much more likely to contract AIDS through sexual activity than from a contaminated hypodermic needle, you should consider the possibility that your child or her friends may be experimenting with drugs. This way, you can expand your warnings about the transmission of HIV through shared needles to include the risks posed by drug abuse in general.

How can you prepare for a conversation about AIDS? First, it's wise to arm yourself with resource material. Books and videos are available from several sources (see page 122), and can provide valuable information on the topics you'd like to cover. Since stories are often more convincing than hard, cold facts, you can make AIDS seem more real by gathering information on some high-profile HIV victims. Magic Johnson and Ryan White are two good examples.

When you're ready to begin your discussion of AIDS, sit down with your child and speak to her eye to eye, preferably without outside distractions. Your undivided attention will help convey the seriousness of the matter. Then, you can begin by asking your child what she already knows about the disease. Her answer will help you decide how much information to offer.

As you start your discussion, you're likely to find that your child is very concerned about her chances of contracting the disease. It's important to reassure her, but it's also important to admit the limits of your own knowledge. If your child asks questions that you cannot answer, offer to track down the missing information. But first, here are some facts about AIDS that everyone needs to know.

- AIDS is a disease that progressively destroys the body's immune system—the system that fights infection. It develops as a result of infection by the as-yet-incurable HIV organism, and it is this organism—not AIDS—that is transmitted from person to person.

- It is well established that HIV can be spread through sexual contact, intravenous drug use, and blood transfusions, and from mother to unborn child or nursing infant. However, since the virus is present in all of an infected individual's bodily fluids, and because there is strong evidence that, in at least one instance, HIV was passed from dentist to patient, it's safe to say that more research needs to be done about the transmission of the virus.

- According to the Centers for Disease Control in Atlanta, Georgia, we are not yet certain as to how long the AIDS virus can live outside the body. Currently, many experts believe that HIV dies within a few seconds, but the fact is that the medical community isn't absolutely sure of this claim. Naturally, a hardier virus would raise many new transmission possibilities, so awareness and caution are quite important.

- So far, there have been no documented cases of transmission of the AIDS virus through deep kissing. Yet, it is known that HIV is carried in the saliva—though in smaller quantities than in other bodily fluids. Therefore, it is not completely clear whether a person can contract the virus while kissing an infected individual. It *is* known that HIV can be transmitted during oral sex, because the virus can enter the bloodstream through cuts or sores in the mouth.

- Birth control pills do not protect the user against the AIDS virus. Condoms can be effective, provided they are the right type, do not break during use, and are worn every time oral, anal, or vaginal sex is attempted. It's important to note that natural-skin condoms and condoms designed solely for sexual stimulation are not effective against the spread of this disease. If a particular condom has been approved as an HIV-preventive by the Food and Drug Administration, the package will state this fact.

- When weighing the risk of contracting AIDS through sexual activity, it's necessary to consider a potential partner's experiences. Even monogamy—an exclusive relationship—cannot offer protection from diseases transmitted by former partners.

- In many cases, teachers and child-care professionals are not advised of the presence of an AIDS victim among their young charges. Some states, in fact, suggest assuming that any child in a class or day-care group could potentially be HIV-positive, and therefore recommend the use of disposable gloves whenever an adult must come in contact with a child's nasal mucus, blood, vomit, or bodily waste.

In addition to educating your child about the transmission of HIV, you can clearly identify practices that will reduce her risk of contracting the virus. Promoting abstinence—the avoidance of sexual activity—can be effective. So can reminding your child that in these days of multiple partners, long-term relationships do not guarantee safety from HIV. You can spell out the horrors of drug abuse and addiction, and even try role-playing with your child so that she can practice saying "No" to risky behavior.

If your child spends part of her day around other small children, it's wise to instill in her a healthy respect for the germs that can exist in blood, tears, saliva, urine, and excrement. You might wish to teach your child from the start that it's safest to avoid any contact with the bodily fluids of others. She should learn to wash her hands after using the bathroom, before eating, and often during the day.

Dealing with a sensitive topic like AIDS may not be easy. It's vital, however, to set aside your feelings of discomfort in order to clearly convey the danger involved should your child become—or continue to be—sexually active or a user of hard drugs. An open discussion of HIV and AIDS will give both of you an opportunity to air your views on such subjects as premarital sex and substance abuse, and can better equip your child to resist the peer pressure that often goes hand-in-hand with risky behavior. Certainly, this discussion may be one of the most important things you can do to safeguard your child's life.

Resources

You can get help in arming your child against HIV from your pediatrician or health-care provider. You can also contact your state or local health department, the March of Dimes, the National Urban League, or the American Red Cross for AIDS information. (Check your local phone directory.) The organizations and other resources listed below can provide assistance, as well.

ORGANIZATIONS

American Foundation for AIDS
  Research
1515 Broadway, Suite 3601
New York, NY 10036
(212) 719–0033

This group raises funds for research into the transmission and treatment of HIV and AIDS, and offers resource information designed to arm the public against AIDS.

American Red Cross AIDS
  Education Office
1709 New York Avenue NW
Washington, DC 20006
(202) 639–3223

This agency promotes education in schools and the community as the best defense against the spread of HIV and AIDS.

National AIDS Information
  Clearinghouse
PO Box 6003
Rockville, MD 20850
(800) 458–5231

This organization helps educate the public about AIDS and AIDS-related diseases by providing information, literature, and referrals to local AIDS resources.

National Women's Health
  Network
1325 G Street, NW
Washington, DC 20005
(202) 347–1140

This group advocates better federal health policies for women and serves as a clearinghouse for women's health information.

Project Inform
1965 Market Street, Room 220
San Francisco, CA 94103
(800) 822–7422 *National Hotline*
(800) 334–7422 *In California*

This organization provides AIDS treatment services through its hotline, advocates early intervention and treatment of HIV carriers, and publishes a newsletter dealing with the latest HIV and AIDS treatment information.

U.S. Public Health Service
(800) 342–AIDS *National Hotline*
(800) 344–SIDA *In Spanish*
(800) AIDS–TTY *For the Hearing Impaired*

This organization offers support materials and information about AIDS, and serves as a national referral network.

BOOKS

Armstrong, Ewan McKay. *The Impact of AIDS.* New York: Gloucester Press, 1990.

Blake, Jeanne. *Risky Times: How to Be AIDS-Smart and Stay Healthy—A Guide for Teenagers.* New York: Workman Publishing, 1990.

Day, Lorraine. *AIDS: What the Government Isn't Telling You.* Palm Desert, CA: Rockford Press, 1991.

Fassler, David, and Kelly McQueen. *What's a Virus, Anyway?: The Kid's Book About AIDS.* Burlington, VT: Waterfront Books, 1990.

Hein, Karen, and Theresa Foy DiGeronimo. *AIDS: Trading Fears for Facts—A Guide for Teens.* Mount Vernon, NY: Consumers Union, 1989.

Taylor, Barbara. *Everything You Need to Know About AIDS.* New York: Rosen Publishing Group, 1988.

Protecting Your Child From AIDS

While it's of paramount importance to talk to your child about HIV and AIDS, there are additional steps you can take to protect her from this life-threatening illness. The ideas below can help you play an active part in arming your child against AIDS.

☐ *Keep abreast of the latest information about AIDS. Newspapers and magazines are likely to contain the most current news. In addition, many school districts and hospitals sponsor workshops on AIDS for community members who want to know the facts about the disease.*

☐ *Ask local school district officials about the inclusion of AIDS education in curriculums at all grade levels. If no programs exist, lobby for the addition of this vital information.*

☐ *Ensure that your child's day-care facility is cleaned and disinfected frequently, and that personnel regularly use disposable gloves when wiping noses, changing diapers, and assisting in the bathroom.*

☐ *Since the American Dental Association currently lacks regulations regarding the sterilization of equipment, consider writing to this organization—based at 211 East Chicago Avenue, Chicago, IL 60611— or to your congressperson, urging action on this important issue.*

☐ *Since traces of blood can linger on improperly cleaned dental instruments, insist that your dentist use an autoclave, which is the most effective sterilizing device available. Keep in mind that you are free to leave his or her practice if your requests are not complied with.*

☐ *Expect other health-care providers to use the same vigilance you expect from your dentist. Sterile conditions are vital, as are properly cleaned instruments. And you should insist on the use of disposable gloves during examinations and procedures, and the proper in-office disposal of used needles, cotton, and other hazardous wastes.*

It's reassuring to know that there are so many ways in which you can decrease your child's chances of contracting the HIV organism. And while you're making the world a safer place for your son or daughter, you'll be making it safer for other children, as well.

24

CONSIDER ORGAN DONATION

The issue of organ donation and transplantation is a sensitive one, and perhaps even more unsettling when a child is concerned. But the fact remains that donor organs, tissue, and marrow are very much in demand. You see, each year, more gravely ill patients are added to the tens of thousands on organ-transplant waiting lists. At this time, more than 1,400 patients awaiting donor organs are children and teen-agers. Learning about organ donation will help you decide if this is the right course for your family to take should your life or your child's life end prematurely.

A generation ago, organ transplantation was a novel and highly controversial idea. But with each passing year, surgical techniques have become more sophisticated, and transplant success rates have increased. Today, the greatest impediment to such lifesaving procedures is the scarcity of available organs. Donor kidneys, hearts, livers, lungs, and pancreases are always in demand for use in patients whose own organs are damaged or malfunctioning. Also needed are eyes, tissue, and bone marrow, which are used to restore the sight of the visually impaired and introduce healthy cells into patients whose own systems are ravaged by diseases such as cancer. The fact that matching or near-matching blood and tissue types—a necessity for organ transplantation—are often difficult to obtain seriously limits some patients' chances of receiving a donated organ. Happily, organs from a single donor can be used to save the lives or restore the sight of several recipients. With these facts in mind, you may wish to examine your own feelings about the possibility of donating organs—your own or your child's—in the event of death.

YOU AS AN ORGAN DONOR

The prospect of having your life cut short is grim, indeed. However, the need for donor organs and tissue is so great that you may wish to consider giving this gift of life should you meet an untimely death. While you cannot request that your organs be donated to a child—recipients are chosen according to medical urgency, size, blood type, and antigen match-ups—adult organs, bone, skin, tendons, blood vessels, and heart valves are often transplanted into children. So although any recipient is surely deserving of a second chance at life, you may in fact end up helping a child when you elect to become a donor. Another possibility to consider is becoming a living donor by providing blood, bone marrow, a kidney, or part of your liver or lung to someone in need who is deemed genetically compatible.

YOUR CHILD AS AN ORGAN DONOR

No doubt, the thought of your child's life ending unexpectedly is even more disturbing than the prospect of your own early demise. But many families who donate their deceased child's organs find that this act gives some purpose to an otherwise senseless tragedy. Often, the family's healing process begins when the agreement is made to donate, for the gift of life or sight is a noble legacy. There is also comfort to be taken from communication with the recipient's family members, who, amid joy and gratitude for their own child's good fortune, recognize and share the grief of the donor's family.

BECOMING A DONOR

You can become a prospective donor by completing a donor card, which can be obtained from a hospital or organ procurement organization. In some states, you can indicate permission to transplant your organs by signing the appropriate place on the back of your driver's license. Be aware, however, that even if the deceased is a registered donor, hospitals generally require the next-of-kin's consent before removing any organs. It's important, therefore, to discuss your decision to donate with your family so that, in the event of a tragedy, they can act in your interest. In your child's case, permission to donate would take the form of your signature on the appropriate hospital documents.

What would become of your or your child's donated organs in the event of sudden death? Because it's important to find recipients immediately, hospital personnel would access a computerized registry of people awaiting transplants. Once a match was made, the organs to be donated would be removed—at no cost to the donor's family—and rushed to their various destinations, where the recipients and their prearranged surgical teams would be standing by. Many families are relieved to know that the removal of the organs and tissues neither disfigures the body nor delays funeral arrangements.

In order to make a choice about organ donation that's right for your family, it's probably wise to consider the issue in advance. Certainly, it is easiest to examine your feelings when tragedy is only a remote possibility. Bear in mind that although most organs and tissues are taken from people under the age of sixty-five, anyone in good health can elect to be a donor. Children under the age of eighteen can do so with a parent's or legal guardian's consent.

It isn't hard to picture the pain of losing a family member or the sense of powerlessness and uncertainty that must accompany the wait for a suitable organ for someone who is very sick. But imagine the elation and gratitude when the organs of one person give a second person a new chance at a healthy, normal life. The topic of organ donation and transplantation is unquestionably a difficult one, but becoming knowledgeable about this issue may someday help you make a decision that will save or immeasurably improve the quality of a young life.

Resources

Transplant service personnel are available at most hospitals to help you examine the possibility of organ donation. Their experience, sensitivity, and knowledge of the transplant issue can make your decision-making process easier. For further information, your health-care provider or hospital referral service can put you in touch with the nearest bone-marrow registry; eye bank; organ bank; regional transplant group; or kidney, lung, liver, or heart foundation. The resources listed below may prove helpful, as well.

ORGANIZATIONS

American Transplant Association
PO Box 822123
Dallas, TX 75382–2123
(214) 340–0942

This organization acts as an information and referral network for transplant patients and their families, and offers financial assistance, support, and emergency transportation.

Children's Transplant Association
PO Box 53699
Dallas, TX 75253
(214) 287–8484

This group provides support for families of young patients in need of organ transplants, as well as transportation, accommodations, funds, referrals, and grief recovery programs.

The United Network of Organ
   Sharing (UNOS)
Suite 500
1100 Boulders Parkway
PO Box 13770
Richmond, VA 23225–8770
(800) 24–DONOR

This organization has been established by law as a clearinghouse for organs used in U.S. transplant operations. UNOS matches patients with donors, arranges for organ transport, formulates and implements national policy regarding organ donation and transplantation, and conducts a number of courses for transplant personnel.

BOOKS

Beckelman, Laurie. *Transplants*. New York: Crestwood House, 1990.

Dowie, Mark. *We Have a Donor*. New York: St. Martin's Press, 1988.

Pekkanen, John. *Donor: How One Girl's Death Gave Life to Others*. Boston: Little, Brown and Co., 1986.

25

KNOW THE FACTS ABOUT IMMUNIZATION

At many times in history, epidemics of bacterial infection have swept through villages and towns, wreaking havoc on whole populations. From these epidemics grew the study of immunology, which has resulted in vaccines that stimulate the production of disease-fighting antibodies, thereby providing protection against some very serious diseases. Thanks to these vaccines, once-dreaded infections such as smallpox and polio have been eradicated, and outbreaks of many other diseases have sharply declined.

The medical community overwhelmingly recommends immunizing today's children against a long list of potentially dangerous infections. The vaccines currently available are considered by doctors to be safe, easy to administer, and largely effective. In addition, immunization is mandatory for your child's enrollment in most day-care settings, public and private schools, and colleges. Therefore, many parents follow a doctor-prescribed schedule of vaccines and tests for their children that is similar, if not identical, to the one that appears on page 133.

Other parents, however, choose not to automatically vaccinate their children. Sometimes, this noncompliance with doctors' recommendations has its roots in religious beliefs. More often, however, these parents cite the questionable success of the measles and pertussis vaccines; reports of injuries related to DTP (diphtheria-tetanus-pertussis), measles, and mumps injections; and other areas of concern regarding the immunization issue. Most of this group believes that a natural immunity to infection—brought on by a child's enduring a mild case of a given disease—is preferable to artificially introducing the germ for the purpose of long-term antibody production, thus causing the child to harbor the infection permanently. Some experts in homeopathy suggest that becoming a "carrier" through vaccination actually decreases a child's ability to respond to other infections.

Then there's the sensitive issue of vaccine injury. While incidents of serious reactions to immunization are relatively rare, vaccines have been linked to such serious conditions as brain damage, encephalitis, convulsions, Guillain-Barré syndrome, meningitis, and nerve deafness. As a result, the 1986 National Childhood Vaccine Injury Act requires the Public Health Service to investigate all reports of vaccine injury.

In light of even the smallest possible risk to their children's health, some parents are simply unwilling to agree to a procedure whose success rate cannot be guaranteed. Although you're likely to meet resistance from school officials and mainstream medical professionals should you decide against immunizing your child, the numbers of parents and health-care experts who object to routine vaccinations are growing.

Where do these conflicting schools of thought leave you, the parent? It's important to realize that requirements and recommendations regarding immunization are ever-changing—and that, as a result, the health risks posed to child recipients are decreasing—because of ongoing research as well as upswings or downturns in the incidence of different diseases. Therefore, you can best serve your child by becoming knowledgeable about the history, purpose, pros, and cons of each vaccine, and by keeping up with the latest immunization information from the health-care and alternative health-care communities. This way, you can be assured of making the choice that's right for your family. Here are some ideas that may help you.

☐ Remember that breastfeeding (see Entry 19 on page 101), as well as general fitness and a healthy diet (see Entry 16 on page 77), can create the strongest possible immune system in a growing child.

☐ Before okaying any vaccine or test, discuss your child's recent health and history of immunization reactions with your doctor or health professional. To avoid subjecting your child to a virus or bacteria while her resistance is poor, also have her examined for current infection.

☐ Ask questions of your health-care professional. Learn the purpose of each immunization, and find out if there are serious risks involved. Also ask what, if any, reaction you can expect in the days ahead.

☐ Be aware that immunization policies at schools and day-care facilities exist to protect all children. However, exemptions from these policies are occasionally granted for religious or health reasons. And parents who teach their children at home often can postpone the immunization issue indefinitely. If you are strongly against having your child vaccinated, investigate the possibility of an exemption or home schooling.

☐ Ask your health-care provider about the possibility of delaying immunizations. While this may make your child more vulnerable to certain infections during infancy, she may tolerate the various vaccines better when she's heavier than twenty pounds or more than a year old.

☐ Watch your child carefully during the forty-eight hours following an injection. Take complete notes about any reactions, and report these to your doctor during the next office visit. If a reaction is unexpected or seems severe, seek medical attention at once. Then investigate alternatives to the procedure that caused the problem.

☐ Keep complete, signed records of your child's immunization history, if any. These can come in handy during emergencies, when traveling, when you change doctors, and when your child enters or changes schools.

☐ Be aware that, due to reports of occasional severe reactions to the pertussis vaccine, more doctors are now willing to give the TD vaccine alone. Discuss this option with your health-care provider.

In very recent years, diseases that were once thought to be well controlled or nearly eradicated—namely, measles, mumps, tuberculosis, pertussis, and hepatitis B—have made a comeback. Children who are not immunized, or who are vaccinated only when they are ready to start school, are unprotected against these serious infections during early childhood, when vulnerability is greatest. Additionally, because the existence of vaccines gives unimmunized children less chance to acquire immunity through natural infection, *their* children may be born without any immunity at all to these diseases.

Nevertheless, experts in the field of homeopathy have raised valid questions about the advisability of routinely vaccinating children—and thereby subjecting them to possible complications—when immunity through natural infection has sometimes proven safer and has always proven more effective. In the end, it's important that you understand *both* viewpoints about vaccinations, and that you obtain the latest information about the immunization issue before making a choice for your child.

Resources

You can get the information you need to make an informed decision about vaccination from the resources listed below.

ORGANIZATIONS

American Academy of Pediatrics
141 Northwest Point Boulevard
PO Box 927
Elk Grove Village, IL 60009-0927
(708) 228–5005
(800) 433–9016

This medical society operates a library of books and journals on pediatric medicine, office practice, and child health-care policies; maintains committees to study more than forty issues in pediatrics; sponsors continuing education programs; and produces a variety of publications of interest to medical professionals and the general public.

American Medical Association
  (AMA)
515 North State Street
Chicago, IL 60610
(312) 464–5000

The AMA provides information on medical and health legislation, cooperates in setting medical school standards, and operates a physicians' library.

Dissatisfied Parents Together
  (DPT)
c/o National Vaccine Information
  Center
128 Branch Road
Vienna, VA 22180
(703) 938–DPT3

Dissatisfied Parents Together works to raise public awareness of the plight of vaccine-injured children, and seeks to change the policy of mandatory vaccinations.

International Foundation for
  Homeopathy
2366 Eastlake, Number 301
Seattle, WA 98102
(206) 324–8230

This alternative-health organization promotes homeopathy and provides the public with a better understanding of the relationship of health and diseases to the natural laws of cure.

National Center for Homeopathy
801 North Fairfax Street, Suite 306
Alexandria, VA 22314
(703) 5487790

This group seeks to promote the art of healing according to natural laws of cure, and to implement and facilitate the study of homeopathy among laypersons and the medical community.

BOOKS

Bindler, Ruth McGillis, Yvonne Tso, and Linda Berner Howry. *The Parent's Guide to Pediatric Drugs*. New York: Harper and Row, 1986.

Coulter, Harris L., and Barbara Loe Fisher. *A Shot in the Dark: Why the P in the DPT Vaccination May Be Hazardous to Your Child's Health*. Garden City Park, NY: Avery Publishing Group, 1991.

James, William. *Immunization: The Reality Behind the Myth*. Granberry, MA: Bergin and Garvey, 1988.

Neustaedter, Randall. *The Immunization Decision: A Guide for Parents*. Berkeley, CA: North Atlantic Books, 1990.

Schmidt, Barton D. *Your Child's Health*. New York: Bantam Books, 1991.

"We can say with some assurance that although children may be the victims of fate, they will not be the victims of our neglect."

—**John Fitzgerald Kennedy**

The AAP-Recommended Vaccination and Test Schedule

Many North American children are routinely immunized and tested for certain infectious diseases. The table below shows the schedule of vaccines and tests currently recommended for children by the American Academy of Pediatrics. This is followed by a description of the various procedures.

Age	Vaccines and Tests
Newborn	First Hepatitis B.
One Month	Second Hepatitis B.
Two Months	First DTP/Hib and OPV.
Four Months	Second DTP/Hib and OPV.
Six Months	Third DTP/Hib and Hepatitis B.
Twelve Months	Tuberculin Test.
Fifteen Months	MMR.
Eighteen Months	Fourth DTP/Hib and Third OPV.
Four to Six Years	Fifth DTP and Fourth OPV, Measles Booster, and Tuberculin Test (where required).
Ten to Twelve Years	Measles Booster and Tuberculin Test (where required).
Fourteen to Sixteen Years	TD Booster and Tuberculin Test (where required).

Considering that vaccines may be accompanied by side effects such as rash, fever, swelling, or irritability, you may well question their purpose. The information below can give you a clearer picture.

The DTP/Hib (Diphtheria, Tetanus, and Pertussis or Whooping Cough/Haemophilus Influenzae type b) Vaccine

For years, DTP and Hib injections were administered separately. Now, however, the vaccines for diphtheria, tetanus, and pertussis—all serious viral infections—are combined with the vaccine that protects against the bacteria Haemophilus b, and are offered as a series of four shots during infancy and toddlerhood. One DTP and one or more TD boosters are given later in childhood to maintain protection. The Hib portion of the vaccine, also identified as HbCV, protects against bacterial meningitis, as well as three other dangerous diseases caused by Haemophilus b: epiglottitis, joint infection, and pneumonia.

Sometimes a small lump persists for several weeks at the site of the DTP/Hib injection. In addition, the pertussis portion of this vaccine can produce crankiness and fever, beginning a few hours after injection and lasting for up to two days. In relatively rare cases, the reaction to the pertussis vaccine is severe, resulting in convulsions or paralysis, and leads doctors to exclude pertussis from that child's future injections. An acellular pertussis (DtaP) vaccine, which carries fewer side effects but provides reduced immunity, is available for children over twelve months of age who have received previous DTP doses. After a child's seventh birthday, pertussis is eliminated from booster injections, in any case. It is important to contact your doctor for advice concerning any immunization reaction exhibited by your child, or about the possibility of avoiding the pertussis vaccine altogether.

The Hepatitis B Vaccine

This immunization is now recommended for all infants, as well as for older children, teen-agers, and adults who may face a high risk of exposure due to immune-system problems or possible close contact with a victim of the disease. The immunization consists of a series of three injections, and provides protection against the hepatitis B virus— a highly contagious and potentially disabling disease that has seen a recent resurgence.

The MMR (Measles, Mumps, and Rubella, or German Measles) Vaccine

This vaccine protects your child from three potentially serious viral diseases in a single shot. In some states, this initial shot is followed by a booster before a child starts school; in all states, it's followed by a booster in early adolescence. Some children exhibit a reaction similar to a mild case of measles—a fever and/or rash that occurs five to twelve days after inoculation and lasts for a day or two.

The OPV (Oral Poliovirus, or Sabin) Vaccine

This vaccine is dropped directly onto the tongue according to the schedule on page 133, and provides protection against the three types of viruses that cause polio, a once-prevalent crippling disease. The OPV vaccine is made from a live virus, and so can be transmitted to anyone who comes in contact with the bowel movement of the vaccinated child. Occasionally, if a family member has a serious illness that lowers his or her resistance to infection, the Salk vaccine—made from an inactivated virus—may be used instead. Neither vaccine carries side effects.

The TD (Tetanus and Diphtheria) Vaccine

This tetanus-diphtheria booster injection is given after a child's seventh birthday, after the pertussis segment has been eliminated from the vaccine.

The Tuberculin Test

This test is being administered with increasing frequency due to a recent resurgence in cases of tuberculosis, a lung disease that is highly contagious and difficult to treat. The test involves compressing the skin of the inner forearm with a set of treated tines, and watching for a skin reaction—redness and swelling—at the site over the next few days. There is no effective immunization available against tuberculosis; therefore, the best protection is early detection through the tine test.

The Varicella (Chicken Pox) Vaccine

This vaccine, which protects children against chicken pox, is currently available only to children whose chronic illness results in an impaired immune system. The vaccine has been tested in the United States and abroad, and is under consideration by the Food and Drug Administration (FDA) for use by the general public.

Doctors agree that inoculating a child—and, sometimes, subjecting him to a day or two of discomfort and irritability—can be traumatic. However, from the medical community's standpoint, nonimmunized children, whose numbers are growing, face the threat of early exposure and increased vulnerability to complications from serious diseases—diseases against which they can be armed by a course of inoculations that may be momentarily unpleasant, but will afford years of protection. On the other hand, many proponents of natural immunity and healing techniques endorse abstinence from routine vaccinations. As a parent, you do have a choice about vaccination, and you'll be doing your child a great favor by basing your decision on research and advice gleaned from experts on both sides of the issue.

"Mankind owes to the children the best it has to give."

—Declaration of the Rights of the Child

26

PROVIDE PREVENTATIVE HEALTH CARE FOR YOUR CHILD

Chances are, you would head for a doctor, dentist, or emergency room if your child's temperature soared to 105°F, or if he dislodged a permanent tooth or bled profusely from a deep cut. The fact is that emergencies of this nature require professional attention. Yet, it can be all too easy to overlook the preventative aspects of your child's health care, such as well-baby visits to a pediatrician or semi-annual teeth cleanings for your older child—particularly when costs are high, insurance coverage is inadequate or nonexistent, and money is in short supply. But each time you neglect or postpone your child's routine medical and dental care, your health professional misses the opportunity to detect problems at an early, easily treatable stage; you, the parent, lose the chance to instill good health habits in your child; and your child has a greater risk of facing such unnecessary handicaps as impaired hearing, as well as a host of other disorders.

There's no question that difficult financial times can make routine health care seem like a luxury. But, as you can see, neglecting preventative care poses a threat to your child's well-being. The list below offers ideas on how you can provide your child with the health care he needs.

☐ Practice preventative health and dental care at home. Make adequate sleep, regular exercise, and a healthy diet family priorities. (See Entry 16 on page 77 for suggestions regarding nutrition and fitness.) Promote good health habits such as hand-washing, and discourage the spread of germs by avoiding shared eating utensils, combs, handkerchiefs, toothbrushes, and face cloths, and by properly disposing of soiled tissues and diapers. Encourage your child to brush his teeth after eating and to use dental floss daily.

☐ Reduce your child's exposure to lead (see Entry 46 on page 239), secondhand smoke (see Entry 20 on page 104), and drugs and alcohol (see Entry 29 on page 153)—substances that can play havoc with his health.

☐ Follow the medical and dental communities' recommendations for preventative care. Seek physical checkups on a monthly basis for an infant, twice yearly for a toddler or preschooler, and once a year for an older child. Become knowledgeable about immunizations. (See Entry 25 on page 128 for information.) Have your child checked by a dentist at age two, and follow up with annual examinations and twice-yearly teeth cleanings.

☐ Follow your doctor's suggestions regarding the consultation of specialists. In certain cases, it is a common and well-advised practice for health-care professionals to refer patients to doctors who have greater expertise in the appropriate area.

☐ If cost is a factor in postponing your child's health care, explore your options. If you have health insurance, contact your insurance company for a listing of participating providers. If you must take your child to a specialist, ask your primary health-care provider to recommend someone from this list. Look into county-run clinics, which sometimes offer reduced-rate health care to qualified families. Seek out a doctor who is willing to accept payment in manageable installments, or who will exchange services with you (e.g., your child's annual checkup for the painting of his or her office or the drafting of his or her next newsletter). Find out if a medical or dental school in your area offers low-cost checkups or teeth-cleaning by students.

☐ Consider qualified alternative health care. Excellent and often less-expensive results have been obtained through homeopathy, the stimulation of the body's natural immune system; chiropractic, the promotion of self-healing by freeing bodily organs of interference from the central nervous system; and naturopathy, the use of therapeutic products and healing techniques based on the healing powers of nature.

☐ Lobby for affordable health care. Entry 53 on page 287 outlines some of the ways in which you can work for better conditions for the next generation.

Proper preventative medical and dental care can make a great difference in the life of your child; yet, parents are often neglectful in this area. By staying mindful of the benefits of routine checkups, investigating alternative health care, and being somewhat creative in the face of financial constraints, you can provide your child with the care he needs, as well as a brighter future.

Resources

The following are some good sources of information on providing your child with proper preventative health care.

ORGANIZATIONS

American Academy of Pediatrics
141 Northwest Point Boulevard
PO Box 927
Elk Grove Village, IL 60009–0927
(708) 228–5005
(800) 433–9016

This society of pediatricians works for child health and safety through research, education, and advancements in the field of pediatric care.

American Medical Association (AMA)
515 North State Street
Chicago, IL 60610
(312) 464–5000

The AMA furnishes information on improvements in health care and health legislation, and operates committees to study various aspects of the medical field.

BOOKS

Anderson, Kenneth, and Lois Harmon. *The Prentice-Hall Dictionary of Nutrition and Health.* Englewood Cliffs, NJ: Prentice Hall, 1985.

Bennett, William I., et al. *Your Good Health: How to Stay Well and What to Do When You're Not.* Cambridge, MA: Harvard University Press, 1987.

World Book Corporation. *The World Book Rush-Presbyterian-St. Luke's Medical Center Medical Encyclopedia: Your Guide to Good Health.* Chicago: World Book, 1991.

Wootan, George, and Sarah Verney. *Take Charge of Your Child's Health.* New York: Crown Publishers, 1992.

Zand, Janet, Rachel Walton, and Robert Rountree. *Smart Medicine for a Healthier Child.* Garden City Park, NY: Avery Publishing Group, 1994.

27

RECOGNIZE THE SIGNS OF DEPRESSION AND SUICIDAL TENDENCIES

Youth suicide is a disturbing topic, to say the least. More than 5,000 people under the age of twenty-five take their own lives each year. Statistically, boys are five times more likely to commit suicide than are girls; but neither gender—and no socioeconomic, ethnic, or racial group—can consider itself safe from this tragedy. Still, while emotional upheaval often goes hand-in-hand with adolescence and young adulthood, there is much you can do to improve communication with and encourage healthy behavior in your child, thereby avoiding circumstances that might cause her to consider suicide. And if you learn about and watch for behavior that signals serious depression or suicidal intent, you'll be able to get your child the help she needs to cope with her problems.

What can be done to improve your child's self-image, stability, and communicativeness? First, it's important to share feelings openly with the family, encouraging the exploration of problems and the airing of grievances. It's also wise to train yourself to be an attentive listener. This sort of support teaches your child that discussing and seeking help with problems is both desirable and healthy. Since physical fitness is closely linked to self-image and state of mind, you can also make it a habit to incorporate exercise, a well-balanced diet, and adequate sleep into the whole family's routine. Encouraging your child's participation in wholesome activities, such as team sports or a service club, can be helpful, as can including religion in everyday life. You might also explore therapy as a way to strengthen the family unit, since suicidal feelings in a child are sometimes related to other problems within the home. Finally, it's wise to avoid placing too many demands on your child, for doing so can create stress. Instead, teach her to keep her expectations realistic and to seek the support of family and friends in working toward her goals—one goal at a time.

Occasionally, despite their best efforts, parents still sense that their child is becoming depressed or withdrawn. If particular books, magazines, TV programs, videos, movies, or games seem to frighten, alienate, or depress your child, show your concern and urge her to avoid them. (See Entry 8 on page 30 for more information.) If her depression is ongoing, or if you suspect involvement with alcohol or other drugs, consider contacting a family therapist or drug treatment center for assistance. There are several suicide hotline numbers included in this section (see page 143) that you might wish to post with your family's other emergency phone listings. Needless to say, a call placed by you or your child during an emotional crisis could be a lifesaver!

Unfortunately, there are many myths concerning youth suicide, and it's important to realize that some of what you hear may be untrue. Contrary to one popular notion, for example, a child who talks about suicide *may indeed* attempt to take her life. In fact, a very depressed child often tries to warn her parents or friends of suicidal intentions. A child who feels suicidal is often undisturbed by the idea of death and dying; but, despite what another common myth would have us believe, this kind of emotional instability doesn't necessarily last forever. Additionally, suicide need not be a forbidden topic between parent and child, because asking a youngster about suicidal intentions will *not* encourage her to make an attempt on her life. In fact, talking over your child's concerns can diffuse the threat of suicide.

This is not to say that you should let down your guard about youth suicide, however. Actually, there are some very clear signs of impending suicide—signs that parents would do well to learn and watch for. Studies have shown that a teen-ager or young adult who is considering suicide may:

- Suddenly appear withdrawn or very depressed.
- Act unusually rebellious or hostile.

- Show marked changes in sleeping or eating habits.
- Be preoccupied with themes of death and dying.
- Talk about suicidal feelings.
- Be upset about the loss of an important relationship.
- Be extremely secretive.
- Suddenly lose interest in grooming and hygiene.
- Begin to give away valued possessions.
- Be heavily involved with alcohol or other drugs.
- Be a victim of emotional, sexual, physical, or psychological abuse.
- Have a history of suicide attempts.

If your child exhibits one or more of the above warning signs, and if the behavior is unusual for her or comes on suddenly, the need for help may be indicated. If your child appears to be in the grip of a suicidal emergency, immediate help is available at the hotline numbers listed on page 143. If your child's situation does not appear to be an emergency, but you would like more information about suicide prevention, see the Resources section beginning on page 143.

A generation ago, there was great shame attached to the act of suicide. Today, a more enlightened population recognizes that emotional instability, severe depression, and suicidal tendencies are increasingly common—and very treatable— conditions. Happily, you can greatly reduce the chance that your child will be affected by problems of this nature by creating a positive, supportive atmosphere at home and exploring counseling as a solution to problems within the family. And if your child's current state of mind seems to demand even more decisive action, it's good to know that help is widely available.

Resources

A family therapist or your community mental health center can furnish additional information about dealing with depression and suicidal tendencies in a child. The following resources may also be helpful.

Hotline Numbers

If your child appears to be in crisis, use the following hotline numbers for immediate assistance.

Childhelp USA
National Child Abuse Hotline
(800) 4-A-CHILD

National Runaway Switchboard
(800) 621-4000

Covenant House
(800) 999-9999

National Youth Crisis Hotline
(800) HIT-HOME

ORGANIZATIONS

American Association of Suicidology
2459 South Ash
Denver, CO 80222
(303) 692–0985

This organization encourages the study of suicide and suicide prevention through programs, publications, and cooperation with similar organizations.

National Committee on Youth
  Suicide Prevention
65 Essex Road
Chestnut Hill, MA 02167
(617) 738–0700

This volunteer committee of parents, professionals, and government officials works to increase public awareness of youth suicide, provides a national information and referral system, and assists in the development of youth suicide-prevention programs in communities.

National Institute of Mental
  Health/Office of Scientific
  Information
Room 15C–05
Public Inquiry Branch
5600 Fishers Lane
Rockville, MD 20857
(301) 443–4513

This agency conducts research on and educates the public and health officials about the causes, diagnosis, treatment, and prevention of depression and other mental disorders.

Youth Suicide National Center
Suite 203
204 East Second Avenue
San Mateo, CA 94401
(415) 347–3961

This group coordinates and supports efforts to reduce youth suicide through educational programs, materials, and services.

In Canada:

Canadian Association for Child
  and Play Therapy
Box 698
Kingston, ON K7L 4X1
(613) 382–1045

*This organization works to understand
and treat childhood depression, as well
as other serious emotional conditions.*

Children's Psychiatric Research
  Institute
600 Sanitorium Road
London, ON N6H 3W7
(519) 471–2540

*This group of medical professionals
conducts research into, educates the
public about, and diagnoses and treats
depression and other mental disorders
in children.*

BOOKS

Chiles, John. *Teenage Depression and Suicide.* New York: Chelsea House, 1986.

Colman, Warren. *Understanding and Preventing Teen Suicide.* Chicago: Children's Press, 1990.

Colt, George Howe. *The Enigma of Suicide.* New York: Summit Books, 1991.

Conroy, David L. *Out of the Nightmare: Recovery From Depression and Suicidal Pain.* New York: New Liberty Press, 1991.

Crook, Marion. *Teenagers Talk About Suicide.* Toronto: NC Press, 1988.

Flanders, Stephen A. *Suicide.* New York: Facts on File, 1991.

Hyde, Margaret O., and Elizabeth Held Forsyth. *Suicide.* New York: Franklin Watts, 1991.

Johnston, Jerry. *Why Suicide? What Parents and Teachers Must Know to Save Our Kids.* Nashville, TN: Oliver-Nelson Books, 1987.

McEvoy, Alan. *Youth and Exploitation.* Montreal: Learning Publications, 1990.

Smith, Judie. *Coping With Suicide: A Resource Book for Teenagers and Young Adults.* New York: Rosen Publishing Group, 1990.

28

RECOGNIZE THE SIGNS OF AN ALCOHOL OR DRUG PROBLEM

It is estimated that one million of today's adolescents smoke marijuana, and nearly five million drink alcohol. Many thousands of teens admit using various stimulants and tranquilizers, and between 5 and 11 percent of male high school students build up their bodies with anabolic steroids. And the result? Studies show that as many as half of teen-agers who use alcohol and other drugs may already be chemically dependent. And, sadly, some of today's children venture into the world of substance abuse at a very early age. Every day, in fact, some five hundred 10- to 14-year-olds experiment with drugs for the first time, while a thousand more take their first drink of alcohol. Some of the substances with which these children experiment are highly addictive, others carry grave physical side effects, most are deadly in large quantities, and all are illegal when used by a child under the age of 21. And it is clear that even occasional substance abuse poses a threat to the health of your child.

Have you reason for alarm if you suspect that your child is involved in substance abuse? Certainly. But you can help your child by being aware of the signs of alcohol and drug use, and by knowing how to best respond if your child does in fact have a problem.

WHY A CHILD MIGHT USE DRUGS OR ALCOHOL

There are several factors that might compel a child or teen-ager to use alcohol and other drugs. Peer pressure has often been found to foreshadow drug experimentation, as adolescents are particularly motivated to "follow the crowd." Boredom also contributes to drug use by children under age eighteen, some of whom view getting high as a form of recreation. Low self-esteem can be a factor, too, because drugs can make a shy teen feel momentarily relaxed and outgoing, can create a sense of belonging for a lonely teen, or, in the case of steroids, can improve the physique, endurance, and speed of a teen who measures self-worth by athletic ability. Lastly, some adolescents turn to drugs as an escape from circumstances that make them unhappy. Getting high can bring a false sense of power to a child who is frightened, angry, or depressed.

HOW TO TELL IF YOUR CHILD USES DRUGS

Most parents hope for a parent-child relationship that is strong enough to allow confidences. But more often than not, an adolescent keeps drug or alcohol use a secret from his family. If this is the case, you can examine four aspects of your child's life for signs of drug involvement: physical appearance, behavior, school performance, and personal possessions.

Physical Appearance

A child who abuses drugs may undergo certain changes in appearance. He may look exceptionally pale and have bloodshot eyes or drooping eyelids. His eye movements may appear to be slow, his pupils may be dilated, and he may wear sunglasses indoors or at night. An adolescent drug user may have unexplained weight loss or sudden muscle development and a rapid onset on acne, or he may demonstrate an increased appetite for sweets. In addition, a child may show signs of neglecting personal hygiene, or marked changes in speech or vocabulary patterns.

Behavior

Certain behavioral changes may also occur if your child becomes a habitual user of drugs or alcohol. You may have cause for concern if your child experiences unexplained moodiness, depression, irritability, or anxiety; or if he begins to violate curfews, balks at telling you his whereabouts away from home, and overreacts to simple requests and mild criticisms. If your child is involved with drugs or alcohol, he may limit communication with family and friends, seem preoccupied, and lose interest in hobbies, sports, and other previously important pursuits. He may act lethargic, sleep for extended periods of time, and, overall, lose his enthusiasm for life. And a drug-involved child may occasionally take money or items of value from family members or friends as a means of paying for drugs. It's important to remember that behavioral changes associated with substance abuse are not always sudden, but are usually marked when compared with a child's customary behavior.

School Performance

Classroom performance problems are another strong indication of a child's involvement with alcohol and drugs. Warning signs include a decreased interest in going to school, withdrawal from sports and school activities, and frequent absenteeism or tardiness. You should also be alert to the onset of problems with your child's concentration, attention span, and short-term memory. A drug-involved child may fall asleep during classes, may experience a marked drop in grades, and may show an increase in or onset of disruptive behavior in school. He may also suddenly acquire new friends and adopt new styles of dress. Like other behavioral changes, these problems will be easiest to see when you compare your child's past and present attitude, interest, and grades.

Personal Possessions

Certain physical evidence can also indicate that your child is drinking alcohol or taking drugs. Certainly, finding marijuana cigarettes, capsules, white powder, or tablets in your child's possession is a warning sign. But drugs themselves are not the only things to look for. You should be alert to the smell of marijuana—described as a sweet, acrid, burned-rope odor—and to the sudden appearance of incense, deodorizers, mouthwash, or eye drops in your child's room or car. Drug paraphernalia is also evidence of substance involvement; look for cigarette rolling papers, clay pipes, screens, strainers, pipe filters, small glass vials, small spoons, straws, and razor blades. A child who uses drugs often has drugs to hide, so you should also be on the lookout for "stash" holders—film cannisters, for instance, plastic sandwich bags, or any container that unscrews at the bottom or top. There may also be cause for concern if your child suddenly has money but cannot or will not explain its source, or if he seems fascinated by drug-related books, music, magazines, or comics.

HOW TO RESPOND TO SUSPECTED DRUG USE

If you have reason to believe that your child is using drugs or alcohol, a wise first step would be to call a toll-free substance-abuse hotline (see the Resources list beginning on page 150) for information and guidance. Some other helpful suggestions are listed below.

☐ Share your concerns with your child in a calm, objective manner.

☐ Involve your family doctor. Ask him or her to examine your child and to provide advice and literature pertaining to substance abuse.

☐ Speak with your child's teachers and with school officials to learn what you can about your child's school performance.

☐ Set an example for your child—and remove temptation—by eliminating tobacco, alcohol, and drugs from your home.

☐ Contact a local treatment facility in your community and ask for advice and assistance.

☐ Impose restrictions that will help to remove your child from circumstances in which drug use may occur. For instance, you can establish a curfew, check to see if parents will be present at parties, and set limits on time spent in friends' unsupervised homes. Entry 1 on page 3 presents additional suggestions to help you keep tabs on your child and get to know his friends.

☐ Investigate family counseling to help your child determine the underlying cause of his drug or alcohol use.

☐ Seek support for yourself through Al-Anon, Nar-Anon, or a similar group. You'll be better able to help your child when you begin to understand and learn to cope with his substance involvement.

If your child's drug problem warrants ongoing treatment, there are several options to explore. The first option, the public substance-abuse program, tends to be centered in urban areas. Because most public programs are government-funded, waiting lists are long, treatment time is brief—in some cases, just a few weeks—and follow-up support is virtually nonexistent. The second option is an intensive inpatient program. A program such as this, usually geared for people who are chemically dependent, costs an average of $9,000 per month and usually lasts two months. The third and often most successful option is an outpatient program, which can provide your child with therapy and support for as long as two years. This type of treatment costs an average of $1,000 to $2,000 per month.

Most substance-abuse hotlines can offer referrals to programs in your area that can treat your child's specific problem for a cost that you can afford. It's important to note that treatment for teens often differs from adult treatment in that it helps a child "catch up" developmentally with the physical and social strides his peers may have made while he was involved with drugs or alcohol. Nutritionists and exercise trainers are often involved.

While the possibility that your child is involved in alcohol or drug abuse is certainly frightening, it should not be disheartening. With your unflagging support, plus the intervention of substance-abuse professionals, your child can relearn healthy habits and discover the exciting, fulfilling life that awaits him outside the world of drugs.

Resources

The organizations and publications that follow can furnish more information about recognizing and responding to a child's drug or alcohol problem.

ORGANIZATIONS

Al-Anon Family Group
  Headquarters
PO Box 862, Midtown Station
New York, NY 10018
(212) 302–7240
(800) 356–9996 *National Hotline*

This twelve-step group helps individuals who have a friend or relative with a drinking problem by providing information on alcoholism and by offering support.

Alcohol Policy Council
PO Box 148
Waterford, VA 22190
(703) 882–3933

This organization works to reduce alcohol-related problems through education, and offers information on alcoholism.

Alcoholics Anonymous World
  Services (AA)
PO Box 459, Grand Central Station
New York, NY 10163
(212) 686–1100

This organization helps members achieve sobriety through a twelve-step program that involves sharing experiences, hope, and strength. AA publishes several informative publications that offer support to members and their families.

Families Anonymous, Inc.
PO Box 528
Van Nuys, CA 91408
(818) 989–7841

This worldwide organization offers twelve-step self-help programs for families and friends of people with behavioral problems associated with drug abuse.

Friendly *Peer*suasion
c/o Girls Incorporated
441 West Michigan Street
Indianapolis, IN 46202
(317) 634–7546

This group provides a twelve-week course that seeks to prevent drug and alcohol abuse in girls from eleven to fourteen years of age.

Hazelden Foundation
Pleasant Valley Road
Box 176
Center City, MN 55012–0176
(800) 328–9000

This organization distributes educational materials and self-help literature for participants in twelve-step recovery programs and for professionals in the recovery field.

Institute on Black Chemical Abuse
2616 Nicollet Avenue
Minneapolis, MN 55408
(612) 871–7878

This group provides training, technical assistance, and programs that address drug issues of concern to African-Americans and other clients of color.

Nar-Anon Family Group
  Headquarters
World Service Office
PO Box 2562
Palos Verdes Peninsula, CA 90274
(213) 547–5800

This organization offers support to friends and family members of people with drug problems.

National Clearinghouse for
Alcohol and Drug Information
(NCADI)
Box 2345
Rockville, MD 20852
(301) 468–2600
(800) SAY–NOTO *National Hotline*

This organization serves as a resource center for information and publications dealing with alcohol and drug abuse, and distributes several free pamphlets on drug abuse and prevention.

National Council on Alcoholism, Inc.
12 West 21st Street
New York, NY 10010
(212) 206–6770
(800) NCA–CALL *National Hotline*

This group provides information about alcoholism through more than 300 local affiliates, and provides a referral service for families and individuals who are seeking help with chemical dependency.

Toughlove, International
100 Mechanic Street
PO Box 1069
Doylestown, PA 18901
(215) 348–7090
(800) 333–1069

This national self-help support group for parents, children, and communities endorses a hard-line approach to initiate and maintain positive behavior changes in young people in trouble. Toughlove publishes a newsletter, brochures, and books, and holds workshops around the country.

BOOKS

Alexander, Clifton Jack. *Kick the Drug Habit: The Basic Guide.* Tucson, AZ: Antler Publishing, 1989.

Alibraneli, Tom. *Young Alcoholics.* Minneapolis: CompCare Publications, 1978.

Chomet, Julian. *Speed and Amphetamines.* New York: Franklin Watts, 1990.

Collins, Lorraine, Kenneth E. Leonard, and John S. Searles. *Alcohol and the Family: Research and Clinical Perspectives.* New York: Guilford Press, 1990.

DeStefano, Susan. *Focus on Opiates.* Frederick, MD: Twenty-First Century Books, 1991.

DuPont, Robert, Jr. *Getting Tough on Gateway Drugs.* Washington: American Psychiatric Press, 1985.

Friedman, David P. *Focus on Drugs and the Brain: A Drug-Alert Book.* Frederick, MD: Twenty-First Century Books, 1990.

Heuer, Marti. *Happy Daze*. Denver: MAC Printing and Publishing Division, 1985.

Hyde, Margaret O. *Know About Drugs*. New York: Walker and Co., 1990.

Lawson, Gary, et al. *Alcoholism and the Family: A Guide to Treatment and Prevention*. Rockville, MD: ASPE Publications, 1983.

McLoughlin, Katharine Delaney, and Jennifer Rice-Licare. *Cocaine Solutions: Help for Cocaine Abusers and Their Families*. New York: Harrington Park Press, 1990.

Madison, Arnold. *Drugs and You*. Englewood Cliffs, NJ: J. Messner, 1990.

Manatt, Marsha. *Parents, Peers, and Pot II (Parents in Action)*. Rockville, MD: U.S. Department of Health and Human Services, 1983.

Meehan, Bob. *Beyond the Yellow Brick Road: Our Children and Drugs*. New York: Farnsworth Publishing, 1984.

Milgram, Gail Gleason. *What, When, and How to Talk to Children About Alcohol and Other Drugs*. Minneapolis: Hazelden Publishing, 1983.

Neilson, Nancy J. *Teen Alcoholism*. San Diego: Lucent Books, 1990.

Perry, Robert. *Focus on Nicotine and Caffeine: A Drug-Alert Book*. Frederick, MD: Twenty-First Century Books, 1990.

Shulman, Jeffrey. *Focus on Hallucinogens*. Frederick, MD: Twenty-First Century Books, 1991.

Steinglass, Peter, et al. *The Alcoholic Family*. New York: Basic Books, 1987.

Talmadge, Katherine S. *Focus on Steroids*. Frederick, MD: Twenty-First Century Books, 1991.

Winn, Mark. *Children Without Childhood: Growing Up Too Fast in the World of Sex and Drugs*. New York: Penguin Books, 1983.

29

HELP YOUR CHILD
GROW UP ALCOHOL -
AND DRUG - FREE

Alcohol and other drugs are widely available to today's children. In fact, growing up drug-free can be one of the greatest challenges facing your school-aged child. Fortunately, a loving family, knowledge of the dangers of drugs, and your personal example can combine to form a powerful deterrent to substance abuse. You can certainly begin to take preventative measures as early as the preschool years, but it's never too late to guide your child toward a drug- and alcohol-free lifestyle. The following discussions examine different ways in which you can help your child resist the pressure to drink or experiment with illegal substances.

☐ *Encourage communication.* Be honest and respectful in your conversations with your child, and give her your undivided attention when discussing something important. Ask open-ended questions to create an atmosphere of give-and-take, and listen carefully to your child's answers. Be aware of your child's body language, eye contact, and facial expressions. Respond in a positive manner—even if your child shares something that upsets you.

☐ *Nurture your child's self-esteem.* Professionals who work with troubled children and teens have noticed a strong link between low self-esteem and drug use. Offer lots of praise. Voice your admiration for your child's special gifts and accomplishments, and let her know that you enjoy spending time with her. (See Entry 7 on page 27 for additional ideas.)

☐ *Get involved in your child's life.* Keep abreast of your child's activities and whereabouts, and get to know her friends. (See Entry 1 on page 3 for more information on this.) Encourage relationships with peers who seem drug- and alcohol-free, and help your child view friendship as a means of sharing, caring, and support.

☐ *Encourage alternative activities to drug involvement.* Support your child's pursuit of sports, hobbies, art, ecology projects, or youth-group activities. A happy, busy child is less likely to turn to drugs and alcohol.

☐ *Teach your child how to manage stress.* Encourage physical activity and the use of relaxation techniques. Avoid overemphasizing good grades or athletic performance, or overscheduling free time. Be available to your child for confidences, and if she *shows* signs of stress, help her to understand the cause and to find an appropriate solution. Set a good example by managing your own frustrations appropriately. (See Entry 6 on page 22.)

☐ *Help your child focus on future goals.* Teach her that drug use can prevent her from fulfilling her potential, and guide her toward a lifestyle that supports her goals, instead.

☐ *Teach your child about drugs.* Learn the hard facts about drugs, and share this information with your child. Obtain age-appropriate books and materials about drugs from anti-drug organizations, the library, or your doctor. Share news items about drug abuse and drug crime with your child. Watch drug-abuse prevention programs together, and use them as a launching point for discussions on substance abuse. Start a conversation about drugs with a family counselor or support group. Finally, campaign for drug education in the schools.

☐ *Set a good example for your child.* Give clear messages about the use of drugs or alcohol in your home. Involve your child in family activities that are alcohol- and drug-free. Take part in community drug education. If a family member or close friend experiences problems with substance abuse, seek help, and discuss the problem openly with your child.

☐ *Help your child practice taking a stand against drugs.* Arm your child against peer pressure with ready answers to offers of alcohol and other drugs. Use role-playing to give her practice with refusal tactics.

☐ *Encourage anti-drug social action on your child's part.* Urge your child to become involved in Drug Abuse Resistance Education (see Entry 31 on page 165) or Students Against Driving Drunk (see Entry 30 on page 161) at his school. Encourage your child's interest in community programs aimed at a drug-free society. Through these activities, your child will not only learn the facts about drugs and alcohol, but will also strike up friendships with other drug- and alcohol-free students.

☐ *Enlist the help of other parents.* Your child is less likely to be tempted by drugs if her friends also avoid them. Encourage other parents to educate their children about drugs and to support their children's efforts to stay drug-free.

Most children who use drugs do so to increase their self-confidence, avoid social pressures and problems, escape from anxiety or unhappiness, feel grown up, or simply satisfy their curiosity. Covering all these bases is no small task for you, the parent. However, you can go a long way toward helping your child stay drug-free by knowing and sharing the facts about drugs, providing a positive role model, nurturing your child's self-esteem, and helping your child build a healthy, active, fulfilling life.

Resources

The organizations and books listed below can furnish additional information to help your child grow up drug-free.

ORGANIZATIONS

American Council for Drug
  Education
204 Monroe Street
Rockville, MD 20850
(301) 294–0600
(800) 488–DRUG

This organization provides information on drug use, develops media campaigns, reviews scientific findings, publishes books and a newsletter, and offers films and curriculum materials on drug education.

Drug Abuse Resistance Education
  (DARE)
Los Angeles Police Department
3353 San Fernando Road
Los Angeles, CA 90065
(800) 223–DARE

This program sends specially trained police officers to elementary schools to teach students about the dangers of drugs. DARE also enlists the help of parents, teachers, peers, and celebrity ambassadors.

Families in Action National Drug Information Center
Suite 204
2296 Henderson Mill Road
Atlanta, GA 30345
(404) 934–6364

This group publishes a quarterly news journal and offers information about preventing drug use.

Just Say No Clubs
Suite 200
1777 North California Boulevard
Walnut Creek, CA 94596
(800) 258–2766
(415) 939–6666

This group provides support and positive peer reinforcement to students through workshops, seminars, newsletters, and community activities.

Mothers Against Drunk Driving
PO Box 541688
Dallas, TX 75354–1688
(214) 744–6233

This organization of concerned parents seeks to raise public awareness of the dangers of drinking and driving and to make the nation's roadways safer for children.

National Clearinghouse for Alcohol and Drug Information (NCADI)
Box 2345
Rockville, MD 20852
(800) SAY–NOTO *National Hotline*
(301) 468–2600

This organization works as a resource center for alcohol- and drug-related information and publications, including a number of informational videos that are available for loan.

National Council on Alcoholism, Inc.
12 West 21st Street
New York, NY 10010
(212) 206–6770
(800) NCA–CALL *National Hotline*

This group provides information about alcoholism through more than three hundred local affiliates.

National Crime Prevention Council
1700 K Street NW
Washington, DC 20006
(202) 466–NCPC

This council develops materials about crime and drug-use prevention for the use of parents and children.

National Federation of Parents for Drug-Free Youth, Inc.
PO Box 3878
St. Louis, MO 63122
(314) 845–7955

This group sponsors the National Red Ribbon Campaign, which is designed to reduce the demand for drugs, and the Responsible Educated Adolescents Can Help (REACH) program, which teaches junior and senior high school students about drug abuse.

National PTA Drug and Alcohol Abuse Prevention Project
700 North Rush Street
Chicago, IL 60611
(312) 577–4500

This PTA project offers kits, brochures, posters, and other publications about drugs and alcohol to parents, teachers, and PTA organizations.

PRIDE Parent Training
Parents' Resource Institute for
  Drug Education (PRIDE)
1240 Johnson Ferry Place, Suite F-10
Marietta, GA 30068
(404) 565–5257
(800) 487–7743

*This national educational association
provides parents with the knowledge,
skills, attitudes, and abilities necessary
to guide children through the high-risk
drug years.*

Students Against Driving Drunk
  (SADD) National Office
110 Pleasant Street, Corbin Plaza
Marlboro, MA 01752
(508) 481–3568

*This organization helps students deal
with social pressures to drink and
drive, and encourages a substance-free
lifestyle.*

In Canada:

Mothers Against Drunk Driving
  (MADD) Canadian Society
704 6th Street, Suite 5
New Westminster, BC V3L 3C5
(604) 524–0722

*This group works to protect children
and teens by eliminating the practice of
drinking and driving.*

Students Against Drinking and
  Driving (SADD)
Saskatchewan Safety Council
140 4th Avenue East
Regina, Sask S4N 4Z4
(306) 757–3197

*This organization publicizes the perils
of drinking and driving, and encourages teen-agers to abstain from the use
of alcohol and other drugs.*

BOOKS

Collins, Lorraine, Kenneth E. Leonard, and John S. Searles. *Alcohol and
the Family: Research and Clinical Perspectives.* New York: Guilford Press,
1990.

Maxwell, Ruth. *Kids, Alcohol and Drugs: A Parent's Guide.* New York:
Ballantine Books, 1991.

Perkins, Nancy McMurtrie, and William Mack Perkins. *Raising Drug-Free
Kids in a Drug-Filled World.* San Francisco: Harper/Hazelden, 1986.

Super, Gretchen. *What Are Drugs?* Frederick, MD: Twenty-First Century
Books, 1990.

Tessler, Diane Jane. *Drugs, Kids, and Schools: Practical Strategies for Educators
and Other Concerned Adults.* Glenview, IL: Scott, Foresman and Co., 1980.

Waggoner, Richard. *Parent's Alliance for Drug Free Children.* Brentwood,
TN: JM Productions, 1988.

Avoiding Childhood Tobacco Habits

Nearly two-thirds of children under the age of eighteen smoke cigarettes at one time or another. Some 3,000 children light up for the first time each day, despite the medical community's warnings. Use of smokeless tobacco is on the rise among teens, as well. You see, many adolescents have a need to appear grown up and to fit in, and this sometimes overpowers their concern for their health. And teens often have a sense of immortality that enables them to disregard any health risks associated with their pastimes and habits. You can help your child avoid the tobacco habit by providing the information and support she needs to stay smoke-free.

The risks associated with tobacco are clear. The cancer death rate of male cigarette smokers is more than twice that of nonsmokers. Among females, the cancer death rate is 67 percent higher for smokers. In fact, it's been shown that smoking causes 90 percent of all lung cancers among men and 70 percent among women. Not just smokers are at risk; the smoke and toxins from cigarettes, cigars, and pipes pose a threat to everyone in the smoker's vicinity. (See Entry 20 on page 104 for details.) And although smokeless tobacco may spare those nearby, its users stand to absorb twice as much nicotine through the mouth tissues as would be absorbed by smoking.

It's a good idea to start your campaign against tobacco early in your child's life, since fully half of today's adult smokers were smoking by thirteen years of age. You can explain to your child that tobacco is legal but harmful due to its addictive powers and its ties to heart disease, lung disease, and cancer. Of course, you may find that your youngster is even more responsive to information about the short-term effects of smoking—stale breath, smoky hair and clothing, stained teeth and fingers, wrinkles, and depleted energy. Here are some more specific suggestions to help your child avoid the tobacco habit.

☐ *Educate yourself about the dangers of tobacco, and share this information with your child. You might also want to enlist the help of your doctor to discuss the dangers of smoking with your youngster.*

☐ *Find out what your child's school is doing to discourage tobacco use, and urge the principal to start an anti-smoking program.*

☐ *Point out the expense of tobacco, and suggest other ways your child could spend her money—on athletic shoes or CDs, for example.*

☐ *Use a friend or family member who smokes as an example of what it's like to be hooked on tobacco.*

☐ *Nurture your child's self-esteem. A strong, confident child can better resist peer pressure to smoke. (See Entry 7 on page 27 for details.)*

☐ *Teach refusal skills. Your child will have an easier time saying "No" if she has a ready answer.*

☐ *Encourage your child to become involved in interesting activities— music, sports, or a hobby, perhaps.*

☐ *Become active against teen smoking. Speak to parent and civic groups about preventing cigarette sales to minors, banning vending machines, and keeping schools smoke-free. Oppose advertising that glamorizes smoking.*

If your child already uses tobacco, she may be less receptive to your anti-smoking message. However, you can still encourage your youngster to quit. Consider banning smoking in your home. Suggest that your child team up with a smoking family member in an effort to kick the habit. Be clear about where your child may not smoke—in her room, in the family car, or at school, for instance. You may also be able to help your child find her own motivation to quit. For instance, you could point out that shortness of breath affects a smoker's athletic performance, or that eight out of ten teen-agers prefer to date nonsmokers.

Although many teen-agers eventually abandon the smoking habit on their own, it is still important to help your child avoid tobacco use. After all, 20 percent of teen smokers go on to smoke daily as adults. In addition, cigarettes have been identified as a "gateway drug"—that is, a habit shared by nearly all children who go on to abuse alcohol and other drugs. And since tobacco is responsible for nearly 400,000 deaths each year, your efforts to get your child to avoid or quit smoking may actually save her life!

Resources

For more information on smoking in adolescence, contact your local chapter of the American Heart Association, American Lung Association, or American Cancer Society—all listed in the white pages of your phone book—or the sources listed below.

ORGANIZATIONS

Doctors Ought to Care (DOC)
5510 Greenbriar, Suite 235
Houston, TX 77005 (Prefers mail
  inquiries.)

This anti-smoking program employs family doctors and other trained leaders to run teen groups that examine the issues of smoking and cigarette advertising.

Stop Teen-Age Addiction to Tobacco
121 Lyman Street, Suite 210
Springfield, MA 01103
(413) 732-STAT

This organization conducts no-smoking programs in schools, and works to raise public awareness of the teen smoking problem.

TARGET
c/o The National Federation of State
  High School Associations
PO Box 20626
Kansas City, MO 64195
(816) 464-5400

This program provides teachers with materials that explore ways in which teens can quit smoking.

Tobacco-Free Teens
c/o American Lung Association
490 Concordia Avenue
St. Paul, MN 55103
(612) 227-8014

This eight-session program uses trained leaders to help teens set goals related to ending the tobacco habit.

BOOKS

Burton, Dee. *The Joy of Quitting: How to Help Young People Stop Smoking.* New York: Macmillan Publishing, 1979.

Hyde, Margaret O. *Know About Smoking.* New York: Walker and Co., 1990.

Krogh, David. *Smoking: The Artificial Passion.* New York: W.H. Freeman, 1991.

Szumski, Bonnie. *Smoking: Distinguishing Betweeen Fact and Opinion.* San Diego: Greenhaven Press, 1989.

30

ENCOURAGE YOUR CHILD TO JOIN SADD

Glance through a newspaper on almost any day of the week, and you're likely to find a report of an alcohol-related traffic accident. Question your child and his school friends, and you'll probably hear several stories about classmates whose involvement with drugs has gotten them into serious trouble. You see, despite the fact that the legal drinking age in most states is twenty-one, injury from alcohol-related car crashes is the number-one health problem facing today's teen-agers. Abuse of other drugs is also a factor in many teen auto accidents, and poses other hazards as well. In fact, drug use exists to a frightening degree among middle-schoolers and high-schoolers. A recent survey of high school seniors revealed that nearly one-third experiment with drugs, and that close to 15 percent of this group had their first drug experience in grade six, seven, or eight. Fully 80 percent of twelfth graders drink alcohol, with nearly 40 percent having had their first drink before beginning high school.

Whether or not your child uses alcohol or other drugs, he may spend time in the company of teen-agers who do. But involvement in SADD (Students Against Driving Drunk or Student Athletes Detest Drugs) will reduce the chances of your child getting involved with illegal substances or being victimized by a friend's impairment. The mission of SADD members is to stop drunk driving and drug abuse among fellow students through education, peer counseling, and public awareness. Each year, an estimated four hundred lives are saved, and thousands of disabilities are prevented, through the efforts of SADD.

STUDENTS AGAINST DRIVING DRUNK

The original SADD—Students Against Driving Drunk—was founded in 1981. There are now SADD chapters in thousands of middle schools, high schools, and colleges across the United States, Canada, Europe, Australia, New Zealand, and Africa. SADD's main goal is to help students deal effectively with social pressures to drink and drive. One successful tactic involves the election of a "designated driver" who, by abstaining from alcohol for the evening, guarantees his friends and himself a safe return home. Another popular idea is a no-questions-asked, any-hour call to parents for a ride home. SADD endorses a no-use policy regarding underage drinking and illegal drugs. SADD asks parents to also discourage these practices, and encourages teens and their families to sign and participate in a Contract for Life (see page 163).

Involvement in SADD can help keep your child safe, of course, but the organization has other objectives, as well. Through SADD, your child will be encouraged to adopt a substance-free lifestyle and use positive peer pressure to persuade classmates to do the same. The program will also provide ongoing opportunities for straight talk between you and your child—about social pressure, trust, and your concerns about underage drinking. The SADD National Office provides local chapters with a twelve-month activity plan to help SADD members organize and sponsor alcohol-and-drug-awareness events in the community. Banners, bumper stickers, and pamphlets make SADD a visible presence at school sporting events, rallies, and dances.

If a SADD program has not yet been established at your child's school, he and his friends can approach the student council and school administration about organizing a chapter. All that is needed is a faculty advisor and a group of concerned students.

STUDENT ATHLETES DETEST DRUGS

Student Athletes Detest Drugs is an extension of the program that shares its SADD acronym, Students Against Driving Drunk. This offshoot program, which focuses on the use of steroids and other drugs by teen-agers, is enjoying the same rapid growth as the original group. The purpose of the new SADD is twofold: to

CONTRACT FOR LIFE

A Contract for Life
Between Parent and Teenager

Under this contract, we understand S.A.D.D. encourages all youth to adopt a <u>no use</u> policy and obey the laws of their state with regards to alcohol and illicit drugs.

Teenager I agree to call you for advice and/or transportation at any hour from any place if I am ever faced with a situation where a driver has been drinking or using illicit drugs. I have discussed with you and fully understand your attitude toward any involvement with underage drinking or the use of illegal drugs.

_____
Signature

Parent I agree to come and get you at any hour, any place, no questions asked and no argument at that time, or I will pay for a taxi to bring you home safely. I expect we would discuss this at a later time.

I agree to seek safe, sober transportation home if I am ever in a situation where I have had too much to drink or a friend who is driving me has had too much to drink.

_____
Signature

_____
Date

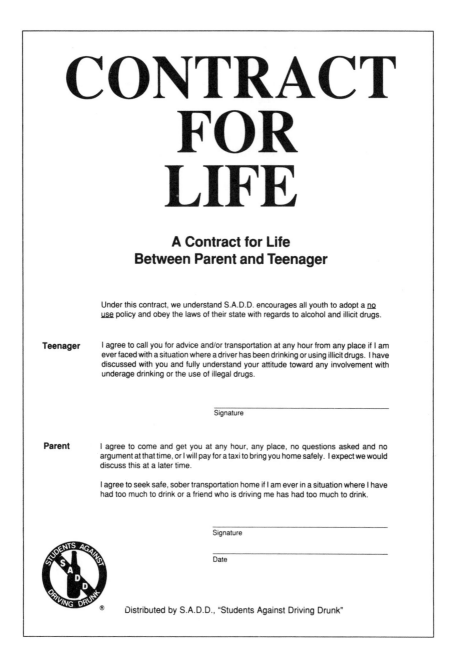

® Distributed by S.A.D.D., "Students Against Driving Drunk"

encourage student athletes to abstain from using illegal drugs, and to encourage athletes to use their leadership qualities to convince their classmates to do the same.

The Student Athletes Detest Drugs program is based on the successful principles of Students Against Driving Drunk. SADD encourages members to take the Athlete's Pledge, a public declaration that the student will abstain from drug use. Athletes also deliver a high-profile anti-drug message through their presence at all school sporting events, both as team members and as SADD representatives.

Your child's principal, athletic coach, or guidance counselor can tell you whether a Student Athletes Detest Drugs chapter exists at your child's school. The SADD National Office (see the address, below) can guide your child in starting a SADD program where none exists.

Encouraging your child to join either SADD program at school can pay big dividends. As your teen-ager helps to promote student awareness of the dangers of drug and alcohol use, he will take pride in his commitment to the safety of his classmates, strengthen his personal resolve to abstain, and enjoy a close association with peers who share his standards and ideals. Urge your child to become involved in SADD.

Resources

For additional information about Students Against Driving Drunk and Student Athletes Detest Drugs, you can contact the SADD National Office at the address listed below.

ORGANIZATIONS

The SADD National Office
110 Pleasant Street
Corbin Plaza
Marlboro, MA 01752
(508) 481–3568

In Canada:

Students Against Drinking and
  Driving (SADD)
Saskatchewan Safety Council
140 4th Avenue East
Regina, Sask S4N 4Z4
(306) 757–3197

31

ENCOURAGE YOUR CHILD TO JOIN DARE

Drug abuse has been a fact of life among students across North America for more than twenty years, and use of alcohol and tobacco for much longer than that. Certainly, drugs of choice have varied through the years as dictated by current fads, substance availability, and the purchasers' finances. Yet, the overall number of students who use these substances has climbed steadily. Today, even some primary grade students are involved with smoking, drinking, and other drug use. Happily, you can reduce the chances of your child's involvement with alcohol, drugs, and tobacco by encouraging her participation in Drug Abuse Resistance Education (DARE).

In the early 1980s, there was a growing awareness that drug use had filtered down into the preteen set. In response, DARE was organized in 1983 by the Los Angeles Police Department and the city's school district in an effort to keep the area's youngest students from getting involved with drugs. DARE—now the most popular anti-drug program in America—started in about 50 elementary schools, and now extends to a quarter of the United States grade schools in some 4,700 communities across the country.

DARE enables specially trained police officers to bring stories about the dangers of drugs directly to students in kindergarten and grades one through six. Although the officers appear in uniform during their talks, the program emphasizes caring and concern, and the idea that the police are the children's friends. In fact, DARE officers continue their interactions with students on the playground and during extracurricular activities.

The DARE program recognizes that peer pressure is a factor in many instances of experimentation with drugs. Therefore, the program enlists the help of parents, teachers, and peers in building the children's self-esteem and developing those skills that will help them resist pressures to conform. Another important part of DARE's mission is the examination of the "gateway drugs"—alcohol, tobacco, and marijuana, for instance—that are widely available and can pave the way to addiction. DARE has also named several celebrity ambassadors who visit DARE schools and urge students not to be sidetracked by drugs in the pursuit of their dreams.

The DARE program seems to be working. A University of Illinois survey of 1,800 sixth- and seventh-grade DARE graduates showed that students in the program tend to have a harsher view of drugs and a more positive attitude toward the police than youngsters not involved in DARE. As an added benefit, DARE graduates tend to get into less trouble at school. The DARE program involves some five million students per year in the United States alone. Perhaps the best measure of DARE's success is the fact that over one hundred other drug education programs now also use the presentation of healthy alternatives and the building of peer-resistance skills as their foundation.

DARE and programs like it have given parents and teachers a positive and truly effective means of halting the spread of drug use among schoolchildren. By encouraging your youngster to participate in the DARE program in her school—or by helping to start a DARE program if her school is not yet involved—you'll make it easier for your child and other children to say "No" to drugs.

Resources

For more information on getting your child's school involved in a DARE program, call the school principal, the parent-teacher organization, or your local police department. You can also contact DARE officials directly at the address listed below.

ORGANIZATION

Drug Abuse Resistance Education (DARE)
Los Angeles Police Department
3353 San Fernando Road
Los Angeles, CA 90065
(800) 223–DARE

32

PROTECT YOUR CHILD FROM MOLESTATION

If you were to believe what you see in movies or on television, you would no doubt picture the typical child molester—or pedophile, to use another term—as a single, trench coat-clad, "thirtysomething" male who cannot relate to other adults and spends his days cruising for children to victimize. But the truth is that neither gender, age, marital status, profession, race, nor religion plays a part in child molestation. Simply put, pedophiles cannot be easily identified. Fortunately, you can lessen the chances of your child becoming a molestation victim by ensuring his supervision, looking out for suspicious behavior, and educating him about personal safety.

Identifying a pedophile is made difficult by the fact that behavior varies from offender to offender. A child molester may or may not seem friendly, have a particular sexual preference, exploit victims more than once, or behave in a seductive manner. However, many *do* share the traits of insecurity, inappropriate anger, abusive relationships with adult family members, and fascination with child pornography and erotica. You should certainly be alert to these characteristics. It also pays to remember that pedophiles are adept at engineering situations that leave them alone with potential victims. A school bus driver, for example, might alter his or her drop-off route to gain access to a particular child. A teacher or care giver might work for weeks or months to earn the trust of an intended victim before creating an opportunity for isolated contact. A friend or family member might lure an unsuspecting birthday party guest to a deserted area of the house. The possibilities are endless, as you can see. Therefore, it's wise to be wary of any man, woman, or child with whom your child spends time alone and who exhibits the following behavior.

- He (or she) expresses a strong interest in your child's physical traits—by taking unnecessary photographs, for instance, or by dwelling on your youngster's beauty or physique.
- He habitually engages your child in play that involves a lot of touching, such as wrestling, dancing, or piggyback rides.
- He gives unwarranted gifts to your child.
- He frequently orchestrates meetings, parties, or play dates that exclude adults.
- He exhibits a strong sense of possessiveness about your child.

In many cases, proper supervision may be enough to shield a child from the attentions of a pedophile. It certainly pays to be choosy when making child-care arrangements (see Entry 47 on page 244), and to keep abreast of your older child's whereabouts and activities (see Entry 1 on page 3). Bear in mind, however, that it's impossible to watch over your youngster throughout every moment of his formative years. For this reason, your child must be taught to protect himself from possible molestation by acting safely when away from home. You may wish to begin by demonstrating ways of maintaining a safe distance from slow-moving or stopped cars or from people in doorways. Encouraging the use of a "buddy system"—movement about the neighborhood only when accompanied by a partner—is another good idea. Naturally, you will also want to teach your child the hazards of public rest rooms, abandoned buildings, and secluded wooded or fenced areas.

Of course, there's still a great deal of value in the age-old warning about not talking to strangers. And you should also teach your child that he needs your permission before going anywhere with an older child or adult, even if he's familiar with the person. But since pedophiles have devised many "lines" designed to override parental instructions—"Your mom's been rushed to the hospital and I'm going to take you to her" is just one example—you might consider inventing a code word that would signal your approval of a departure or outing with someone out of the ordinary.

When teaching your child to avoid molestation, impress upon him—through word and deed, and from the very start—that his body is private property worthy of respect. Depending on your child's age and maturity level, he should be made aware of appropriate physical boundaries. Even toddlers can be taught the difference between "good" and "bad" touching. Your child should also be helped to understand that he has the right to say "No" to any contact with any person who makes him uneasy or uncomfortable. You might also consider practicing with your child responses to offers of money, candy, or other gifts in exchange for physical contact. If a "safe house" exists in your neighborhood (see Entry 38 on page 200), it's important that your child know its location and understand its function. Finally, it is wise to get in the habit of asking questions about your child's experiences during his time away from home. Listen carefully to his answers, and make it a point to express your belief in what he tells you so that he will feel free to talk about his day and to share his feelings with you.

There's no question that teaching your child about personal safety can be tricky. It's vital to strike a balance; that is, to urge your youngster to be cautious without raising him to fear unfamiliar places and people. Just as when teaching your child about crossing the street or avoiding gun play, it's not particularly helpful to dwell on the terrible things that might happen to him. Instead, focus on giving your youngster age-appropriate rules to follow. For example, you can instruct your two-year-old that he must never let go of your hand in a crowd. You can teach your preschooler to go directly to a police officer, security guard, or store clerk if he is lost or in trouble. And you can discuss with your grade-schooler the difference between friendliness and suspicious behavior in the people he meets on the street. Asking hypothetical questions— "What if someone asked you to help him search the woods for his lost dog?" or "What if someone wanted to show you something that was in his car?"— can tell you a lot about how your child would handle an inappropriate overture. In addition, this practice will pinpoint topics that require additional discussion.

Quite often, the media seem to offer more than their share of frightening stories about child molestation. But by becoming knowledgeable about the habits of pedophiles, by teaching your child to avoid circumstances in which molestation could take place, and by staying abreast of your youngster's activities through supervision and healthy communication, you will do a great deal to keep your child safe and sound.

Resources

You can get additional information about protecting your child from molestation from the following sources.

ORGANIZATIONS

Kidsrights
10100 Park Cedar Drive
Charlotte, NC 28210
(704) 541–0100
(800) 892–KIDS

This organization offers a large selection of books, tapes, and videos to parents and professionals who work with children, including materials on the prevention of sexual abuse.

National Center for Missing and
  Exploited Children
2101 Wilson Boulevard, Suite 550
Arlington, VA 22201
(703) 235–3900
(800) 843–5678 *National Hotline*
(800) 826–7653 *For the Hearing Impaired*

This agency offers free brochures on preventing the exploitation of children.

Project for the Advancement of
  Sexual Health and Safety, Inc.
Maine State Prison Sex Offender
  Project
PO Box 272
Thomaston, ME 04861–0272
(207) 354–2535, Extension 234

This group offers information about sex offenders from inmates who are serving time for sex crimes against children.

The Tennis Shoe Brigade
PO Box 12157
Tacoma, WA 98412
(206) 472–7920

This grass roots movement is dedicated to creating stronger laws and safer communities for children.

BOOKS

Colao, Flora, and Tamar Hosansky. *Your Children Should Know.* Indianapolis: Bobbs-Merrill, 1983.

Haden, Dawn C., editor. *Out of Harm's Way: Readings on Child Sexual Abuse, Its Prevention and Treatment.* Phoenix: Oryx Press, 1986.

Hagans, Kathryn B., and Joyce Case. *When Your Child Has Been Molested: A Parent's Guide to Healing and Recovery.* Lexington, MA: Lexington Books, 1988.

Kraizer, Sherryll Kerns. *The Safe Child Book.* New York: Dell Publishing, 1985.

Know When a Sex Offender Is Living in Your Neighborhood

In forty-nine of the fifty United States, a convicted sex offender can, upon release from prison, quietly reintegrate himself into community life. Unfortunately, many of these offenders take up residence in a new city or town, assume new identities, and begin to prey upon children once again.

The State of Washington, however, is working to make it harder for sex criminals to find new young victims. Washington's Community Protection Act of 1990 mandates residence registration and, in some cases, school and public notification within twenty-four hours of a sex offender's release from prison. In Spokane County, for example, close to 500 sex offenders—an estimated 8 percent of whom are pedophiles (child molesters)—are currently registered with the sheriff's department as required by Washington State law.

Washington's sheriff's departments rank each newly released offender according to criminal history. When a Level One offender registers his new address, local law enforcement agencies are notified of his where-abouts. If the offender is ranked Level Two, area schools are notified, as well. In the case of Level Three offenders, this notification extends to the media and the general public. For instance, it's not unusual for area schools to distribute a Level Three offender's picture—accompanied by a descriptive memo—to teachers, children, and parents.

Surely, children in other parts of the country have the right to the same sort of protection from potential sexual abuse. One idea under consid-eration concerns the formation of a national registry to monitor the whereabouts of all persons convicted of crimes against children. A registry such as this could be used as a nationwide employee-screening device, and could offer protection from sex offenders who escape the attention of authorities by moving to another state after leaving prison.

How can you safeguard your child from convicted sex offenders who may be living in your area? Entry 32 on page 167 offers several suggestions. And you can go a step further by increasing public awareness of current policies regarding the release of sex criminals from prison, and by working to replace these policies with ones that offer better protection. Here are a few ideas.

☐ Learn about your school district's policies regarding background checks on new employees. Make parents' groups aware of the need to screen administrators, teachers, cafeteria aides, bus drivers, clerical workers, and custodial staff for criminal history information.

☐ If you learn that a convicted sex offender has moved into your neighborhood, make sure your child—and the parents of your child's friends—knows what the offender looks like, where he lives, and what type of car he drives.

☐ Contact your local political representatives to voice your outrage over the inadequacy of current child-protection laws. Urge them to follow the lead of Washington State by mandating public notification whenever a sex offender is released from prison.

Washington's Community Protection Act was largely a response to demands made by citizens' groups. By becoming involved in this important issue, you can make sure your child has the best protection the law can provide.

"If our American way of life fails the child, it fails us all."

—Pearl S. Buck

33

TAKE ACTION AGAINST CHILD PORNOGRAPHY

Child pornography—or sexually explicit photographs, books, magazines, films, and videos featuring children—made its first appearance in North America in the late 1960s. Unfortunately, the market for child pornography has proven to be lucrative, and there are now over 300 pornographic publications and literally thousands of videos involving children and sex. Moreover, there are organizations in existence that actively promote sex with children. These include the North American Man-Boy Love Association (NAMBLA), the Rene Guyon Society, the Childhood Sensuality Circle, and the Paedophile Information Exchange (PIE). Happily, there are steps you can take to decrease the chance that your child—or any child—will be exposed to child pornography or, worse, become one of the hundreds of thousands of children each year who are coerced into becoming participants.

The use of pornography was once thought to be a victimless crime. However, it is now known that many sex offenders and child molesters are actively involved in pornography, both for sexual stimulation and to break down a potential victim's defenses. The production and distribution of pornography is illegal, yet explicit publications from all over the globe make their way into the underground sales network that supplies North American users.

There are several ways in which you can take action against the use of child pornography. Since it is obvious that the current laws regarding pornography are not completely effective, you can ask your political representatives what they are doing to crack down on the continued production, sale, and use of sexually explicit material. You may also wish to join forces with one of the many organizations working for tougher legislation against pornography. (A list of such groups begins on page 175.) Bear in mind that the possession of pornography is illegal in many states. If you see or hear of child pornography in someone's possession, a call to your police department will tell you whether that individual is breaking the law and whether action can be taken against him.

There are other ways to lessen the spread of child pornography. Naturally, if your youngster has contact with friends of any age who use child pornography, you should terminate that relationship at once. There is certainly no benefit to your child's viewing such material, and there is always the risk that she will be personally exploited. (Often, children are coerced into posing for pornography after seeing pictures of other children doing the same.) Also encourage your child to tell you if someone shows her pornography, or if they photograph, approach, or touch her inappropriately. And finally, be aware that, illegal or not, many video and bookstores sell or rent child pornography. If there is a store of this kind in your area, you may choose to boycott the establishment and expose it within the community. Peaceful demonstrations, newspaper advertisements, calls to police and local news stations, and word of mouth are some of the techniques that have proved effective in closing down businesses that are involved with child pornography.

There is no question that child pornography threatens the well-being of those youngsters who pose for the contraband material. Moreover, the existence within your own town or county of sexually explicit photos, videos, and magazines involving children increases the chance that your child and her friends may be exposed to, or become involved with, pornography. It is important, therefore, that you take immediate action if you learn of someone producing, selling, or using material that violates the law and exploits children in this manner. In doing so, you'll be preventing sexually explicit material from leaving its mark on your child—and you'll be helping to clean up your community in the bargain.

Resources

The resources listed below can furnish additional information on taking action against child pornography.

ORGANIZATIONS

American Family Association
PO Box 2440
Tupelo, MS 38803
(601) 844–5036

This group works for the elimination of vulgarity, immorality, violence, and profanity in the media.

Citizens for Community Values
11175 Reading Road
Cincinnati, OH 45241
(513) 733–5775

This organization works to uphold family values by promoting public awareness and fighting the proliferation of obscenity in today's society.

The Clean Up Project
2875 Snelling Avenue North
St. Paul, MN 55113
(612) 633–1864

This group seeks to educate and alert the public to the problem of pornography and urges vigorous enforcement of obscenity laws.

Coalition Against Pornography—
   Kansas City
8301 Lanar
Overland Park, KS 66207
(913) 381–1808

This organization seeks to halt the sale of pornographic magazines and to stop the production and distribution of other pornographic materials.

Dallas Association for Decency
13643 Beta Road
Dallas, TX 75244–4585
(214) 239–8128

This group seeks to educate the public about problems linked to obscenity and immorality in the media, and works to halt the spread of pornography.

Feminists Fighting Pornography
PO Box 6730
New York, NY 10128
(212) 439–6449

This organization combats pornography by lobbying the federal government.

Focus on the Family
420 North Cascade Avenue
Colorado Springs, CO 80903
(713) 531–3400

This group seeks to enact and enforce laws, statutes, and regulations controlling obscenity, pornography, and material harmful to juveniles.

Morality in Media
475 Riverside Drive
New York, NY 10115
(212) 870–3222

This organization is composed of individuals concerned about the circulation of pornography and its dehumanizing effects.

National Coalition Against Pornography
800 Compton Road, Suite 9248
Cincinnati, OH 45231
(513) 521–6227

This group focuses on reducing sexual abuse by eliminating child pornography and removing obscenity from the open market.

BOOKS

Burgess, Ann Wolbert. *Child Pornography and Sex Rings.* Lexington, MA: Lexington Books, 1984.

Campagna, Daniel. *The Sexual Trafficking in Children: An Investigation of the Child Sex Trade.* Dover, MA: Auburn House Publishing, 1988.

Reisman, Judith A. *Soft Porn Plays Hard Ball: Its Tragic Effects on Women and Children and the Family.* Lafayette, LA: Huntington House Publishers, 1991.

Stanmeyer, William A. *The Seduction of Society: Pornography and Its Impact on American Life.* Ann Arbor, MI: Servant Publications, 1984.

"Everyone is the Child of his past."

—Edna G. Rostow

34

Use a car seat

No matter how safely you drive, it's impossible to guarantee the safety of a young passenger unless that child is secured in an approved car seat. Conditions might cause you to swerve or brake your vehicle without warning, or you might become involved in a collision—either of which could cause your car's occupants to be violently tossed around or ejected onto the roadside. However, correct use of an appropriate car seat virtually eliminates your child's risk of injury from sharp turns and sudden stops, and provides excellent protection during crashes, as well.

How does a car seat protect your child? When a seat is correctly placed, its harnesses restrain your child during sudden stops and minimize the chance of injury from striking the dashboard, windshield, or floor, or another passenger. Car seats are constructed to absorb some of a crash's violent energy, while spreading the rest of the energy over the strongest parts of your child's body. Securing your child in a car seat further guarantees his safety by enabling you, the driver, to keep your eyes on the road—and your hands on the wheel—at all times.

It's important to realize that most car accidents allow you less than half a second to react. If seated in your lap or cradled in your arms at the time of impact, your child is likely to be flung forward or crushed between you and the dashboard. Despite your best intentions, you see, it's simply not possible to protect your unrestrained child during a crash.

Child passenger safety laws are in effect in all fifty states and throughout Canada, which makes it doubly important to insist that your child is properly protected during all car rides. You can learn the particulars of the laws in your area by calling your county's traffic safety board, which is listed in the blue pages of your phone directory.

Because a child's size and muscle control change continually as he moves from infancy to school age, there are various types of car seats—and special recommendations for each seat's use—to guarantee your youngster the safest possible ride until he is old enough to use only seat belts. Each of the sections below pertains to one phase of a child's development, and explains the proper use of a car seat during that period.

CAR SEATS FOR INFANTS

Infants up to twenty pounds in weight should face the rear of the car and recline at a forty-five-degree angle when fastened into a car seat. If your baby's head flops forward, you can wedge padding under the base of the seat beneath his feet—just enough so that his head stays upright. Shoulder straps should be placed in the lower slots at first, and raised as your baby grows. The harness retainer clip, when present, should rest on your baby's chest at armpit level. Your child's buttocks and back should be flat against the back of the seat. If your infant slides forward, a rolled diaper or thin blanket can be placed under his knees between his crotch and the seat's crotch strap. For a snug fit, additional rolled blankets can be placed along the sides of the seat, outside the straps. Be aware that to provide maximum protection, your child's safety seat must be properly anchored to the car. Follow the manufacturer's installation instructions carefully.

CAR SEATS FOR TODDLERS

For children between twenty and forty pounds in weight who can sit up without support, you can turn a convertible car seat to face forward, or you can switch to a toddler seat. Some models contain a harness to protect your child's upper body; others have a padded swing-arm shield for this purpose; and still others have both. When switching your car seat to the forward-facing position, it is important to check the manufacturer's instructions to be sure that the harness is threaded through the proper slots and that the seat itself is properly anchored to your car.

CAR SEATS FOR PRESCHOOLERS

Booster seats, designed for use by children over forty pounds in weight, provide far better protection than ill-fitting seat belts. Some boosters make use of a car's existing lap-and-shoulder belt system; others use the lap belt over a padded swing-arm shield. In either case, a booster seat elevates your child so that the car's lap belt fits across his hips and pelvic bones—or the booster shield—rather than his stomach. Only when your child has out-grown safety seats is he ready to graduate to your vehicle's belt system. And then, until your child is tall enough for the shoulder belt to fit across his chest, he is safest sitting in the rear seat of your car and using the lap belt only.

CAR SEATS FOR SPECIAL-NEEDS CHILDREN

Children with orthopedic, neuromuscular, or respiratory problems often have difficulty using conventional vehicle restraint systems. But it is important not to alter a safety seat to meet your child's needs without first checking with the manufacturer to see whether such a modification will be crash-safe. If your child has poor head control, select a convertible seat that can be semi-reclined when facing forward. A seat with a five-point harness—that is, with separate anchors behind the shoulders, across the chest, and below the waist—provides good upper-torso support. Rolls of cloth can be used alongside your child's trunk and head or beneath his knees to reduce slouching and sliding. If a conventional seat does not meet your child's positioning needs, your pediatrician should be able to guide you in choosing more appropriate equipment. Specially modified seats, belted vests, and car beds are available from various manufacturers.

GENERAL GUIDELINES FOR CHOOSING AND USING A CAR SEAT

The following are some general suggestions that will help you properly select and use a car seat, thereby offering your child maximum protection while traveling.

☐ Choose a seat that fits your child's height and weight, and try it in your car to make certain that it fits properly.

☐ Never use a seat that has been involved in an accident, as seats are constructed to withstand the force of one crash only.

☐ Check the car seat for a label certifying that the seat meets current federal safety standards. Seats manufactured before January 1, 1981, don't have such a label, and may not meet the same strict standards.

☐ Follow the manufacturer's instructions to the letter. If you use a car seat in the wrong way, your child may not be protected. Keep the instructions handy—perhaps in the glove compartment—and refer to them periodically for any changes that must be made as your child grows.

☐ For optimum safety, securely fasten your child's car seat to the middle of the rear seat.

☐ Check your automobile owner's manual for specific instructions on using the vehicle's seat belts to anchor a car seat. In order to prevent injury, the car seat must be correctly placed within the car.

☐ Adjust the car seat's over-the-shoulder harness according to the bulk of your child's clothing, as well as his changing weight. Two fingers' width of slack between the straps and your child's collarbone is recommended.

☐ Be aware that even such simple modifications as the placement of a protective pad between the car seat and the seat of your automobile can affect a seat's performance in a crash. Make no such modifications to the car seat unless you've been assured by the manufacturer or the National Highway Traffic Safety Administration (see page 181) that the seat will still be safe.

☐ Many makes and models of car seats have been recalled during the past decade. Whether the car seat your child uses is new or a hand-me-down, periodically call the U.S. Consumer Product Safety Commission (see page 181) or the manufacturer to see if it has been involved in a recall.

☐ Many toddlers rebel against restraint. Teach your child that the car does not move unless everyone is buckled. You might also store a special toy in the car—one that your child can have only after he is in his car seat.

Car accidents are the principal cause of death and injury to young children. However, proper use of the right-sized child safety seat and your car's lap-and-shoulder belt system can give your child the best available protection from trauma in the event of a crash. For your child's sake, teach him to remain secured whenever he is a passenger in an automobile, and set a good example by using your own seat belt whenever you drive. Your whole family will be safer—and you, the parent, will have greater peace of mind.

Resources

Additional information about the use of car seats is available from the following resources.

ORGANIZATIONS

American Academy of
  Pediatrics
141 Northwest Point Boulevard
PO Box 927
Elk Grove Village, IL 60009–0927
(708) 228–5005
(800) 433–9016

This professional medical society of pediatricians publishes reports, guides, handbooks, and a newsletter covering all aspects of pediatric care, and maintains a task force on Accident and Poison Prevention as one of over forty committees concerned with the health and well-being of children.

American Seatbelt Council
3319 Tates Creek Road
Lexington, KY 40502
(606) 269–4240

This organization works for the enactment and enforcement of passenger restraint laws as a means of improving the safety of travel on our nation's roadways.

National Highway Traffic Safety
  Administration
Office of Occupant Protection, NTS–10
U.S. Department of Transportation
400 7th Street, SW
Washington, DC 20590
(800) 424–9393 *National Hotline*

This agency seeks to promote highway safety through enforcement of regulations and education.

U.S. Consumer Product Safety
  Commission (CPSC)
Office of Information and
  Public Affairs
Washington, DC 20207
(301) 392–6580
(800) 638–CPSC
(800) 638–8270 *For the Hearing
  Impaired*
(800) 492–8104 *For the Hearing
  Impaired, Maryland Only*

The CPSC monitors the market for dangerous products and has the power to make labeling regulations and demand recalls.

One-Minute Safety Checkup

*Using a car seat correctly makes a **big** difference. Even the "safest" seat may not protect your baby in a crash, so take a minute to check to be sure ...*

☐ ***Do you have the instructions?***
Follow them and keep them with your seat for use as your child grows older.

☐ ***Is your child facing the right way, for both weight and age?***
- *If you use a seat made only for infants (A), **always** face it backward.*
- *A baby should ride facing the back of the car up to 20 pounds, and as close as possible to age one (B).*
- *A child over 20 pounds faces forward (C).*

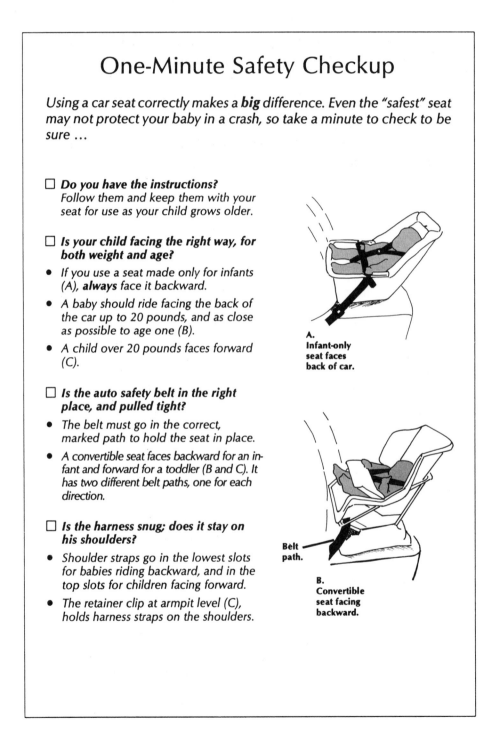

A.
Infant-only seat faces back of car.

☐ ***Is the auto safety belt in the right place, and pulled tight?***
- *The belt must go in the correct, marked path to hold the seat in place.*
- *A convertible seat faces backward for an infant and forward for a toddler (B and C). It has two different belt paths, one for each direction.*

☐ ***Is the harness snug; does it stay on his shoulders?***
- *Shoulder straps go in the lowest slots for babies riding backward, and in the top slots for children facing forward.*
- *The retainer clip at armpit level (C), holds harness straps on the shoulders.*

Belt path.

B.
Convertible seat facing backward.

☐ **Does your child use a booster seat, if he is close to 40 pounds and has outgrown his convertible seat?**

• *A booster seat helps the safety belt protect your child until he grows big enough to fit the belt alone.*

• *A booster seat with no shield is used* **only** *with a lap and shoulder belt (D). Use a booster with a shield (E) if your car has only lap belts.*

☐ **Have you fixed your child's car seat, if it has been recalled?**
Call the Auto Safety Hotline (number below) for a list of recalled seats that need repair.

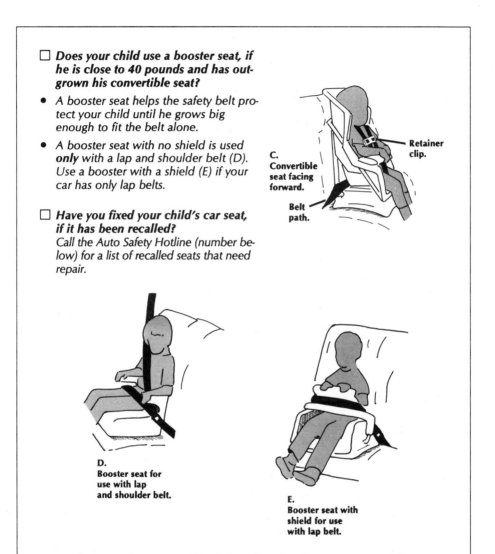

C. Convertible seat facing forward.

Retainer clip.

Belt path.

D. Booster seat for use with lap and shoulder belt.

E. Booster seat with shield for use with lap belt.

Questions? Ask your pediatrician, local safety group, or the Auto Safety Hotline, 800–424–9393.

Brought to you by:

American Academy of Pediatrics, PO Box 927, Elk Grove Village, IL 60009. Supported with a grant from the National Highway Traffic Safety Administration. This flyer may be reproduced in its entirety. The information contained in this publication should not be used as a substitute for the medical care and advice of your pediatrician. There may be variations in treatment that your pediatrician may recommend based on the individual facts and circumstances.

35

HAVE YOUR CHILD WEAR PROTECTIVE SPORTS GEAR

When parents buy their child a bicycle or skateboard or enroll her in an organized sport, they usually don't expect her to come to any great harm. But falls, collisions, and blows from bats, racquets, and balls are a fact of life when children play hard—and so are injuries. Fortunately, by wearing the appropriate protective gear when she plays, your child can avoid many sports-related injuries. The sections below, each of which focuses on a specific type of protection, will help you properly equip your child for the sport of her choice.

HELMETS

The purpose of a sports helmet is to prevent brain damage by spreading the force of a collision across the entire head area. Helmets have long been used in organized sports like football, baseball, hockey, and lacrosse. Nowadays, lightweight, comfortable head protection is also available for bicycling, rock climbing, horseback riding, skiing, skateboarding, and roller blading. A properly fitting bicycle helmet can reduce your child's risk of serious injury by 85 percent. Yet, nine out of ten riders go helmetless, as do many other sports enthusiasts. Unfortunately, this results in several hundred thousand avoidable head injuries each year.

Since sports helmets are designed to protect the wearer from the types of impact associated with a particular sport, it's important to make sure the helmet you buy is suited to your child's activity. A bicycle helmet, for example, should cover half of your child's forehead. In fact, to ensure maximum protection, *all* helmets should sit level on your child's head. A snug fit is also crucial, for loose-fitting headgear may well fall off on impact. Many helmets come with adjustable chin straps and foam inserts that help in this regard and also enable the helmet to grow with your child. Be certain to follow the manufacturer's instructions to the letter. The following are some additional tips for buying and using sports helmets.

☐ Purchase only those sports helmets that meet the standards of the American Society for Testing and Materials (ASTM). ASTM-approved helmets will bear a label to that effect on the packaging.

☐ Look for a bicycle helmet that meets American National Standards Institute (ANSI) or Snell Memorial Foundation specifications. Again, ANSI and Snell labels appear on the packaging of approved products.

☐ Remember that helmets deteriorate over time. Replace even undamaged bicycle helmets after five years, and replace other sports helmets after ten. Immediately replace any helmet that has been in an accident. (Many manufacturers will replace accident-damaged helmets at no charge.)

EYE PROTECTION

It is estimated that nearly 40 percent of children who play ball and puck sports will receive an injury at some point between the ages of five and fourteen. Baseball, ice hockey, racquet sports, football, basketball, and golf appear to pose the most risks to a child's eyes. Prolonged periods spent staring into the sun—on a ballfield or golf course, for example—or submerged in a pool can irritate the eyes, as well. Many eye injuries can be avoided with the use of proper protective equipment, but such protection is mandated only for professional athletes—not for children. As a parent, it is up to you to choose the right eye gear for your child. Here are some suggestions.

☐ Consider eye protection as part of your child's sports uniform, and promote it to your child as such.

☐ If your child wears glasses, shop around for scratch- and

shatter-resistant polycarbonate lenses. These cost only about ten dollars more than regular lenses. Ordinary frames are fine for non-impact sports, but your child needs protective goggles for contact and high-speed sports.

☐ Look for protective goggles that meet the ASTM's standards for sports protection. (The box or package will bear the ASTM label.) These goggles are available with regular and prescription lenses.

☐ If your child swims, consider providing her with properly fitting swim goggles that will protect her eyes from chemicals and irritants in the water.

☐ If your child plays an outdoor sport, provide her with sunglasses or, if necessary, with polycarbonate goggles that filter out the sun's ultraviolet rays.

☐ If your child plays baseball, suggest that her team use a "soft" baseball, which may help prevent eye injuries.

OTHER PROTECTIVE GEAR

Impact injuries to the mouth, knees, shins, and elbows are also common occurrences in children's sports. For years, football, hockey, and lacrosse helmets have been made with cage-like face guards. Now, even baseball batting helmets are available with a polycarbonate guard that covers the nose, mouth, and jaw. Knee pads, elbow pads, shin guards, mouth guards, padded gloves, and other types of protection are also easy to find for use in soccer and other impact sports, as well as for skateboarding and roller blading. And you might be surprised by the variety of other protective equipment that is available to prevent or reduce sports injuries. Consider browsing in a sporting goods or toy store for new and different ways to equip your child for sports. And always look for the ASTM label on any protective equipment you buy.

Naturally, protective equipment can't do its job if your child doesn't wear it. Make it a rule that your child must properly equip herself before riding or playing. Then set a good example by outfitting your whole family with the appropriate gear. Your child is more likely to go along with those safety measures that you yourself follow. As an added incentive, tell your child about professional athletes who wear protective equipment. Finally, talk to other parents about the importance of protective helmets, goggles, pads, and guards, and convince team organizers and school personnel that this equipment should be worn during both practice and competition. Everyone's children will play in greater safety as a result.

Resources

Listed below are some good sources of information about sports safety.

BOOKS

Figelman, Alan R., and Patrick Young. *Keeping Young Athletes Healthy.* New York: Fireside, 1991.

Glover, Bob, and Jack Shepherd. *The Family Fitness Handbook.* New York: Penguin Books, 1989.

Griffith, H. Winter. *Complete Guide to Sports Injuries.* New York: Perigee Books, 1986.

Schreiber, Lee R. *The Parent's Guide to Kids' Sports.* New York: Time, Inc. Magazine Company, 1990.

Bicycle Safety Tips

Every child wants a bicycle. And some of today's bicycles are small enough for even a two-year-old to mount and pedal with a little help from training wheels. Remember, though, that more than 1,000 deaths and 70,000 disabling injuries occur each year as a result of collisions between bicycles and motor vehicles. And these figures do not include nonvehicular accidents, spills, and unreported injuries. Certainly, children derive a great deal of pleasure and healthy exercise from cycling. But before allowing a child of any age to take to the streets on her bicycle, consider the following suggestions.

☐ *Make sure that your child's bicycle is the proper size. Your child should be able to sit on her bicycle seat and balance her bicycle—without leaning to one side—on the tips of her toes. A bicycle that is too large or too small for your child's height is dangerous.*

☐ *Equip your child's bicycle with front and rear brakes; front, rear, side, and pedal reflectors; a warning bell or horn; handle grips; a chain guard; and a neon-colored safety flag.*

☐ *As a general rule, prohibit your child from riding after dark. However, for those times when your child must be out at night, make certain that her bicycle has a white front light and red rear light. Insist that your child walk the bicycle and that she remain as far as possible from the street.*

☐ *A helmet is a must, but to further ensure your child's safety, consider buying her pants clips, a reflective vest, and brightly colored clothing.*

☐ *Ride with your child until you are sure she knows how to:*

- *stop and look for traffic before entering a street*
- *ride with traffic*
- *keep to the right side of the street*
- *obey all traffic signals and signs*
- *use hand signals*
- *exercise caution around parked cars*

☐ *Discourage your child from carrying books or packages in one arm while she rides. Provide her with a bicycle basket or back pack, instead. Also, do not permit your child to carry a passenger on her bicycle.*

To most children, a bicycle is as much a source of fun as a means of transportation. A well-equipped bike, the proper protective gear, and the establishment of a few safety rules can keep your child out of harm's way whenever she travels on two wheels.

36

TEACH YOUR CHILD TO RESPOND TO EMERGENCIES

Part of the job of being a parent is to ensure your child's safety and well-being. But it's important to realize that your child may one day have to face an emergency alone. Therefore, one of the best forms of protection you can offer your child is knowledge of the proper handling of emergencies. A quick and appropriate response may actually save a life if your child or the adult caring for him ever needs help.

Quite often, a telephone is available when danger or injury strikes, and your child can call for the help he needs. The section directly below explains what your child should know about dialing 911 or 0. And since emergencies sometimes take place where telephoning for aid is not an option, a section on other types of responses has also been included.

Naturally, a child's ability to handle a discussion of possible emergency situations depends on temperament and maturity level. Since you certainly don't want to terrify your child in the process of teaching him what he needs to know about responding to a crisis, it's important to give him only as much information as you feel he can handle and to use discretion in its presentation. Let your knowledge of your child serve as your guide.

DIALING 911 OR 0 FOR EMERGENCY ASSISTANCE

The 911 emergency number is used in most populated areas throughout the United States and Canada. By dialing 911, a caller reaches a police department operator who asks about the nature of the emergency and can dispatch a squad car, rescue vehicle, fire engine, or ambulance to the scene within minutes. In rural areas, similar calls for help can be made by dialing 0 for operator. The operator, in turn, either connects the caller with the appropriate emergency service switchboard or makes a request for help on the caller's behalf.

Any child who is old enough to recognize numbers can place a call for help in an emergency. You can practice with your child on a toy phone that dials in the same manner as your real phone. Or you can hold down the disconnect button while your child practices on the phone he'd actually use to place a call for help. You might choose to step out of sight and play "operator," so that your child becomes used to responding to a voice, rather than a face. Changing your tone of voice and rephrasing the operator's questions each time is also helpful. Most important, be sure your child can recite his full name, address, and phone number. With lots of practice, even two- and three-year-olds may be able to memorize much of this information.

Once your child has learned to place a call for help, he should be taught when to do so. Naturally, a call to 911 or the operator is to be made only during a true emergency. A good way to help your child learn to make this determination is to describe hypothetical situations—a fire at a neighbor's house, a lost cat, gunfire in the street, a flat tire, and the like—and talk about the differences between emergency circumstances and lesser problems. You can explain to your child that most emergencies fall into three categories: fire, the threat of personal harm, and illness or injury that prevents a person from helping himself. Reassure your child that if serious trouble looms and he has access to a phone, a call to 911 or 0 *costs nothing*—even from a pay telephone—and will bring help to his side within minutes.

RESPONDING TO AN EMERGENCY WHEN A PHONE IS NOT AVAILABLE

Certainly, many emergencies take place far from a private telephone. And public telephones aren't always the answer for a child in trouble. Even when there is a public phone nearby, it may be out of order or too visible to be used safely. Therefore, it's important to teach your child how to respond to any crises he may face on his own. It's often helpful to sit down with your child, suggest different predicaments, examine possible responses, and determine the most appropriate course of action for each situation. The following list of common emergencies and responses can serve as guidelines for such a discussion with your child.

If Your Child Gets Lost

Make sure your child understands the function and knows the location of any safe houses in your area. (See Entry 38 on page 200 for additional information.) Explain to your child that he is safest seeking assistance from an adult in charge—a police officer, naturally, but barring that, a security guard, store personnel, or someone in management. Of course, your child may become lost out of doors where there is no one in the vicinity to help him. In this case, it is imperative that your child not wander, but remain in one place where searchers can locate him. Get him in the habit of carrying a pocket mirror and a whistle if he plays in wooded or sparsely populated areas. Either can summon help. It's a good idea to reassure your child that you'll never give up looking for him should he ever get lost.

If Your Child Is Caught in a Fire

Naturally, your child's aim in a fire should be to get to safety after first yelling "Fire!" to alert other occupants of the house or building. Depending on your child's age, he can then ask a neighbor to call for help or can simply wait in a designated meeting place for the rest of the family. Convince your child to let others see to saving his family members, rescuing his possessions, and alerting the fire department. At home, it's vital to have a planned, rehearsed escape route from every room. Your child should also know about fighting panic, feeling doors before opening them, staying close to the floor, and cooperating with rescuers. Entry 37 on page 194 gives additional information on appropriate behavior during a fire.

If Your Child or a Companion Is Injured or Seriously Ill

It's wise to make your child aware of basic first-aid rules as soon as he is old enough to understand. Just as an inappropriate response to a burn, laceration, fracture, seizure, or fainting or choking incident can make matters worse, the right action can speed healing and, in some cases, save a life. In addition, you should teach your child the importance of immediately seeking help whenever it is possible to do so. You can also explain to your child how to stay visible to rescuers if he cannot physically go for help or cannot leave the side of an injured party.

If Your Child Is Chased, Followed, or Threatened

It's important that your child knows what to do if he runs into trouble on the street. Stress the importance of immediate adult intervention, and teach him the value of a safe house, if there is one in the area (see page 200). You can also explain the need to run toward a populated area if your child is in a desolate spot and is chased or threatened. You might wish to practice ways of attracting the attention of passersby, for this may cause a pursuer to give up.

You may wonder whether discussing your child's responses to various emergencies might make him unnecessarily fearful about being alone. Indeed, he may feel a bit nervous at first. But along with any unease will come a healthy awareness of the predicaments in which he might someday find himself. Moreover, your discussions about responding to emergencies will give you the chance to convince your child that his well-being is worth more than any material possessions—thereby reassuring him, for instance, that it's okay to break a window to escape a fire, or to leave behind a book bag that is impeding his flight from a threatening stranger. In the end, your child's knowledge of the best responses to illness, injury, and danger will help him handle emergencies swiftly, properly, and with a clear head. Preparedness is the key.

Resources

Your child can learn a lot about handling unforeseen dangers by joining a youth group such as the Boy Scouts or 4-H Club (see pages 39–40). You can get additional literature and information on responding to emergencies from your local police and fire departments. The following resources may also be helpful.

ORGANIZATIONS

American Academy of Safety Education (AASE)
Central Missouri State University
Safety Center/Humphreys Building
Warrensburg, MO 64093
(816) 429–4830

This group of elected fellows promotes safety education and accident prevention throughout the nation.

National Children's Safety Council
4065 Page Avenue
Jackson, MI 49204
(517) 764–6070

This organization furnishes complete child safety education programs through local law enforcement agencies and schools.

National SAFE KIDS Campaign
111 Michigan Avenue NW
Washington, DC 20010–2970
(202) 939–4993

This long-term program uses education and literature to help keep children safe from the dangers they may face in everyday life.

The Safety Society (TSS)
1900 Association Drive
Reston, VA 22091
(703) 476–3430

This group of teachers and other professionals involved in emergency preparedness, safety research, curriculum development, and other educational aspects of safety encourages the development of safety concepts and behavior among its members.

BOOKS

Fleischer, Gary R. *Barron's First Aid for Kids.* Hauppauge, NY: Barron's Educational Series, 1987.

Vanderberg, Mary Lou. *Help! Emergencies That Could Happen to You, and How to Handle Them.* Minneapolis: Lerner Publications, 1975.

37

TEACH YOUR CHILD THE RULES OF FIRE SAFETY

For centuries, fire has helped to provide homes and businesses with heat, light, and power. But to the 27,000 families each year whose homes are damaged by accidental fires—and to the 1,000 or more whose misfortune turns to anguish with the death of a child—fire is also a source of horror. Certainly, there are ways to keep your family from being victimized by fire. By practicing and teaching the rules of fire safety, you can convince your child to view fire with a healthy respect, and to react swiftly and appropriately if she should ever find herself in its path.

HOW TO PREVENT FIRES IN AND AROUND YOUR HOME

You need only read your local paper or watch a TV news program to realize that fires in and around the home happen with surprising frequency. Of course, conditions such as drought, old wiring, and careless storage increase the likelihood of fire, but fire can occur in *any* home. Malfunctioning appliances, space heaters, damaged or dirty chimneys and flue pipes, overloaded electrical systems, flammable substances, cigarettes, cigars, and curious children are all common causes of fires at home.

Whatever the cause, a large number of accidental fires are entirely avoidable. Unfortunately, many families realize this only after smoke, fumes, and flames have left their mark. The following safety guidelines can help you prevent fire from striking your home.

☐ If you smoke, never do so in bed or while lying down. Use large ashtrays, and be sure the contents are cool before emptying.

☐ Use fireplace screens to contain sparks.

☐ Have your chimney cleared of creosote and ash once a year to avoid a chimney fire.

☐ At bedtime, check that fireplace fires have been extinguished and that all appliances have been turned off.

☐ Store lighter fluid, kerosene, gasoline, and other flammable substances in a locked storage area away from your house.

☐ Avoid careless storage. Do not pile items or objects near doors or on stairways, or store flammable materials near heat sources. Keep candles, lighters, and matches well beyond your child's reach.

☐ Keep heat-producing appliances—heaters, irons, and coffee makers, for instance—away from upholstery, drapes, and other flammable items.

☐ Do not overload electrical outlets or extension cords, and do not run cords beneath carpeting. An extension cord that is hot to the touch is overloaded and therefore dangerous.

☐ Read labels to be certain that your children's clothing, holiday decorations, curtains, slipcovers, and other interior fabrics are fire-resistant.

☐ If you use a space heater, make sure that the heating element is covered and that the unit bears a UL or AGA label of approval.

☐ Make sure that relatives, friends, and your child's care givers follow your family's fire-safety rules.

WHAT TO DO WHEN FIRE STRIKES

Of course, there are no guarantees that an accidental fire will not strike. Therefore, it's important to prepare your home—and your child—for the possibility of fire. Doors and windows, for instance, can stick, shrink, or swell in various types of weather. To ensure your family's hasty exit or temporary protection during a fire, it's a good idea to periodically check every door and window in your home to be sure that it opens and closes easily. Safely store escape ladders in every room above ground level. Discuss and practice with your family two possible escape routes from each room, and designate an outside meeting area—a tree in the yard, perhaps, or a corner mailbox—to be used in the event of a fire. Other good fire-preparation ideas include the posting of emergency numbers at every telephone in your house, and the installation of smoke detectors and fire extinguishers (see page 199). It's also wise to avoid stacking toys or laundry on stairs or in doorways, and to think twice before removing the key from the inside lock of a double-dead-bolted entry door. Either practice could dangerously hamper your exit from a pitch-black, smoke-filled home. Also consider keeping a flashlight at your bedside.

Fire preparedness is just one way to maximize your family's safety in the event of a blaze. Knowing what to do during a fire is equally important, and can keep your child from becoming a needless victim. It's important, for example, to teach and practice with your child the "stop, drop, and roll" technique that can be so effective when clothing catches fire. Also practice summoning help in the event of a blaze, whether by phone or by fire alarm box. And teach your child the following procedure, which should be followed during any fire.

1. Alert those nearby by shouting "Fire!"
2. Leave the premises immediately without pausing to gather possessions or fight the fire.
3. When escaping a fire, feel each door before opening it. If the door is hot, find another escape route. If none exists, stuff clothing or a towel beneath the door and wait for help. Close doors behind you as you leave.
4. Stay close to the floor, where there is the least amount of smoke. If possible, cover your face with a wet cloth and take short breaths through the fabric.
5. Once outside, summon help from a telephone or alarm box.

If the fire still appears small and contained after you have called the fire department and seen to your family's safety, you might consider fighting it with an extinguisher—from outside the doorway if the fire is in a closet, attic, or small room. If the fire is in your yard or a wooded area near your property line, close all windows and doors and—having made sure that a safe escape route exists—rake, dig, or wet down a four-foot path around your house to prevent the fire from spreading to your home. Also wet down the house and shrubbery, and keep a shovel or broom on hand to beat down flames. Naturally, your child should not take part in this effort, nor should she attempt to fight a fire on her own. And, of course, every family member should heed evacuation orders during a fire of major proportions.

Certainly, the idea of a house catching fire is frightening to any parent. But by setting examples of fire safety during everyday life and teaching all household members how to respond to an accidental fire, you will do a great deal to make the occurrence of a fire unlikely and to ensure that if a fire does take place, your family will remain unharmed.

Resources

Your local fire department can provide booklets and additional information about fire safety. The resources listed below may also be helpful.

ORGANIZATION

National Fire Protection Association
Batterymarch Park
PO Box 9101
Quincy, MA 02269–9101
(617) 770–3000

This organization sets fire-safety standards, sponsors school and community programs, and publishes literature aimed at reducing the incidence of personal injury and property damage caused by fire.

BOOKS

Chlad, Dorothy. *When There Is a Fire, Go Outside.* Chicago: Children's Press, 1982.

Feagin, Clairece. *Safe at Home.* Chicago: Contemporary Books, 1991.

Owen, Howard R. *Fire and You: The Plan to Get You and Your Family Out of the Inevitable Fire—Alive.* Garden City, NY: Doubleday, 1977.

Vandenburg, Mary Lou. *Help! Emergencies That Could Happen to You and How to Handle Them.* Minneapolis: Lerner Publications, 1975.

Williams, Sandra J., John Downey, and Lois Cohen. *We're Responsible: A Children's Guide to Fire Safety.* Dobbs Ferry, NY: Oceana Educational Communications, 1987.

Teach Your Child to Respect Fire

Even more horrifying than accidental fire is the blaze that was deliberately set. In the United States alone, there are more than 100,000 intentional and suspicious fires each year. A full 40 percent of these fires are set by children and teen-agers, with one in every thirteen being set by a child under the age of ten.

You can certainly expect your youngster to express an interest in fire at various points during her childhood. Of course, your child is much less likely to act on this curiosity when she is well supervised and has restricted access to lighters, matches, and other incendiary devices. But it's also important to balance her normal childhood fascination with the unusual properties of fire with a clear understanding of its potential for destruction. Share stories and pictures of fires with your child, and use each incident to launch a discussion of how the sustained damage or injury might have been avoided. Teach her that heat can be painful, and that there is a difference between "good" fires and those that are out of control and dangerous. Stress fire-safe behavior, such as avoiding ovens and stoves, keeping a safe distance from open fires, and not playing with matches, lighters, or electricity. Under controlled conditions, show your child the destruction that smoke and flames can cause to paper, wood, and fabric.

It's often helpful to calmly voice your concern for your child's ongoing safety, and to explain the importance of having similar regard for the well-being and property of others. Make sure your child understands what arson is, and that a purposely set fire is grounds for arrest even if no damage occurs. Above all, don't hesitate to seek professional intervention if you suspect that your child's fascination with fire might be unhealthy. If she collects matches or lighters, for example, or continues to experiment with fire despite repeated discussions and warnings, contact your family doctor or community mental health center for advice and assistance.

Buy and Maintain Fire-Safety Devices

A large number of house-fire deaths occur at night, when families are asleep. Many such fires smolder for an hour or more before smoke and flames grow intense enough to be noticed from outside. You can go a long way toward making your family fire-safe by keeping the following devices available and in good working order.

Smoke Detectors

It's vital to install at least one smoke detector on each floor of your home—particularly near your family's sleeping area and in the vicinity of heat sources and the kitchen. Check smoke-detector batteries monthly, and replace the batteries at least once a year.

Fire Extinguishers

There are several types of fire extinguishers available that cool, smother, or react chemically with flames until they die out. Both liquefied gas and multipurpose dry chemical extinguishers are effective on most home fires. Your extinguisher should have a UL (Underwriters Laboratories) approval label, be inspected yearly, and be accessible during an emergency. Be aware that some older, inverted-type extinguishers are no longer used. To check the safety of your older extinguisher, contact your local fire department.

Fire Alarm Boxes

The purpose of a fire alarm box is to summon help quickly in the event of a fire. If alarm boxes are in use where you live, make sure that you and your family know where they are and how they work. If you see a nonfunctioning alarm box, notify your fire department immediately. And if you ever send in an alarm, remember to stay put—in a safe area, of course—until firefighters arrive so that you can direct them to the blaze.

Fire is a possibility in any sort of dwelling. Certainly, it pays to arm your home and family with high-quality, well-maintained fire safety devices.

38

CREATE A "SAFE HOUSE" IN YOUR NEIGHBORHOOD

Wouldn't it be reassuring to know that there was a place your child could go for help if he were ill, injured, lost, or threatened, and couldn't make his way home? How wonderful it would be to have carefully screened and easily identifiable adult assistance available to your child in an emergency! By registering your own home in a "safe house" program—or by creating a safe house elsewhere in your community—you can provide this sort of help and protection for all the children in your neighborhood.

A safe house, identified by a sign placed in a window that is easily seen from the street, does for a child just what its name implies: it provides a haven from situations that might prevent him from reaching home safely. A child—and his parents—can be certain that the adult in charge is caring and trustworthy and will respond to emergencies by phoning a child's parents and, if necessary, the appropriate medical personnel or law enforcement authorities. Many parent-teacher and civic associations provide safe houses through "child watch" or "block parent" programs, and there is a well-known national program as well.

The National Crime Prevention Council uses the familiar "McGruff" character to popularize their program. McGruff is a large, streetwise dog in a wrinkled beige raincoat whose face adorns television commercials and posters countrywide, and whose life-size version makes appearances at elementary schools from coast to coast. Since a recent study showed that McGruff has an 89-percent recognition rate among schoolchildren, the council's publicity campaign has obviously been successful. And just as many children—and adults—can recite the program's growled slogan: "Take a bite out of crime!"

McGruff Houses are registered with the police department and display a large yellow-and-black profile of the McGruff character. As part of the National Crime Prevention Council's program, children are taught not to approach a McGruff House for any reason other than an emergency, but not to hesitate to appeal to the residents if trouble should arise. McGruff House applicants and their families undergo a background check by the police department since, naturally, their character and reliability are of primary importance. People with a record of domestic violence, substance abuse, or child-related arrests, for example, would not qualify as McGruff House sponsors. In fact, as an additional safeguard, McGruff House registrants are required to reapply to the program each year. Upon approval, the adults in the household receive updated instructions on the handling of emergencies.

Council officials—and, certainly, parents—would eventually like to see one or more McGruff Houses on every residential block. Stay-at-home parents and retired persons are ideal candidates to run these havens. Since most safe-house programs are coordinated through area schools, you can get an application or additional information through your district's central administration office. If you are not at home often enough for your residence to be a viable safe house, but nevertheless wish to further ensure your child's safety, you might try publicizing these programs at an upcoming community, school board, or parent organization meeting. You can also make an effort to recruit at-home neighbors to register their homes as safe houses by telling them about McGruff House and other similar programs.

In the best of all possible worlds, your child's safety on the street would never even be in question. However, the growing number of two-income families means that, these days, your neighborhood may be nearly deserted between eight a.m. and five p.m.—the very hours that your child travels to and from school and plays outdoors. This fact, along with an ever-increasing crime rate, makes child safety an important issue. By creating a safe house on your block or within your community, you will make a tremendous difference in the life of a child in trouble. Just as important, you'll make it possible to send your own child forth each morning with a strong sense that he'll remain safe and sound till he walks back through the door at day's end.

Resources

To find out whether any safe houses currently exist in your community, or for more information about volunteering your own home, you can contact your local school principal, parent-teacher organization, or the police department. You can learn more about the McGruff House program from the National Crime Prevention Council at the following address.

ORGANIZATION

The McGruff House Program
Suite 180
1879 South Main Street
Salt Lake City, UT 84115
(801) 486–8768

"Children are the parents' riches."

—William Shakespeare

39

KEEP YOUR CHILD SAFE FROM FIREARMS

When your child plays at home, is there a gun anywhere in the vicinity? Do the parents of your child's friends keep firearms in their homes? These days, gun ownership is in no way limited to hunters, target shooters, and would-be criminals. Actually, many of the 200 million registered firearms currently in American homes are handguns that were purchased for protection. Yet, studies show that guns in the home are much more likely to kill a family member than an intruder. Sadly, hundreds of children die in accidental shootings each year. But you can minimize the risk of your child being involved in such an incident by taking specific safety precautions and by being aware of her activities.

It may be difficult to imagine your child handling a loaded weapon—or worse, placing herself, a friend, or a family member in the path of a bullet. However, this scenario is more common than you would think. The fact is that more than half of all domestic shooting accidents involve guns that were found in bedrooms and living rooms by children under age fourteen. And it is safe to assume that many hundreds of additional gun firings by children go unreported because no injuries are sustained. Not surprisingly, parents are not at home during the majority of accidental shootings.

Opinions are divided about the need for more stringent gun control laws. On one hand, proponents believe that practicing gun safety is not enough, and that the best way to protect children from firearms is to ban weapons from areas where children live and play. However, opponents of stricter gun control cite the ineffectiveness of the tens of thousands of laws that already exist, and support education and parental responsibility as keys to reducing firearm accidents. There are several points to keep in mind when considering your own position on guns and children. First, your child may have a deep fascination with guns that stems from their use by television and fictional heroes. (See Entry 8 on page 30 for information on monitoring children's TV viewing habits.) Also, it may be difficult for your child to distinguish between a toy gun and the real thing. Your practice of gun safety can certainly help protect your child, but there is always the chance that your teachings will be disregarded if your child gets deeply involved in a game or becomes extremely upset. Finally, and perhaps most thought-provoking of all, the safest storage of a handgun purchased for protection at home—unloaded, inaccessible, and locked—may well defeat the very purpose of owning the weapon.

Whatever your feelings about current gun-ownership laws, you have an immediate responsibility to safeguard your child against any firearms stored in your home and in any home she visits. The guidelines listed below should help.

☐ Remember that many of the guns used by children are taken from drawers and closets. Therefore, storing a gun out of *sight* is not enough. If you have a gun in your home, keep it unloaded and securely locked away, out of your child's reach.

☐ Equip any guns you own with trigger locks and other child-proofing devices.

☐ Store ammunition separately from guns, locked up, and away from heat sources that could cause it to become activated.

☐ When handling guns at home, keep them unloaded, and avoid demonstrating unsafe practices that your child might copy.

☐ Consider storing recreational firearms at a gun club. If you must keep them at home, unload and disassemble them elsewhere before entering your house.

☐ Load your recreational gun at the shooting range or in the field, rather than at home.

☐ If your child is going to participate in recreational shooting, enroll her in a course in gun safety.

☐ Explain to your child the dangers of guns stored in other

people's homes. Teach her never to handle these items, and to leave the premises if her friend wishes to use them.

☐ Don't hesitate to ask the parents of your child's friends whether they keep guns in their homes. If they do, inquire where the guns are located and whether they are loaded. The answer you receive will help you decide whether to permit your child to play in that home. Share any pertinent information with your child.

In the long run, your best defense against your child's involvement in an accidental shooting is vigilance. Make it a point to stay informed of your child's whereabouts and activities, and to get to know her friends and their parents. (Entry 1 on page 3 presents additional ideas for staying knowledgeable about your child's activities.) And if you're interested in making far-reaching changes, contact an organization that's involved in changing gun-control legislation, raising gun-safety awareness in the community, or lobbying for gun-responsibility laws that target gun owners whose unsecured weapons cause injury at the hand of a child.

Whatever your personal opinion about firearms, they remain a fact of life in many homes. If you teach your child about the danger of firearms and take steps to remove guns from her play environment, you'll both have greater peace of mind.

Resources

The following organizations and books can furnish helpful information about keeping your child safe from firearms.

ORGANIZATIONS

Center to Prevent Handgun
  Violence
1225 Eye Street NW, Suite 1150
Washington, DC 20005
(202) 289–7319

This organization works to educate the American public about the risks and responsibilities of owning a handgun.

Coalition to Stop Gun Violence
100 Maryland Avenue NE
Washington, DC 20002
(202) 544–7190

This national coalition of educational, professional, and religious organizations seeks a ban on the private sale and possession of handguns in America.

Educational Fund to End Handgun
  Violence
PO Box 72
110 Maryland Avenue NE
Washington, DC 20002
(202) 544–7227

This organization offers public educa-
tion on handgun violence in the United
States.

Gun Responsibility in Every
  Family (GRIEF)
PO Box 743
Naugatuck, CT 06770
(203) 729–1708
(203) 729–3636

This organization seeks to change fire-
arm laws that protect the gun owner at
the expense of the victim.

Gun.Owners, Inc.
3304 Viking Drive
Sacramento, CA 95826
(916) 361–3109

This group advocates harsher punish-
ment for criminal misuse of firearms.

Handgun Control, Inc.
1225 Eye Street NW, Suite 1100
Washington, DC 20005
(202) 898–0792

This group advocates stricter gun-con-
trol legislation.

BOOKS

Harris, Jack C. *Gun Control.* Mankato, NH: Crestwood House, 1990.

Landau, Elaine. *Armed America: The Status of Gun Control.* Englewood
Cliffs, NJ: J. Messner, 1991.

Newton, David E. *Gun Control: An Issue for the Nineties.* Hillside, NJ:
Enslow Publishers, 1992.

VIDEOTAPE

Don't Touch That Gun. Crawford Productions, 1990.

40

CHILDPROOF YOUR HOME

Babies grow and change quickly. And with the passing of each developmental milestone comes the acquisition of new skills that allow your baby to more easily explore the world with his eyes, his mouth, his hands, and his feet—and to get into a lot of trouble in the process! By childproofing your home, you'll provide your little one with a *safe* environment in which to reach, crawl, stand, and eventually walk.

It's vital to childproof your house before your baby even begins to move around. Keep in mind that his transition from sedentary to mobile will happen quickly—perhaps even unexpectedly. It makes sense to clear your child's path of hazards before that inevitable day when you turn your head for a moment only to find your little explorer upending a tool kit or gnawing on a lamp cord. In addition, there is a first time for every accomplishment. You can never be sure when your baby will first gain access to the items on your coffee table or successfully pry open a cabinet.

Far from a quick scan of your table tops, thorough childproofing is a time-consuming process. Listed directly below are some general guidelines that are applicable to nearly every room of your house. Following that are more specific suggestions for the nursery, kitchen, bathroom, and family room.

GENERAL SAFETY TIPS

☐ Take a crawling tour of your home. Traveling through your house on your hands and knees will turn up hazards unseen to an adult, but perfectly visible—and attractive—to a baby.

☐ Make sure that all windows contain latches and guards to prevent your baby from climbing out. Don't rely on screens to prevent falls, as they're not strong enough. Open double-hung windows from the top only, and move any furniture that could provide window access. Remember that a child can fall out of a window that's open only five inches.

☐ Use safety gates to fence off doorways that lead to off-limits rooms and stairs. Avoid diamond-shaped accordion gates and gates with openings large enough to entrap a child's neck.

☐ To prevent pinched fingers, climbing accidents, and other mishaps, invest in safety latches for cabinets and drawers in every room of the house.

☐ Rather than trying to train your baby not to touch items displayed on tables or shelves, consider temporarily removing breakables and sharp or dangerous items.

☐ To prevent painful, dangerous electrical shocks, cover unused electrical outlets with mock plastic plugs or safety plates. Many electrical appliances are now sold with flat plugs that are difficult for a baby to pull from an outlet. Or you can invest in outlet guards that completely cover traditional plugs. It's also wise to shorten or hide electrical cords so that they remain as much out of reach as possible.

☐ Keep dangerous substances—plastic bags, poisonous chemicals, cleaning supplies, and sharp tools, for example—in a locked cabinet. (See Entry 45 on page 234 for more suggestions.)

☐ Check all wooden surfaces for splinters by running a dry sponge over furniture, molding, and floors. Look for and repair chipped paint—especially when it may contain lead. (See Entry 46 on page 239 for a discussion of lead.)

SAFETY TIPS FOR THE NURSERY

☐ Make sure all baby toys and equipment meet current safety standards. (See Entry 41 on page 212 for details.)

☐ Keep playpens and cribs away from drapery and venetian blind cords, radiators, and shelves.

☐ Leave pillows and stuffed animals out of the crib, as they present a suffocation hazard to young babies. Also attach bumper pads securely to the rails. Remove mobiles and crib gyms from playpens and cribs once your baby can sit; take away bumper pads and large toys on which your child might gain a foothold once he can stand.

☐ If your child has a walker, keep it only on smooth surfaces and away from stairs, and *never* leave him alone in it.

☐ Store baby products out of your child's reach.

SAFETY TIPS FOR THE KITCHEN

☐ Cover stove dials and front burners with protective shields.

☐ Cook only on the rear burners when possible, and turn pot handles inward.

☐ Substitute place mats for tablecloths, and push chairs completely underneath the table to discourage climbing.

☐ Store dangerous items and substances in high locked cabinets.

☐ Keep your step-stool out of sight.

☐ Position highchairs away from radiators and appliances.

☐ Do not attach clamp-on chairs to pedestal tables, counter tops, or any other object with a vertical surface that your baby can push with his feet, possibly causing the chair to become dislodged.

SAFETY TIPS FOR THE BATHROOM

☐ Purchase childproof fasteners for toilet seats, and cover tile floors with a rubber-backed throw rug.

☐ To prevent scaldings, keep your water heater set at 120°F or less, and install temperature-sensing shower heads and faucets that automatically shut off too-hot water.

☐ To prevent falls and head injuries, apply nonskid grips to the tub bottom, buy a padded cover for the tub spout, and consider a side-wall cushion for the rim.

☐ Keep electrical appliances, razors, medicines, and cleansing products out of reach in locked cabinets.

SAFETY TIPS FOR THE FAMILY ROOM

☐ Remove hazardous items from table tops and shelves.

☐ Dispose of any poisonous houseplants. (See page 238.)

☐ Roll up phone cords, drapery and venetian blind pulls, and lamp and appliance cords.

☐ Cover sharp table edges with slit lengths of PVC piping.

☐ Secure bookcases, telephone tables, and television and VCR stands.

☐ Cover fireplaces and fans.

☐ Designate a hook for jackets and purses—both of which may be filled with unseen dangers.

When you take your baby to someone else's home, continue your practice of childproofing. Ask your host's permission to remove any dangers that lurk within your baby's reach. Of course, there is no substitute for parental supervision. But even the most diligent parent sometimes turns away. With some careful preparation, you can make infancy and early childhood times of joyful discovery for your child, and make your home a safer place for the entire family.

Resources

The following resources can furnish additional information on childproofing your home.

ORGANIZATIONS

American Academy of Safety
  Education (AASE)
Central Missouri State University
Safety Center/Humphreys Building
Warrensburg, MO 64093
(816) 429–4830

This organization promotes safety education and the prevention of accidents in communities throughout the nation.

National SAFE KIDS Campaign
111 Michigan Avenue NW
Washington, DC 20010
(202) 939–4993

This program is dedicated to raising public awareness of the need for accident prevention, and to making child safety an important consideration in homes and communities across the country.

The Perfectly Safe Company
7245 Whipple Avenue NW
North Canton, OH 44720
(800) 837–KIDS

This company seeks to educate parents about the importance of child safety, and specializes in safety devices.

U.S. Consumer Product Safety
  Commission (CPSC)
Office of Information and
  Public Affairs
Washington, DC 20207
(301) 392–6580
(800) 638–CPSC
(800) 638–8270 *For the Hearing Impaired*
(800) 492–8104 *For the Hearing
  Impaired, Maryland Only*

This agency monitors the market and seeks recalls of hazardous items, investigates complaints, and offers publications on childproofing.

BOOKS

Arena, Jay, and Miriam B. Settle. *Child Safety Is No Accident*. New York: Berkley Publishing Group, 1991.

Cole, Joanna. *Safe From the Start: Your Child's Safety From Birth to Age Five*. New York: St. Martin's Press, 1991.

Fise, Mary Ellen R., and Jack Gillis. *The Childwise Catalog*. New York: Pocket Books, 1986.

Hill, Barbara Albers. *Baby Tactics: Parenting Tips That Really Work*. Garden City Park, NY: Avery Publishing Group, 1991.

Lansky, Vicki. *Babyproofing Basics: How to Keep Your Child Safe*. Deephaven, MN: Meadowbrook Press, 1991.

Miller, Jeanne E. *The Perfectly Safe Catalog for Parents Who Care*. North Canton, OH: Perfectly Safe, 1991.

Miller, Jeanne E. *The Perfectly Safe Home*. North Canton, OH: Perfectly Safe, 1991.

Stewart, Arlene. *Childproofing Your Home*. Reading, MA: Addison-Wesley Publishing, 1984.

---

*"Give a little love to a child
and you get a great deal back."*

—John Ruskin

41

PROVIDE SAFE TOYS AND NURSERY FURNISHINGS

A well-made toy or piece of nursery furniture can last for many years, which is one of the reasons parents often rely on hand-me-downs for their babies. A single crib may serve a dozen or more children during its lifetime; a farm play set may be lovingly stored to be passed on from one generation to the next. However, government safety standards are always changing, and a baby item that was considered safe even five years ago may no longer meet suggested guidelines. In addition, the majority of hand-me-downs come without the manufacturer's age recommendations and guidelines for use, and use of a nursery item or plaything at too young an age can result in serious injury. Fortunately, most accidents of this type are preventable. By ensuring that the equipment and toys your child uses are safe, age-appropriate, and in good repair, you can do a great deal to keep her out of harm's way.

How are safety standards determined? The U.S. Consumer Product Safety Commission (CPSC) works with manufacturers' engineering departments to inspect and test products, collect performance data, and institute necessary changes in product design. In addition, the CPSC investigates consumer complaints and reports of injury, and monitors the domestic and import market for products that violate current standards. If a product is deemed hazardous, the CPSC can mandate corrective action or recall.

The work of the CPSC is ongoing, yet there are those who feel that the commission is overburdened and that government safety standards are not strict enough. For example, many marketed toys just barely exceed the dimensions set by the government to prevent choking. Legally, these toys are considered safe, yet they caused 165 choking deaths and countless "close calls" between 1980 and 1990. As a parent, you cannot assume that every product you buy for your baby has been tested by the CPSC, nor can you conclude that a particular toy or piece of equipment is completely safe simply because it satisfies government safety standards. And if you make use of nursery furnishings that are secondhand, you must bear in mind that over the years, a number of items have been recalled or changed to meet revised standards.

Ultimately, your baby's safety rests in your hands. It's important to be aggressive in your assessment of the playthings and furnishings she uses. The suggestions listed below can help you protect your child from accidents that can occur through misuse of a baby product or through use of toys or equipment that are poorly designed.

☐ Always follow the manufacturers' instructions for assembly and use of nursery equipment. If the instructions are missing, be sure to obtain duplicates from the manufacturer.

☐ Heed the manufacturers' size, weight, and age recommendations carefully. It is often mistakenly assumed that age guidelines refer to a child's intellectual capabilities when, in fact, these recommendations are made with child safety in mind.

☐ Consider warning labels carefully, and leave all labels intact to protect future users of your child's baby equipment.

☐ Check all secondhand nursery furnishings carefully for paint chips, cracks, holes, and missing screws or parts. Be aware that old paint may contain lead, and that older vinyl can be easily bitten and torn by a teething child. (For more information on the dangers of lead, see Entry 46 on page 239.) If you feel that repairs may affect a damaged product's durability, replace the item instead of fixing it.

☐ Before using a secondhand product that is in good condition, compare the item with its currently manufactured counterpart. If you note differences that seem related to child safety, you may want to change your mind about using the hand-me-down.

☐ Request a set of safety guidelines for nursery equipment from the Juvenile Products Manufacturers Association (JPMA) or the CPSC (see page 215). Check the toys and furniture you're interested in purchasing—or already own—against these guidelines to ensure that the products meet current safety standards.

☐ Make it a practice to consult recall listings on a regular basis. *Consumer Reports* and *Consumers' Research Magazine* are just two of the magazines that supply monthly listings of newly recalled products. Many toy stores also post recall notices.

☐ Check on earlier recalls of hand-me-down baby items by noting model numbers and calling the CPSC hotline with the information.

☐ Obtain a choke-test cylinder, used to determine the safety of small toys and parts, for one dollar by calling Toys To Grow On at (800) 542–8338.

Be aware that new safety regulations are always under discussion. Some current considerations, for example, have to do with walkers, play sand, warning flags on riding toys, and lead-crystal baby bottles. Aside from these standards, perhaps the most important suggestion regarding your child's safety at home and in day care pertains to supervision. Young children are explorers by nature, and often use toys and other nursery items in ways that surprise their parents and defy manufacturer's suggestions! By keeping up with current safety information, following established guidelines in the selection of toys and furniture, using common sense, and keeping your eye on your child, you'll be able to stimulate your child's curiosity and encourage creative play while keeping her safe and sound.

Resources

The organizations and literature listed below can help you in your quest for current information about safety standards for toys and nursery furnishings.

ORGANIZATIONS

American Academy of Pediatrics
141 Northwest Point Boulevard
PO Box 927
Elk Grove Village, IL 60009–0927
(708) 228–5005
(800) 433–9016

This professional society of pediatricians publishes materials concerning advancements in the medical field, and maintains more than forty committees to study different aspects of pediatric care, including accident prevention.

Institute for Injury Reduction
  (IIR)
PO Box 1621
Upper Marlboro, MD 20773
(301) 249–0090
(800) 544–3694

This nonprofit educational and research organization, founded by trial attorneys but open to all individuals, is dedicated to reducing deaths and injuries caused by product defects.

Juvenile Products Manufacturers
  Association (JPMA)
Two Greentree Centre, Suite 225
PO Box 955
Marlton, NJ 08053
(609) 985–2878

This association of manufacturers of nursery furniture, baby equipment, and other juvenile products maintains a safety certification program through which the JPMA seal of approval is awarded to products that have passed safety tests.

Toy Manufacturers of America
200 Fifth Avenue, Suite 740
New York, NY 10010
(212) 675–1141
(800) 851–9955

This organization is dedicated to improving all aspects of the design, manufacture, marketing, and performance of toys.

U.S. Consumer Product Safety
  Commission (CPSC)
Office of Information and Public
  Affairs
Washington, DC 20207
(301) 392–6580
(800) 638–CPSC
(800) 638–8270 *For the Hearing Impaired*
(800) 492–8104 *For the Hearing
  Impaired, Maryland Only*

The CPSC is mandated by the government to set safety standards, monitor the market for potentially dangerous products, and seek modifications and recalls of hazardous items. This agency also offers free booklets about product safety.

BOOKS

Fise, Mary Ellen, and Jack Gillis. *The Childwise Catalog.* New York: Pocket Books, 1986.

Jones, Sandy, with Werner Freitag. *Guide to Baby Products.* Yonkers, NY: Consumer Reports Books, 1991.

Kelley, Benjamin, Hubert C. Kelley, and Cynthia Raffles. *The 1992 Toy Safety Report.* Upper Marlboro, MD: Institute for Injury Reduction, 1992.

Terry, Debra, and Juli Plooster. *Creative Nurseries Illustrated.* Radnor, PA: Chilton, 1987.

42

CONSIDER CHILD SAFETY WHEN AWAY FROM HOME

For many families, weekends and vacations are a time to visit new and interesting places. Exciting? Yes. Challenging? Certainly, for it can be difficult to keep your family safe at a popular attraction or play area, in unfamiliar lodgings, or in a car that is unlike your own. Safety standards may be inadequate or poorly enforced, and crowds, noise, and confusion can make it hard for you and your child to keep your minds on being careful. Fortunately, there are steps you can take to ensure that your trip—whether an afternoon visit to a carnival or a three-week stay at a seaside resort—is as safe as it is fun.

☐ When visiting a fair or theme park, make sure your child is dressed appropriately. Insist upon closed shoes that provide good traction, and do not permit hanging jewelry, a shoulder purse, dangling clothing, or long, loose hair.

☐ Plan ahead to make it easier to keep track of your child in a crowd. Have your child wear brightly colored clothing or a unique hat. Tie an unusual scarf or balloon to your stroller handle. Consider using Velcro wrist cuffs that link parent and preschooler with an elastic cord.

☐ Locate the lost-children's facility upon entering any park. Point out an attendant's uniform to your child, and instruct him to find an attendant if he gets lost. Carry a photograph of your child for faster identification.

☐ Teach your child how to avoid contact with the toilet seat—or how to line the seat with paper—when using a public rest room. Also insist that he scrub his hands thoroughly when finished.

☐ Make sure that your child is accompanied on trips to the rest room or snack bar, and that he play or stroll with a partner at all other times.

□ Inspect picnic and playground areas for such hazards as broken equipment, exposed screws, broken glass, trash, and hard, unforgiving surfaces before allowing your child access. Supervise playground activities at all times.

□ When renting a car, van, or camper, request a vehicle that is equipped with front-seat air bags. Be sure to obtain a copy of the operator's manual, and familiarize yourself with the dashboard and controls before starting your trip.

□ Before settling into your hotel or motel room, note the two fire exits nearest to your room and show them to your child. Also note the location of the nearest fire alarm. Keep your room key and a flashlight at your bedside. During an emergency, the key will permit re-entry into your room if escape routes are impassable.

Above all, be vigilant when you and your youngster are away from home. If your child is old enough to go places unescorted, teach him to observe the same safety precautions you routinely follow. If your child is young, there is no substitute for watchfulness. While you may not be able to guarantee that every family outing is problem-free, you *can* help ensure that everyone returns home safe and sound.

Resources

You can obtain additional information about away-from-home safety from the resources listed below.

ORGANIZATIONS

American Automobile Association (AAA)
1000 AAA Drive
Heathrow, FL 32746–5063
(407) 444–7000

This federation of automobile clubs provides domestic and foreign travel services, and works for improved travel conditions and transportation safety.

National SAFE KIDS Campaign
111 Michigan Avenue NW
Washington, DC 20010–2970
(202) 939–4993

This program is dedicated to raising public awareness of the need for accident prevention, and to making child safety an important consideration in homes and communities.

BOOKS

Arena, Jay M., and Miriam B. Settle. *Child Safety Is No Accident*. New York: Berkley Publishing Group, 1991.

Comer, Diana E. *Developing Safety Skills in the Young Child*. Englewood, CO: DelMar, 1987.

Sanders, Pete. *Outdoors With Pete Sanders*. New York: Gloucester Press, 1989.

Vanderburg, Mary Lou. *Help! Emergencies That Could Happen to You and How to Handle Them*. Minneapolis: Lerner Publications, 1975.

Teach Your Child How to Safely Cross the Street

Children playing near the roadside and crossing neighborhood streets are quite ordinary sights. And a good many of these children are able to safely deal with traffic. If your child is younger than eight years old, however, or if he is inexperienced in the matter of street safety, it's important to teach him to be wary of moving vehicles.

Children who are between the ages of five and nine face the greatest risk of getting hit by a car because they are given to darting into the street whether to cross, chase a pet, or retrieve a toy. Certainly, preschoolers occasionally make their way into the street as well, but their toddling or meandering gait often gives surprised drivers an extra second or two to stop. Other factors that lead to pedestrian accidents involving young children are their height, which makes them easily concealed by parked cars and shrubbery; their poor judgment of speed and direction of sound; and a trusting nature that leads many youngsters to believe that drivers will always see them and be able to stop in time. The very young may even think of cars as friendly creatures that would never hurt them.

Your child must learn to respect the street as soon as he is old enough to toddle around outdoors. But he needs you to model and teach him traffic safety. Here are a few ideas that can help.

☐ Train your child to always stop at the curb, even when the street is empty of traffic. This habit will decrease the chance of his darting into the street when preoccupied.

☐ Teach your child to look and listen for approaching cars by turning left, then right, then left again. (Or, for very young children, "this way," "that way," and "this way again.")

☐ Show your child how to wait until the street is clear, and then walk briskly and directly across to the opposite side. Make it clear that there's to be no running, as this can lead to falls, and no dawdling or crossing on the diagonal, as this can lead to extra time spent in the road.

☐ When your child is old enough to walk along the street alone, teach him to use sidewalks. Where none exists, your child is safest walking along the left side of the street, facing oncoming traffic. Train him to wear light-colored clothing or reflective tape whenever he walks on the street at night.

Perhaps the best way to prepare your child to handle street traffic is to practice crossing together—dozens of times, hundreds of times, or for as long as it takes to convince you that he's become a careful pedestrian. This way, when your child is playing or walking near the road, you can rest a bit easier, knowing that he is street smart.

43

LEARN FIRST AID

Most parents quickly become adept at extracting splinters, icing bruises, swabbing scrapes, and applying adhesive bandages after a child's minor accident. But occasionally, your child may suffer a more serious injury. In this case, a swift and appropriate response can be crucial to both the healing process and your child's comfort. Correctly judging the need for professional medical assistance is important, as well. If your child ever faces a life-threatening emergency, however, there may be no time to seek help. In this case, you or your child's care giver can save your youngster's life by knowing how to prevent choking and how to perform cardiopulmonary resuscitation (CPR).

It's important, and relatively easy, for you to get the information you need to handle your child's medical emergencies. The American Heart Association (AHA) gives a Pediatric Basic Life Support Course on home safety and emergency techniques. Your local American Red Cross chapter also offers instruction in the various types of first aid. Both organizations are listed in the white pages of your phone directory. The fee for participation in a Red Cross or AHA course is usually nominal, and completion of a course often entitles you to a certificate of proficiency. Fire departments and hospitals are also good sources of information on handling children's medical situations, as are adult education courses held in community centers, local schools, and colleges.

The following discussions on general first aid and procedures to help a choking child can give you a better idea of what sort of emergency-aid knowledge you need, or can help to refresh your memory if you've already taken a course on emergency techniques. (Information on childproofing your home to prevent these emergencies is provided in Entry 40 on page 207.) Because of the complexity of the CPR process, we have chosen not to present the procedure here, but to urge parents to seek qualified instruction. In this case, there is no substitute for taking a course and practicing on a mannequin.

PROVIDING GENERAL FIRST AID

As every parent knows, because children are so physcially active and so impulsive—and because they often are so unaware of possible dangers—they are also particularly accident-prone. The suggestions listed below will guide you in taking the best possible action the next time your child needs first aid.

Poisoning

If you think your child has swallowed a poison, remove whatever remains in her mouth. Do not induce vomiting at this time. Take the poison container to the phone and call Poison Control for instructions. (This number is listed on the inside cover of your phone directory.) If you suspect that your child has been poisoned by gas or fumes, take her into the fresh air immediately, and call for help. Perform rescue breathing (see pages 223 and 225) or CPR as needed. Entry 45 on page 234 gives additional information about poisons.

Wounds

If a wound is small, wash the area with soap and water, apply antibiotic ointment, and cover the wound with a bandage. For large wounds or cuts that bleed heavily, apply direct pressure to the area to slow the bleeding, and seek immediate medical assistance. Cover your child with a blanket or jacket while you wait for help, and try to keep her calm.

Burns

Cool minor burns under cold water for ten minutes. Do not apply ointments or creams of any kind, but cover the burn with nonadhesive gauze. If the burn is large, blistered, or in a sensitive area of the body, seek medical assistance. While you wait, give your child liquids. Do not break or cover the blisters, and do not remove your child's clothing, as blistered skin may stick to the fabric.

Falls

Apply ice to any bruises sustained in a fall. If you suspect a head or neck injury, or if your child loses consciousness, suffers seizures, or seems disoriented, get medical help at once. If your child is unconscious, do not move her. Keep her warm with a blanket or coat, and perform rescue breathing as necessary while you await assistance. (See pages 223 and 225.) Also see a doctor for treatment of sprains or strains, or if your child complains of pain after a fall.

DISLODGING OBJECTS IN A CHOKING CHILD

Choking occurs when the airway is obstructed by an object or a piece of food. Babies and small children are particularly susceptible to choking because of their tendency to place inappropriate items in their mouths. If your child sputters and coughs or cries, she is getting air and is probably not in danger. In this case, it is best to allow your child to expel the object on her own. Back-slapping and using your fingers to probe your child's mouth can force the object farther into the throat.

If your child cannot speak or cough, if she cannot draw a breath or breathes with a hoarse or crowing sound, or if her lips begin to turn blue, you can be reasonably sure that something is lodged in her airway. Send someone for help if you can. However, if you and your child are alone, do not take the time to use the phone. Instead, look carefully in your child's mouth for the obstruction—again, do not probe blindly with your fingers—and extract the object if you can see it. If you cannot see the obstruction, further action is necessary. Remember that the correct response to a choking incident differs according to your child's age and size. The guidelines below can help you take appropriate action.

Infants

Abdominal thrusts, such as the Heimlich maneuver, can cause injury to the abdominal organs of children under twelve months of age. Instead, do the following:

1. Straddle the infant over your arm, with her head lower than her chest. Support her head with your hand.

2. Using the heel of your other hand, give four sharp blows to your baby's back, between the shoulder blades. (See figure A.)

3. If the object has not been expelled, turn your baby onto her back and, using two fingers of one hand, give four chest thrusts one finger-width below the nipple line. (See figure B.)

4. If the object has not been expelled, repeat the process.

 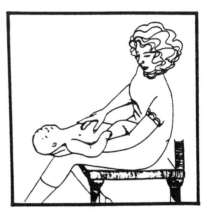

A. Using the heel of your hand, deliver four sharp blows between the shoulder blades.

B. Using two fingers, deliver four chest thrusts one finger-width below the nipple line.

If Your Infant Loses Consciousness:

1. Look for any foreign material in your child's mouth, and remove it if you can see it. *Do not blindly probe your child's mouth.*

2. Tip your baby's head back by lifting her chin up gently with one hand while pushing her forehead down with the other. Her head should be positioned as if she were trying to sniff something. (Be careful not to exaggerate the tilt, as this may completely close the airway. See figure C.)

3. Cover your infant's mouth and nose with your mouth, and attempt to deliver two *small* puffs of air. (See figure D.)

4. Watch to see if your baby's chest rises and falls as in normal breathing. If she is not breathing, *call 911*. Then repeat the entire sequence—back blows, chest thrusts, and rescue breathing—until help arrives.

C. Gently tip your baby's head back.

D. Cover your baby's mouth and nose with your mouth, and deliver two small puffs of air.

Children Over Age One

Respond to choking in your larger child just as you would if she were an adult—with the Heimlich maneuver.

1. Stand or kneel behind your child and wrap your arms around her waist, between her navel and her rib cage. (See figure E.)

2. Make a fist, cup it in your other hand, and make four quick upward thrusts.

3. Repeat the procedure as necessary until the object is expelled.

E. Wrap your arms around your child's waist between her navel and rib cage.

If Your Child Loses Consciousness:

1. Place your child on her back, and kneel next to her.

2. Look for any foreign material in your child's mouth, and remove it if you can. *Do not blindly probe your child's mouth.*

3. Tip your child's head back by lifting her chin up gently with one hand while pushing her forehead down with the other. Her head should be positioned as if she were trying to sniff something. (See figure F.)

4. Pinch your child's nostrils closed, cover her mouth with yours, and deliver two slow breaths. (See figure G.)

F. Gently tip your child's head back.

G. Pinch your child's nostrils closed, and deliver two slow breaths into her mouth.

5. Watch to see if your child's chest rises and falls as in normal breathing. If not, *call 911.* Then kneel at your child's feet or astride her thighs (for a larger child), and place the heel of one hand on the abdomen, midway between the navel and the rib cage. Place the second hand on top of the first, and press into the abdomen with six to ten quick upward thrusts. (See figure H.)

6. Repeat the entire sequence of abdominal thrusts and rescue breathing until help arrives.

It's important to remember that many choking incidents can be avoided by taking precautions beforehand. Entry 16 on page 77

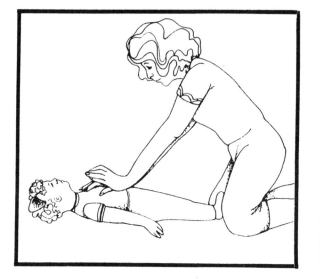

H. Place your hands midway between your child's navel and rib cage, and give six to ten quick upward thrusts.

provides information on foods that can cause choking in small children. Also see Entries 40 and 41 on pages 207 and 212 for information on keeping small objects and inappropriate toys out of your child's reach.

CARDIOPULMONARY RESUSCITATION (CPR)

If your child should suddenly stop breathing, her heart may stop as well because her body is not receiving the oxygen it needs. Electric shock, drowning, and sudden infant death syndrome are all situations that can cause cardiac arrest—heart stoppage—and the cessation of breathing. Because permanent damage to vital organs can occur after only a few minutes without oxygen, you must act immediately to breathe for your child. As discussed earlier, the limits of this book do not allow for a presentation of the complex CPR process. By all means, seek qualified instruction so that you will be ready if your child requires CPR. And bear in mind that you should never practice CPR on anyone. For the hands-on practice that's so vital to learning this procedure, you must use a mannequin under the guidance of a certified instructor.

It's essential that not only you, but also your child's other care givers, receive training in lifesaving techniques. After all, your child can have an accident at any time. Her well-being—her very life—may one day hinge on the ability of those around her to provide swift, clear-headed, appropriate medical assistance.

Resources

The following books and videotapes can provide valuable information about emergency care for your child.

BOOKS

American Heart Association. *Textbook of Pediatric Basic Life Support.* Dallas: American Heart Association, 1988.

Cooper, Martin J. *First Aid for Kids: An Emergency Guidebook for Parents.* Deerfield Beach, FL: Health Communications, 1991.

Fleisher, Gary R. *Barron's First Aid for Kids.* Hauppauge, NY: Barron's Educational Series, 1987.

Hill, James A., and Stanley M. Zydlo, Jr. *The American Medical Association Handbook of First Aid and Emergency Care.* New York: Random House, 1990.

Manhoff, David H., and Stephen N. Vogel. *Emergency Medical Treatment—Children: A Handbook of What to Do in an Emergency to Keep a Child Alive Until Help Arrives.* Oshkosh, WI: RPM, Inc., 1984.

Merenstein, Noel. *Baby and Life: Help Your Child in a Life-Threatening Emergency and Learn What You Can Do to Prevent One From Happening.* New York: Doubleday, 1990.

Reader's Digest Association. *Emergency: What to Do in an Emergency: Reader's Digest Action Guide.* Pleasantville, NY: Reader's Digest, 1988.

Vandenburg, Mary Lou. *Help! Emergencies That Could Happen to You and How to Handle Them.* Minneapolis: Lerner Publications, 1975.

VIDEOTAPES

Baby Alive. Port Washington, NY: Action Films and Video, Ltd., 1988.

How to Save Your Child's Life. Santa Monica, CA: Xenon Video, Inc., Simitar Entertainment, 1986.

44

TEACH YOUR CHILD THE RULES OF WATER SAFETY

Swimming, boating, and ice skating are sources of delight to most children. Naturally, proximity to any body of water—be it a swimming pool, ocean, bay, lake, pond, or stream—enables your child to revel in water sports whenever weather permits. And when toddlers and preschoolers are involved, water-filled buckets, bathtubs, spa tubs, wading pools, and even toilets act as an additional lure. But no matter how careful and comfortable your child seems to be in and around water, you and he must never ignore the risk of drowning. Hundreds of North American children drown each year; in fact, drowning is the third leading cause of death among five- to nine-year-olds. Fortunately, whatever your child's age, you can help keep him safe by observing the rules of water safety and by insisting that he do the same.

Perhaps the surest way to respect the potential danger of water is to remember this: drowning can happen whenever a victim is submerged and cannot breathe. Death can occur quickly if no one is nearby, and the crisis doesn't always end even after a rescue. You see, the human brain suffers permanent damage after three to five minutes without oxygen. So while a near-drowning victim may live, he could suffer irreversible physical harm from the experience. Bear in mind that drowning doesn't always take place in deep water. If an injury or blow to the head renders a victim unconscious, or if a small child topples forward and cannot right himself, *drowning can occur in as little as two inches of water.*

Drowning is certainly a frightening possibility, but many millions of children each year enjoy swimming, boating, and other water play without incident. To that end, it pays to teach your child a healthy respect for water and, at the same time, brush up on the rules of water safety, yourself. This knowledge, plus watchfulness, may be enough to spare your child a "close call" or worse in the water. To help you, the following discussion addresses four different aspects of water safety—boating, ice skating, childproofing your pool, and childproofing your home. Following that is a list of water safety rules that you and your child should memorize and practice whenever you're near the water.

BOATING

A boat can keep your child safe from drowning only as long as it remains upright and your child stays on board. Allow no horseplay while on the water, and make sure that the person rowing or steering the craft is competent to do so and is not using alcohol or other drugs. Spare yourself any unpleasant surprises by checking the weather forecast before heading out. Finally, make sure your child wears a properly fitting, Coast Guard-approved life jacket, and that there is at least one adult swimmer for each nonswimming child on board.

ICE SKATING

If you live in an area where lakes and ponds typically freeze over during the winter months, it's important for your child to understand how deceiving ice can be. Few bodies of water ever freeze solid—or evenly, for that matter—and what appears to be a strong surface may actually not sustain your child's weight. Teach your youngster to check ice for holes, cracks, and transparency, all of which are signs of weakness. Demonstrate how to test the strength of ice by depressing the edge with a hand or foot before shifting your entire body weight forward, and by hurling a heavy stone upward and outward toward the center of the lake or pond—often the weakest part—to see whether the surface holds up beneath the force of the stone's fall. Also show your child how to spread his weight across weak or cracked ice by lying down and inching toward safety on his stomach. Perhaps most important, teach your child to use the buddy system when skating on, playing on, or crossing a frozen surface. Many tragedies have been avoided because a friend was available to run for help after a mishap.

CHILDPROOFING YOUR POOL

A backyard pool is a sure way to make hot summer days more enjoyable. But along with the fun comes a responsibility to ensure the safety of family, neighbors, and friends. Install a self-locking, self-closing five-foot picket fence around the entire perimeter of your pool. Chain link is easy to climb, and therefore is not an effective barrier. Make sure that the pool is well-lit when used during nighttime hours, and that the gate is securely locked whenever the pool is not in use. Avoid using a free-floating pool cover, or permitting use of a pool when the cover is partially in place, as swimmers may become trapped beneath it. You're safest using a cover that anchors to the pool's sides, or using no cover at all. Do not allow riding toys on the pool deck, as they can cause falls. It's wise to keep a telephone and a list of emergency numbers on the deck, along with a Coast Guard-approved flotation device and a long pole for rescues. Also consider hanging a CPR poster on the pool fence. Most important of all, *never leave young swimmers unattended.*

CHILDPROOFING YOUR HOME

While most parents don't think of their home when considering water safety, the fact is that a large proportion of drownings and near-drownings occur indoors. Never leave your young child unattended near an open toilet, or near or in a bucket, wading pool, spa tub, or bathtub that contains water. Apply rubber appliqués to the bottoms of pools and tubs to prevent slipping. Also be aware that some older spa tubs have a suction drain that can entrap hair firmly enough to hold a head beneath the water. (Call the Consumer Product Safety Commission at (800) 668–CPSC to determine whether your make and model meet new safety standards.) Finally, empty all pails, pools, and tubs immediately after use.

GENERAL WATER SAFETY RULES

Your preschooler may be completely fearless when water is concerned, simply because he cannot accurately perceive depth. In addition, young children often misjudge their own capabilities in water. In the past, swim classes for babies were quite popular. However, the American Academy of Pediatrics (AAP) reminds parents that the ability to swim is not instinctive to humans, and that "lessons" for babies can lead to ear infections and other health problems, and to overconfident parents, as well. The AAP therefore recommends that you not enroll your child in swimming lessons before three years of age. Children ages three and over *should* be given swimming lessons by a qualified instructor, so that they can become as competent as possible in the water. Here are a few additional suggestions regarding water safety and your young child.

☐ Buy only Coast Guard-approved flotation devices for use by your child. (Look for a statement to this effect on the package.)

☐ Restrict your child's sand or pool-side play to an area between you and the water. Never leave your child unattended near the water.

☐ Avoid taking your child to beaches or pools during peak hours, and always have him swim and play near the lifeguard station.

☐ Be aware that ocean tidal changes happen quickly. Keep your young child and his toys away from the water's edge.

☐ When visiting an ocean beach, ask the lifeguard if there are any areas where undertow is a problem, and keep your child away from those spots.

☐ Learn cardiopulmonary resuscitation (CPR) in case of an emergency.

Even if your child is older and knows how to swim, it's important that he follow water safety rules. While your youngster may be a fairly good judge of water depth, he may be a poor judge of his ability to tread water for extended periods and to swim against currents or the ocean's undertow. He may also be distracted from his usual safe practices by the presence of friends or an exciting water game. Ongoing swimming lessons are a good idea, particularly if you live where swimming is a seasonal pursuit and your child's skills can get rusty from one summer to the next. In addition, there are several guidelines that can make the time your child spends at any waterfront less dangerous and more fun. Consider teaching your child the following.

☐ Before swimming, learn all swimming facility rules.

☐ Always swim with a partner, so that help is at hand if needed.

☐ Never swim where you won't be visible to lifeguards and others.

☐ Never swim near boats, docks, pilings, or other hazards.

☐ Before diving or jumping into any body of water, always slide in feet first to do a depth check.

☐ Always be mindful of the tide. At the shore, the waterline can change very quickly.

The keys to your child's water safety are knowledge, prevention, and vigilance. Your child can enjoy the water without fear of harm if the area he swims and plays in is supervised, free of hazards, and equipped with necessary lifesaving equipment. In addition, it is wise to instill in your child a healthy respect for the water, while enrolling him in swimming lessons that will help ensure his safety. As an extra precaution, make it a point to learn CPR by calling your local American Heart Association or American Red Cross for information on available classes.

Resources

The following organization and books are good sources of additional information on water safety.

ORGANIZATIONS

American Academy of Pediatrics
141 Northwest Point Boulevard
PO Box 927
Elk Grove Village, IL 60009–0927
(708) 228–5005
(800) 433–9016

This organization of pediatricians maintains some forty committees, one of which focuses on accident and injury prevention.

National Water Safety Congress
PO Box 60
Vicksburg, MS 39180–0060
(601) 631–5095

This group seeks to promote safe usage of the nation's waters and waterways.

BOOKS

American National Red Cross. *Swimming and Diving*. St. Louis: Mosby Year Book, 1992.

Sanders, Pete. *Near Water*. New York: Gloucester Press, 1989.

Usborne Books Staff. *Teach Your Child to Swim*. Tulsa, OK: EDC, 1989.

Rescuing a Drowning Child

Occasionally, a child gets into serious trouble in the water despite the best safety precautions. If this should occur, you can help him to safety by following these steps.

☐ *Get your child out of the water as quickly as possible. Handle him with extreme caution if you suspect injury.*

☐ *Before jumping into deep water to effect a rescue, try to reach your child with your outstretched arm or a pole. If you can pull him to the water's edge, you'll be better able to lift him to safety from above.*

☐ *If you are a poor swimmer, attempt a deep water rescue from within the water only as a last resort. If possible, try to keep your child afloat while you call for help from a more experienced swimmer.*

☐ *Have someone phone for medical assistance at once. Relay to the dispatcher your child's age and condition, and the circumstances of the mishap. Provide your location and phone number. If you are alone and your child is not breathing, give one minute of rescue breathing (see pages 223 and 225) before running to a telephone.*

☐ *Provide rescue breathing or CPR as necessary until help arrives.*

☐ *Even if breathing is restored immediately, take your child to the nearest emergency room for evaluation.*

Remember the vital role that watchfulness plays in water safety. Teach your child never to swim alone, see that the water play of your youngster and his friends is supervised, and learn CPR in case an emergency arises. By being vigilant and prepared, you can help your family get the most from water sports and activities.

45

KEEP POISONS OUT OF YOUR CHILD'S REACH

Even if you've diligently removed every small, sharp, or potentially dangerous object in sight, your home *still* may not be safe for your child. Why? If you take a look around, you'll probably find poison in some form—medication, garden chemicals, cleaning products, or painting materials, perhaps—in almost every room. And chances are, those rooms that for lack of a closet or medicine chest seem at first to be poison-free are, in fact, adorned with house plants—many of which are poisonous if eaten. (See the inset on page 238.) Not surprisingly, tens of thousands of children each year are treated or hospitalized for accidental poisoning, with the majority of poisonings occurring in the home. Fortunately, most of these accidents can be prevented. The following guidelines will help you safeguard your child and make your home a healthier place for the whole family.

MAKING YOUR HOME A SAFER PLACE

The Kitchen

Because kitchens offer so much storage space, they are often home to a wide range of dangerous products. Naturally, it's important to store all caustic and poisonous substances well beyond a child's reach in a locked closet or cabinet. These substances include drain cleaner, plant food, pesticides, and cleaning products. It is also a good idea to look for child-resistant lids on the household products you buy.

Although it's sometimes tempting to transfer the remaining

contents of a near-empty box or bottle to something smaller, all potentially dangerous products should, in fact, be stored in their original containers, giving you ready access to labels that list ingredients and first aid instructions. If you must replace a box or bottle because of leakage, transfer the label information to the new container, and avoid using a jar or bottle that might cause a child to handle or ingest the substance if she accidentally gained access to it. Confusion of this type is also a possibility when hazardous products are stored next to edible items—a good reason to keep poisons locked up and well away from foods.

The Bathroom

The bathroom is another common storage place for poisonous substances. In this room, medicines and cleaning products are the principal threats to a child's safety. Perhaps your best safeguard against poisonings in a bathroom is a locked closet or cabinet that contains *all* of your drugs and medications. It's important to remember that even cold formulas and child-strength pain relievers can be poisonous when swallowed in quantity. It's a good idea to check for child-resistant caps on all of your medications. Your pharmacist can replace standard pop-off caps at your request. And while you're at it, make it a point to check expiration dates on both prescription drugs and over-the-counter medications. As medicines age, you see, they undergo chemical changes that can make them ineffective or unsafe. Therefore, it's wise to flush outdated drugs down the toilet, and then rinse and discard the containers. Just as with household products, it is important to retain each medication's original labeled container. The information on the label may prove vital if the contents are ever swallowed by the wrong person or in the wrong quantity.

The Garage, Basement, or Storage Area

Even ordinary home maintenance requires the use of a great many potentially hazardous substances. Such products as lighter fluid, paint, turpentine, antifreeze, pesticides, and fertilizers are often stored side by side in a storage area. Needless to say, these dangerous items should be locked away from your child's reach. Even so, when you purchase new home-maintenance products, it's a good idea to consider only those with child-resistant caps. It's also important to store these products in their original labeled boxes, bottles, jars, or cans so that a list of the contents and any manufacturer's warnings are immediately available during an emergency. If you transfer a small amount of a dangerous product to a bowl or jar during use, be sure to discard any remains of that small amount in a responsible fashion. And, of course, it's vital that the bowl or jar be either cleaned or disposed of with care.

Additional Safety Tips

There are other steps you can take to reduce the chance of your child being accidentally poisoned or to minimize the damage from a poisoning incident. Supervision is the best defense against a youngster's handling or ingesting something dangerous, of course, so it's imperative that you keep an eye on your baby or small child. Older children can be educated about the dangers of the toxic substances in your home, and even toddlers can be taught to respect the black skull-and-crossbones or "Mr. Yuk" symbol that is so often used to signal poison. You may wish to draw a larger, more-visible version on each container in black marker. You might also consider buying organic cleaners, fertilizers, and pesticides whenever possible, because these products are formulated to be nontoxic. Checking your house greenery against the poisonous plants list on page 238—identifying them through photographs in books, if necessary—is another sound idea. Don't hesitate to discard or give away any plant that is dangerous if eaten. It's also wise to check your yard regularly for mushrooms and fallen berries or leaves.

IF YOUR CHILD SWALLOWS
A POISONOUS SUBSTANCE

But what if your child accidentally swallows a medication or another dangerous substance in spite of your precautions? Often, a parent's first thought is to induce vomiting in order to remove the poison from the child's system. But this can be extremely dangerous, because many caustic substances will cause just as much damage to the esophagus and mouth when vomited as they did when swallowed. Certainly, it is wise to keep a bottle of Ipecac syrup on hand in case you are advised to induce vomiting. But, if you suspect that your child has swallowed a poison, *your first step must be to call your local poison control center.* This number is listed on the inside cover of your telephone directory. Be prepared to name the substance involved, to estimate the amount swallowed, and to give your child's age and weight. The volunteer will then tell you the best course of action.

Accidental poisonings are particularly horrifying when they happen to children. It's reassuring to know that you can do much to safeguard your child against this possibility, and that you will be prepared to act swiftly and effectively should an accident ever occur.

Resources

The following books contain information that will help you keep poisonous substances out of your child's reach.

BOOKS

Dreisbach, Robert Hastings. *Handbook of Poisoning: Prevention, Diagnosis, and Treatment.* Norwalk, CT: Appleton and Lange, 1987.

Kramer, Jack. *1,000 Beautiful Houseplants and How to Grow Them.* New York: Harry N. Abrams, 1982.

Lifton, Bernice. *Bug Busters: Safe, Natural and Effective Controls for Common Household and Garden Pests.* Garden City Park, NY: Avery Publishing Group, 1991.

Stewart, Arlene. *Childproofing Your Home.* Reading, MA: Addison-Wesley Publishing, 1984.

Poisonous Plants

It may surprise you to know that plants are among the household items most often responsible for home poisonings. Dangerous house plants should either be placed out of your child's reach or removed from your home. Dangerous garden plants, such as rhubarb, can be contained in a fenced area, while mushrooms and potentially harmful berries and leaves should be removed from your yard or play area.

If you can't identify a particular house or garden plant, borrow a plant book from the library and compare your plant with those in the photographs. If you are still uncertain, break off a leaf and take it to one of the experts at your local garden center.

The following list of poisonous plants should prove helpful as you childproof your house and garden.

Acorns
Arrowhead asparagus
   berries and shoots
Azalea
Baneberries
Begonia, sand
Bleeding heart
Bulbs (many are
   poisonous)
Buttercup
Caladium
Carrot tops
Castor beans
Chinese lantern
Christmas pepper
Christmas rose
Crown-of-thorns

Daphne berries
Deifenbachia
Devil's ivy
Elephant ear
Foxglove
Grape ivy
Holly
Horse chestnuts
Iris
Ivy
Jerusalem cherry
Laurel
Mistletoe berries
Mushrooms
Nightshade
Philodendron

Potato leaves and
   stems
Pothos
Privet berries and
   leaves
Rhododendron
Rhubarb leaves
Rubber vine
Shamrock
Snowberries
Sweet pea
Tomato leaves and
   stems
Vinca
Water hemlock
Yew

You'll be taking a big step toward preventing accidental poisonings by making dangerous plants inaccessible to your child. Moving—or eliminating—the plants listed above will give your child greater freedom around your home, while giving you greater peace of mind.

46

Reduce your child's exposure to lead

Was your home or your child's school constructed prior to 1978? If so, the paint on the exterior walls, radiators, and indoor stairway, window, and door trim may contain enough lead to slowly poison your child. And old paint is not the only culprit. Your child may be exposed to dangerous lead levels in the air he breathes, the water he drinks, the soil on which he plays, and the crockery from which he eats and drinks. However, knowing the facts about lead and lead poisoning—also called plumbism—can help you greatly reduce the amount of lead that enters your child's bloodstream and threatens his health.

Once inhaled or ingested, lead from any source accumulates in the body, posing a danger to the brain and nervous system. Developing fetuses and growing children are particularly at risk. Studies show that lead ingested by an expectant mother crosses the placenta, and, in toxic amounts, can cause premature delivery or low birth weight. In children, ongoing exposure to lead can cause behavioral problems, poor muscle coordination, learning disabilities, brain damage, and mental retardation. At the highest levels, lead in the bloodstream can lead to convulsions, coma, and even death.

REDUCING THE RISKS OF LEAD POISONING

A number of steps can be taken to eliminate lead from your child's environment. First, remember that paints manufactured before 1978 did not have to conform to current lead-content regulations. Exterior house paint and paint used on window wells and frames is particularly suspect, so if your home was built before 1978, you may wish to ask a contractor or your state or local health department about having your paint tested for lead. The health department can recommend an experienced abatement contractor to safely remove any lead paint that does exist. You may wish to discard older painted toys and furniture. Newer furnishings, as well as interior walls and floors, can be kept free of lead-contaminated dust from nearby window and door frames with frequent washings using a high-phosphate detergent or trisodium wash.

Your drinking water, too, may contain lead if it passes through pipes containing lead or lead solder. Be sure to use cold tap water for drinking and cooking, since hot water picks up lead from pipes more quickly. Bear in mind that water containing more than fifteen parts per billion of lead is considered dangerous. You can ask your water company to recommend an independent laboratory that tests water, usually for a fee of fifteen to thirty-five dollars. A water purification system that specifically filters out lead is another good idea.

It's also wise to check your kitchen and china closets for imported porcelain, pottery, collectible dinnerware, and painted glassware, since most pottery and some older or foreign-made items contain dangerous amounts of lead. Bright green- and orange-glazed pieces are particularly suspect. An antiques dealer or a book on collectible dishes can help you determine if your crockery falls into this category. And you can test for lead in dishes, glassware, and many other household items with your own lead test kit. Kits cost approximately twenty-five dollars, and can be purchased from Frandon Enterprises and Hybrivet Systems, both of which are listed in the Resources section beginning on page 242.

Some hobby supplies like paint and solder may also be hazardous due to lead content. Look for the Art and Craft Materials Institute's safety seals (*CP Nontoxic* or *AP Nontoxic*) on the hobby supplies you buy. A list of art and craft materials considered safe for children can be obtained from the Center for Safety in the Arts. (See page 242.)

The air and soil around your home can also be contaminated by excessive fuel emissions and lead by-products from nearby factories. Here, again, your department of health can help arrange necessary tests. Finally, since so many North American schools were built prior to 1978, and because regulations concerning lead testing vary widely, you might consider talking to your child's principal about the presence of lead in school classrooms and drinking water. Find out what he or she knows about the building's water fountains, plumbing, and construction, and whether tests for lead have ever been conducted.

IF YOU SUSPECT LEAD POISONING

What can you do to lessen already existing effects of lead absorption or ingestion by your child? Perhaps the most important defense against this type of poisoning is an awareness of its symptoms. If your child regularly experiences fatigue, sleeplessness, irritability, loss of appetite, stomachaches, inattentiveness, vomiting, or constipation, lead poisoning may be responsible. Keep in mind that children who are underweight or live in homes that are either deteriorating or under renovation face a greater risk of lead poisoning.

Fortunately, there are medical tests that can tell whether your child has an unsafe level of lead in his system. One test, called a "blood lead measure," typically costs between twenty-five and fifty dollars, and registers lead levels in the blood as low as 5 micrograms per deciliter (5 mcg/dl). (Currently, 24 mcg/dl is considered the danger level; however, new discoveries about lead's toxicity have prompted the Centers for Disease Control to consider revising this figure to 10 mcg/dl.) A second, less-expensive measure, the zinc protoporphyrin (ZPP) test, also determines the presence of lead in the bloodstream, but only at levels of 25 mcg/dl or higher. It's important to note that neither the blood lead measure nor the ZPP test is conducted routinely. Nevertheless, the Consumer Product Safety Commission recommends screening your child for lead poisoning at twelve months and twenty-four months of age, because a missed early-stage diagnosis can lead to long-lasting health problems. And, naturally, a test should be ordered by your pediatrician any time you suspect lead poisoning.

If tests show elevated lead levels in your child's blood, you can ask a health-care provider about the advisability of a low-fat diet, since fats promote lead absorption. Your child's doctor may also recommend calcium and iron supplements, because a diet deficient in these two elements may cause the body to absorb more lead. A process called chelation therapy may help your child if his tested lead level is dangerously high. Hospitalization is required for this procedure, during which a chemical is introduced into the body to promote the secretion of lead.

Many medical experts believe that lead poisoning is the biggest environmental problem facing today's children. But even if your child is one of the millions with measurable blood lead levels, it is comforting to know that you can take steps to minimize his exposure to this toxic substance and to reduce the amount of lead already in his bloodstream. And by staying informed about this environmental hazard, you will be able to keep your entire family healthier.

Resources

Your state or local health department can provide additional information about lead poisoning and lead hazards in your child's environment. Or, you can refer to one of the sources listed below.

ORGANIZATIONS

Center for Safety in the Arts
5 Beekman Street, 10th Floor
New York, NY 10038
(212) 227–6220

This organization promotes the risk-free use of art, craft, and hobby supplies in accordance with the safety standards of the Art and Craft Materials Institute. The center offers a list of child-safe arts and crafts materials.

Citizens for a Better Environment
4075 Dearborn, Suite 1775
Chicago, IL 60605
(312) 939–1530

This group works to reduce exposure to toxic substances in the air, water, and land through research, public information, and advocacy.

Frandon Enterprises
511 North 48th Street
Seattle, WA 98103
(416) 293–4955
(800) 359–9000

This company offers kits that test for the presence of lead in water, as well as in paints, glazes, and other surface materials.

Hybrivet Systems
PO Box 1210
Framingham, MA 01701
(508) 651–7881
(800) 262–LEAD

Hybrivet specializes in contaminant-checking products, and offers information, brochures, and a do-it-yourself swab test to detect lead in paint, dust, soil, pipe solder, and household items.

Lead Free Kids, Inc.
110 East 31st Street, Box 8595
Minneapolis, MN 55408–0595
(612) 641–1959

This organization seeks to protect children from lead poisoning by educating the public about lead prevention techniques. It publishes several free lead-prevention guides.

National Alliance to End
  Childhood Lead Poisoning
Suite 100
600 Pennsylvania Avenue SE
Washington, DC 20003
(202) 543–1147

This group works with policy makers, environmental groups, manufacturers, and consumers to guarantee every child a lead-free environment. A free pamphlet is offered about the dangers of lead poisoning.

U.S. Consumer Product Safety
  Commission (CPSC)
Office of Information and
  Public Affairs
Washington, DC 20207
(301) 392–6580
(800) 638–CPSC
(800) 638–8270 *For the Hearing Impaired*
(800) 492–8104 *For the Hearing Impaired, Maryland Only*

This agency monitors the market for hazardous products and seeks changes in and recalls of dangerous items. The CPSC also publishes a free pamphlet about the problem of lead-based paint.

Washington Toxics Coalition
4516 University Way NE
Seattle, WA 98105
(206) 632–1545

This group is dedicated to better health through a cleaner environment, and offers a booklet on reducing exposure to lead.

BOOKS

Cooper, Kathy, and Barbara Wallace. *The Citizen's Guide to Lead: Uncovering a Hidden Health Hazard.* Toronto: NC Press, 1986.

Levenstein, Mary Kerney. *Everyday Cancer Risks and How to Avoid Them.* Garden City Park, NY: Avery Publishing Group, 1992.

47

KNOW HOW TO CHOOSE
SAFE CHILD CARE

The parents of yesteryear rarely worried about child care. Grandparents and other extended family members were often nearby to lend a hand when parents had work or errands to attend to. In addition, at-home mothers were in plentiful supply in many neighborhoods, making it easy—and cost-free—to leave your child in the care of someone you trusted. But things are different today. The high cost of living has kept many grandparents on the job well into what used to be the retirement years and has sent others out of town or out of state in search of employment or affordable housing. Rising costs have left at-home mothers in short supply, as well. Today's parents still need child care, but more and more families must entrust their youngsters to strangers. For the sake of your child's happiness and well-being, it's important to know how to choose safe, stimulating, and loving child care.

CHOOSE AN ARRANGEMENT
THAT'S APPROPRIATE FOR YOUR CHILD

Can a day-care center or other arrangement provide your child with quality care? Absolutely! The keys to making the right selection for your child are the establishment of priorities and a thorough check of available child-care options. You can start by determining your needs. Does your child require full-time or part-time care? Do you need someone to live in? Will household duties and transportation be part of the job? What are your feelings about the presence of other children? What can you afford to pay?

After you've taken stock of your needs and resources, carefully look at the available child-care options. Depending on your priorities, your child's age and personality, and your budget, you can consider a nanny, an au pair, an in-home care giver who leaves at day's end, a family day-care home, or a day-care center. When considering these options, it's a good idea to talk to friends, relatives, coworkers, and your child's pediatrician about their experiences and recommendations. You can also get ideas and information from the International Nanny Association and other resource organizations listed at the end of this entry, your town or county day-care licensing center, and your city or state child-care resource center. If you're still not sure of what child-care route to take, try visiting each setting and picturing your child as a participant. It might be a good idea to take your child along on these visits so that you can see her reaction to the different places and people.

Once you have a good idea of what you want, the following tips should help you finalize the arrangements, create a smooth period of transition, and make sure that your and your child's relationships with her care givers remain positive.

NARROW THE FIELD

Your first step should be to narrow the field by carefully comparing policies and qualifications. Is the person or center you are considering licensed, accredited, or bonded in accordance with state regulations? Can you agree upon a manageable payment schedule? Also find out about policies regarding the handling of sick children and payment for missed days, as well as arrangements in times of caregiver illness. If more than one child is to be cared for, ask about the makeup of the group and how new entrants are selected. Also learn about the child-to-adult ratio. It is generally recommended that there be no more than three children under twenty-four months of age for each care giver, while four or five two-year-olds per adult is acceptable. By age three, seven children per adult is recommended; after that, the ideal child-to-staff ratio increases by one for each year of a child's age. If more than one care giver will be involved in your child's care, find out how additional staff is chosen and whether background checks are done.

DO YOUR HOMEWORK

Speak personally to all parties listed as references. Make it a point to determine whether a prior employer's or client's child-care needs were similar to yours. For a single care giver, verify any information given about duties, hours, and salary. For a day-care center or home, ask about reliability, supervision, safety, and cleanliness. For either arrangement, ask about provisions for occasional solitary play, as well as policies regarding TV viewing, employee smoking, meal- and naptime supervision, and unannounced parental visits. Ask specific questions about relationships between the care giver or center's personnel and the children served, as well as the care giver's punctuality, professionalism, and availability for discussions. Find out exactly what each family liked and disliked about the care giver or center under consideration.

CONDUCT THOROUGH INTERVIEWS

Meet face-to-face with your top candidates. Take note of each care giver's appearance, and carefully watch his or her interactions with your child—provided that your child is present, of course. Is the person responsive? Does he or she seem warm, talkative, and friendly? Have a detailed job description on hand to weed out those candidates who might not be willing to do as much as you're asking. Consider asking each prospective care giver to fill out a questionnaire, as this tactic will help you get the background information you need, and will tell you a lot about the candidate's literacy, as well. Ask why each person has chosen child care as a field of employment, and ask plenty of "how would you handle" questions to help you gauge each candidate's ability to handle matters of discipline and medical emergency. Question any gaps in a candidate's employment history.

CLEARLY ESTABLISH YOUR TERMS

If you have selected in-home care, prepare a written contract that spells out hours, responsibilities, salary, and provisions for overtime and vacations. Set up regular times to talk about your child's activities and behavior, and be clear about the types of enrichment and stimulation your care giver is expected to provide. If you wish, ask your prospective care giver to go for a physical examination at your expense.

ESTABLISH A BREAKING-IN PERIOD

For in-home care givers, schedule a few days during which *you'll* remain at home, as well. For day-care centers or homes, make arrangements to visit with your child several times. Then gradually increase the amount of time you leave your child with the care giver. If your care giver will be living in, pay for an advance weekend visit that can serve as adjustment time. With an eye toward adequate supervision and safety, call or drop in without notice during the first weeks of your child-care arrangement, and ask a friend or family member to stop by, as well.

KEEP YOUR CHILD-CARE ARRANGEMENT
RUNNING SMOOTHLY

If your child spends part of the day at a center or day-care home, avoid rushing her away at pick-up time. Instead, chat with her and her care giver about how the day was spent. Treat your child's care giver with respect, and allow him or her room to make some of the decisions regarding your child's activities. Be courteous by being on time and giving as much notice as possible of lateness or illness. Avoid giving your care giver additional responsibilities without additional pay, and remember to add a few "perks" to the job—unexpected time off with pay, a souvenir from your business travel, or birthday and holiday gifts.

Some 23 million American children use some form of child care each day. If your child is one of this rapidly expanding group, it's important to be certain that her day-care environment is healthy, safe, and enriching. By devoting some time to researching your child-care options, carefully checking the qualifications of all candidates, and taking pains to keep your parent-care giver relationship positive and mutually respectful, you'll be able to enjoy peace of mind as your child enjoys stimulating and nurturing care.

Resources

The following organizations and publications can provide the information necessary to fill your child-care needs.

ORGANIZATIONS

AuPair/Homestay USA
1015 15th Street NW, Suite 750
Washington, DC 20005
(202) 408–5380

This organization places European young women and men with American families requiring live-in child care.

Au Pair in America
102 Greenwich Avenue
Greenwich, CT 06830
(800) 727–2437

This agency matches young adults from Europe with American families for a year of child care in exchange for room, board, and a weekly stipend.

International Nanny Association
PO Box 26522
Austin, TX 78755
(512) 454–6462

This organization offers nanny training, placement, and nannies interested in upgrading their profession, as well as a directory of nanny schools.

National Association for the
   Education of Young Children
1834 Connecticut Avenue NW
Washington, DC 20009-5786
(202) 232–8777
(800) 424–2460

This organization provides resources for the professional development of those working for and with young children. The association works to increase public knowledge of and support for appropriate early childhood programs and to create legislation that raises the quality of education.

National Association of Child Care
   Resources and Referral Agencies
2116 Campus Drive SE
Rochester, MN 55904
(507) 287–2220
(800) 424–2246

This national organization of community-based child-care resource and referral agencies is committed to building a high-quality child-care system.

BOOKS

Buhler, Danalee. *The Very Best Child Care and How to Find It*. Rocklin, CA: Prima Publishing, 1989.

Olds, Sally Wendkos. *Working Parents' Survival Guide*. Rocklin, CA: Prima Publishing, 1991.

Solomon, Charlene. *The Parent/Child Manual of Daycare*. New York: Tom Doherty Associates, 1989.

Spaide, Deborah. *The Day Care Kit: A Parent's Guide to Quality Child Care*. New York: Carol Publishing Group, 1990.

Woolever, Elizabeth. *Your Child: Selecting Day Care (Birth to 12 Years)*. Des Moines, IA: Meredith Corporation, 1989.

48

PROTECT YOUR CHILD FROM ABDUCTION BY A STRANGER

Many of the innocent young faces that appear on milk cartons, posters, and missing-children flyers across North America belong to youngsters who have been abducted by strangers. In fact, this frightening fate befalls thousands of children each year. But by taking steps to protect your child, and by teaching him how to protect himself, you can greatly reduce the risk of your child's becoming a kidnapping victim.

HOW YOU CAN PROTECT YOUR CHILD

Just as in all aspects of his safety, your very young child depends upon you for protection from abduction. And perhaps the best defense you can offer is proper supervision at home, in public places, and at day care, either by you or by another responsible individual. It is unwise—perhaps even dangerous—to leave your child alone in a parked car. It may be equally risky to expect an older sibling to watch over your young child, unless you are absolutely sure that he or she can handle this responsibility. Consider warning at-home care givers against opening your door to strangers, volunteering family information over the telephone, and leaving your child unattended in the yard. It may also pay to be on the lookout for unfamiliar faces where your child plays, particularly if you notice a stranger who is alone, but nevertheless appears to be interested in the children at hand. And it's wise to teach the same wariness to your child as soon as he is old enough to discriminate between friends and strangers.

As your child gets older, instruct him never to volunteer his name to telephone callers or salespeople. Similarly, label your child's belongings—lunch boxes, back packs, and the like—in *small letters* on the article's interior, and avoid having your child wear personalized shirts, hats, hair bands, and jewelry. You see, it's not unusual for abductors to employ a child's name to quickly win his trust, for such knowledge suggests familiarity even when none exists.

Since an abduction can take place in a matter of seconds, it is wise to keep close track of your child's friends and activities. (See Entry 1 on page 3.) If your child were ever kidnapped, his last-known whereabouts would become crucial information. Moreover, keeping abreast of your child's free-time pursuits will help you to know whether he might be vulnerable to abduction. For example, if you were to learn that your youngster had been riding his bicycle in a deserted park, playing alone in a school yard, or exploring an empty building, you could help him find safer places to play. It's also a good idea to designate several community "safe houses," where your child and other children can go if they are followed or approached while on the street. (See Entry 38 on page 200 for details.)

HOW YOUR CHILD CAN PROTECT HIMSELF

Naturally, your child will take on more of the responsibility for his personal safety as he grows older and spends more time away from adult supervision. Promoting safe, watchful behavior from the time your child first leaves your side is the best way to help him handle his growing independence.

In almost any circumstances, your child is most vulnerable to kidnapping when he is alone. Therefore, it's important to teach your child the value of the buddy system, and to explain why it is best to avoid parks, fields, and other deserted places where he is most vulnerable to abduction. Public bathrooms can also be trouble spots, as can shopping malls, video arcades, and amusement parks—places where everyday noise and confusion can easily mask a confrontation between your child and a stranger. Also instruct your child never to deviate from his usual route to and from school or a friend's house. First, the detour he chooses may not be completely safe. Second, you can best watch out for your child when you can accurately anticipate his arrival home.

It's wise to post emergency numbers near your telephone and to make sure your child knows how to phone for help when he is at home. In particular, make sure your youngster understands when and how to dial 911 or 0. (See Entry 36 on page 189 for details.) You may also wish to have him practice making a long-distance collect call. Your child should also make it a habit to carry change so that he can use a pay telephone to reach you at home or work. Naturally, your child should memorize his full name, address, and home phone number as early as possible, as this may bring help more quickly if it's ever needed. Teach your child to be aware of and report to you the presence of any strangers loitering near home, school, or his usual play areas. Help him to understand the difference between friendly and inappropriate overtures on a stranger's part, and explain the importance of reporting to you any behavior that seems unusual.

Finally, make sure your child knows what to do if he is ever confronted by a stranger. Teach him that making a huge fuss can attract the attention of a nearby adult, and that it's acceptable—even desirable—to run, scream, hit, or kick in order to bring help or break free. You may choose to have your child carry a whistle or learn martial arts. Explain that it is never a child's fault when someone tries to hurt or frighten him, and that children have the right to ignore or refuse adult attention that makes them uncomfortable or uneasy.

Can you help your child feel safe without unduly alarming him? Yes, provided you teach him the facts about kidnapping from a very young age and in a calm, matter-of-fact way that conveys your ongoing concern for his safety. Playing a "what-if" game, during which you and your child invent possible situations and determine the best reactions, can help put the topic of stranger abduction in less-threatening terms. Discussing personal safety in general can help to convince your child that watchfulness and safe play practices are always important. You need not dwell on specific dangers or the possible consequences to a child who isn't vigilant. Instead, make caution the focus of your message. Your conversational tone, also, will reassure your youngster that your concern for his safety is rooted in love, rather than fear. In the end, arming your child with realistic, age-appropriate safety information will help make the hours he spends on his own more enjoyable and worry-free for both of you.

Resources

The following are sources of additional information on keeping your child safe from stranger abduction.

ORGANIZATIONS

Find the Children
11811 West Olympic Boulevard
Los Angeles, CA 90064
(213) 477–6721

This group distributes photographs of missing children, educates parents and children on child safety, assists other child-locating agencies, conducts media campaigns to raise social awareness concerning missing children, and supports legislation about child-safety issues. Find the Children also participates in a project that benefits recovered children and their families.

The Jacob Wetterling Foundation
32 First Avenue, NW
PO Box 639
St. Joseph, MN 56374–0639
(612) 363–0470
(800) 325–HOPE *National Hotline*

This support organization for parents of missing children helps to organize searches, contacts the media, and offers a toll-free hotline. The group endorses community education as a solution to stranger abductions of children, and is active in seeking legislation designed to protect children from abduction.

The Kevin Collins Foundation for
  Missing Children
PO Box 590473
San Francisco, CA 94159
(800) 272–0012

This organization focuses on preventing stranger abduction through education, and lobbies for legislation supporting missing children and their families. Services include searches, and help for families in dealing with law enforcement agencies and the media.

National Center for Missing and
  Exploited Children
2101 Wilson Boulevard, Suite 550
Arlington, VA 22201
(703) 235–3900
(800) 843–5678 *National Hotline*
(800) 826–7653 *For the Hearing
  Impaired*

This organization serves as a clearinghouse of information on missing children and provides assistance to law enforcement agencies and others involved in missing-child searches. The center offers training programs, distributes photographs and descriptions of missing children, coordinates child-protection efforts, and provides information on legislation aimed at protecting all children.

The Roberta Jo Society, Inc.
329 E. Main Street
PO Box 916
Circleville, OH 43113
(614) 474–5020

This national clearinghouse collects data on missing children, publishes a missing-child report, seeks to educate the public about child abduction, and assists families in their search for missing children.

Vanished Children's Alliance
1407 Parkmoor Avenue, Suite 200
San Jose, CA 95126
(408) 971–4822
(800)–VANISHED *National Sighting Line*

This group is dedicated to the recovery of missing and abducted children. The alliance, which publishes an annual directory of missing children, has assisted the families of over 10,000 children since 1980.

BOOKS

Girard, Linda Walvoord. *Who Is a Stranger, and What Should I Do?* Niles, IL: Albert Whitman, 1985.

Hubbard, Kate. *Help Yourself to Safety: A Guide to Avoiding Dangerous Situations With Strangers and Friends.* Edmonds, WA: Charles Franklin Press, 1985.

Jance, Judith A. *It's Not Your Fault.* Edmonds, WA: Charles Franklin Press, 1985.

Schwartz, Linda. *What Would You Do: A Kid's Guide to Tricky and Sticky Situations.* Santa Barbara, CA: Learning Works, 1990.

An Abducted Child Tells How He Could Have Been Found

On December 4, 1972, 7-year-old Steven Stayner was walking home from school. Two men in a car told him they were collecting money for the church. He agreed to show them the way to his house.

For the next 7 years, Steve grew up as an abducted, sexually abused child. Some people knew, but didn't do anything. Some suspected, but would not get involved.

Most people didn't see the signs that could have saved him. And so it went on.

At the age of 14, when his abductor had grabbed another 5-year-old boy, Steve took the child and brought him to the local police.

After 7 years, a shattered family was reunited.

Now Steven Stayner shares his insights into finding abducted children.

"When it comes to finding abducted children, most people think of posters and milk cartons. Photographs are very important in finding abducted children. But to depend on pictures alone is a big mistake.

First, because they may not get to the isolated areas where abductors take children. But also because children change and abductors can easily change a child's appearance.

I believe the single most important thing you can do to help find abducted children is to be aware of the problem and keep an eye out for suspicious 'family' situations around you.

For starters, many abductors are men appearing as single parents, with one child. They intentionally choose to live in isolated areas and are generally not socially active.

You should know that the first thing abductors often do is convince the child that their parents don't want them. My abductor faked phone calls to my parents. He actually told me he went to court to get legal custody. I was 7. I had nowhere else to turn. I eventually accepted the lie as reality.

The next stage was adapting for survival. This meant doing anything to avoid punishment. I actually helped my abductor keep the secret.

So don't expect abducted children to come up and ask for help. They're totally dependent on their abductors. And if they're being sexually abused, which is usually the case, the last thing they want is to draw attention to it.

I trusted no one. My greatest fear was that someone would find out the truth and confront my 'father.' I didn't know what he'd do. As bad as things were, I knew it could get worse.

To survive, abducted children must learn to lie. When people would ask me about my past, I made it up. I now assume people knew I was lying, but no one ever tried to find out why.

Throughout the 7 years, we were constantly moving. We lived in 5 different towns, in a dozen houses and trailer homes. The minute my abductor felt people were getting too close, we'd pack up. That kind of movement is typical of abductions. So is a child who's not enrolled in school.

My abductor was careful and made sure I was always enrolled.

If people paid attention to my relationship with my 'father' there were clues that something was wrong. It was not a normal father-son relationship. And among other things, at 13, I was taller than, and looked nothing like, my 'father.' You should know that most abductors are pedophiles, not psychotic killers. They don't have good relationships with adults. They start out molesting children and graduate to longer abductions. And when they murder children, often it's to get rid of evidence.

As is often the case, there were people involved with my abductor who knew the truth. These people could have saved me at any time but were afraid of legal trouble. You should know that in other cases where people have come forward to save a child, they have not been prosecuted. These people often hold the power of life and death.

Before I was grabbed, my abductor had been convicted of child molesting. Throughout my abduction he never stopped molesting other children. Even so, after taking me from my home, abusing me for 7 years and abducting another 5-year-old, he served only $3\frac{1}{2}$ years in jail. He's now one of the 65,000 registered sex offenders free, in California alone.

Today, no one knows how many missing children are dead or how many now live as I did.

But if you're going to help, you have to be aware of the real nature of stranger abduction. And be committed to helping children. While it may be hard for you to tell an abducted child from an abused child, it's not hard to tell a child in trouble. And it's not hard to do something about it.

If you know of, or suspect, there's a situation where a child is in trouble, please call the police."

If you have any information on a stranger abduction or want more information on what you can do, contact the Kevin Collins Foundation, Post Office Box 590473, San Francisco, California 94159. Or just call the phone number listed below.

Help Us Find Abducted Children 1-800-272-0012.

"In every child who is born,
under no matter what circumstances,
and of no matter what parents,
the potentiality of the human race
is born again."

—James Agee

49

ENCOURAGE YOUR CHILD TO READ

Most small children love to hear stories, and parents who regularly read to their children know both the emotional and academic benefits of curling up together with a rhyme, a poem, or a tale. Yet, it's easy for busy families to overlook the importance of time spent together in this leisurely fashion. And on their own, children often choose visual entertainment over reading. Did you know, for example, that there are five times as many video stores across North America as there are public libraries? Or that the average schoolchild watches between twenty-three and twenty-eight hours of television each week? Fortunately, whether your child is still too young for school or already in her teens, there are a number of steps you can take to help her develop a love for reading and literature.

Why is reading so important for your child? To begin with, the world of literature provides a youngster with an unlimited variety of information and entertainment. And studies have shown that children who are read to are often the earliest independent readers, and go on to have an easier time with school work. You see, reading develops a child's vocabulary and attention span, expands her bank of general knowledge, and sharpens her critical thinking skills. And once your child has learned to "decode" the printed word—that is, to sound out or otherwise transform the printed word into a spoken word—the act of reading for pleasure will improve her reading level and boost her academic confidence.

Moreover, your child's growth in reading will erase the possibility of a future limited by illiteracy—a problem that dogs the footsteps of many thousands of today's adults.

There are several ways to foster a love of reading. You can set a wonderful example by reading for pleasure yourself. Small children love to imitate their parents' behavior, and your child is more likely to read for amusement if she sees that *you* consider it a worthwhile activity. Television may well be your principal competition here, so you might wish to limit TV viewing to certain times of the day or evening. It's also a good idea to have an ever-changing variety of appealing reading materials readily available to your child. Exchange books with other families and display a few at a time in your family room. Give books as gifts to your child and her friends. Clip and share newspaper photos and articles on topics that interest your youngster. Borrow or subscribe to children's magazines, and invest in some quiz and puzzle books. Also, make frequent, regular trips to the library, where a vast collection of reading material can be enjoyed for free. Your child is likely to show more interest in the many different types of literature and the book selection process itself if she feels at home in the library. Therefore, it pays to introduce her to the children's librarian, to acquaint her with the different sections of the library and its array of materials and resources, and to teach her to use the card catalog. Remember, too, that most libraries offer story times and a host of educational and cultural enrichment programs. These special events will help make the library an exciting place for your child.

But perhaps the surest way to help your child fall in love with reading is to make the enjoyment of literature an eagerly anticipated, high-priority event on your family's daily schedule. Your young child may like to curl up close to you and lose herself in the magic of the stories you read aloud to her. Your older child may prefer to read to herself. But whatever your child's age, you can help her enjoy reading as a pastime by turning off the TV, phone, and radio, putting out the dog, and similarly eliminating other distractions. You can help your child find a sofa, a chair, or a place on the carpet where she feels relaxed and comfortable, and can suggest reading at times of the day when she seems most receptive to a quiet activity. The sections that follow offer more specific suggestions for encouraging your child's love of reading.

READING AND YOUR YOUNG CHILD

It's never too early to begin reading to your child. Even a baby enjoys being held, listening to her parent's voice, and looking for new and different pictures at each turn of a page. And this enjoyment of stories and rhymes will increase as your child grows older and develops a longer attention span and an interest in different types of literature. Your preschooler may delight in poems or fairy tales, for instance, while your primary-grade child may prefer books of riddles or a series of stories centered on a familiar character. But whether your youngster is six months or six years of age, when the sharing of books and stories becomes part of your daily routine, your child will begin to associate reading with your loving attention. Here are some ideas to help you build these positive feelings toward reading in your child.

☐ If your child is very young, choose familiar books that will provide the repetition she loves. If she wants to hear the same story night after night, or if she wants you to read only stories about fire trucks, so be it. Your child is likely to be most attentive to books of her own choosing, and she'll let you know when she's ready for variety.

☐ If your youngster seems restless, give her some control. Let her help decide what to read. Suggest that she hold the book and turn the pages. Ask whether she would like to take a turn reciting a story to you.

☐ Enjoy the whole book. Comment on the cover and title, read the synopsis and the "About the Author" blurb, and examine the illustrations.

☐ Read with expression. You can create the proper mood by changing the volume, pitch, and speed of your voice to suit the action of the story. Assigning different voices to different characters can further hold your child's attention.

☐ Don't be afraid to ad-lib. Young children may lose interest in flowery prose or text that is overly long. If the illustrations are what grab your child's attention, let her indulge her fascination while you shorten the story to a line or two per page.

☐ Don't limit your story times to books alone. Sing songs together, read poetry and rhymes, invent tales of your own, and tell stories about your own childhood.

READING AND YOUR OLDER CHILD

You needn't stop reading to your child once she is able to read to herself. Some children continue to enjoy hearing adventure stories or humorous tales throughout the grade-school years. Of course, this is not always the case. Many children like to sit and listen only when they're tired or feeling down in the dumps. Still others—particularly those who have reached the preteen years—forsake the activity altogether, simply because they find solitary reading much more enjoyable. But whatever your child's feelings about being read to, there are many ways to help her increase her overall enjoyment of reading. Here are a few examples.

☐ Promote reading as a family activity. Set aside a time of day when everyone selects a book or magazine and settles down for some quiet reading.

☐ Help make reading time pleasurable for your child. Don't quiz her on the material, don't scold her if she has trouble sitting still, and be willing to end the activity if she begins to resist. Your child might get more from two ten-minute reading periods than from a single longer session.

☐ If your home reading times are successful, ask your child's teacher about instituting a similar routine in the classroom—say, ten or fifteen minutes during which your child and his peers could enjoy a book or magazine of their own choosing.

☐ Keep your child supplied with a variety of reading materials. Clip interesting magazine and newspaper articles, seek out books on topics that interest her, and borrow or subscribe to a selection of children's periodicals. You can also keep an ever-changing collection of unusual books—joke and riddle books, photographic essays, or pop-up science and adventure books, for instance—on display around your home.

☐ Show your child the movie version of a book you think she'd enjoy, and follow up with the book itself.

☐ Encourage your child to read—and, perhaps, collect—other books written by authors whose stories she enjoys. Also, ask a children's librarian whether there are other authors who use a similar writing style or write about similar topics.

WHEN LEARNING PROBLEMS HAMPER YOUR CHILD'S READING

Occasionally, learning problems get in the way of a child's efforts to read. Certainly, reading can't be enjoyable if the very process of concentrating on a story or deciphering the printed word proves to be a struggle. The good news is that help is readily available if you suspect that your child might have a problem with reading—say, if she can't seem to focus on even the simplest picture book, if she holds books very close to her face or rubs her eyes frequently, or if she fails to progress toward independent reading as a schoolchild. If your child attends school, you should certainly share your concerns with her teacher and find out if an evaluation is advisable. In fact, help may be available through your local school district even if your child is a preschooler. In many cases, *all* district children are eligible to be tested for vision problems, an attention-deficit disorder, or a learning disability. You can also seek guidance from your child's health-care provider, who will be able to refer you and your child to a specialist if further evaluation or treatment is warranted. Entry 51 on page 270 provides additional information about pinpointing and treating learning problems.

An exciting world awaits the young reader. A child who reads with ease and pleasure is likely to develop a love of language, stockpile a broad range of information, and expand her personal horizons long before she is old enough to experience action and adventure firsthand. Certainly, the love of reading is a gift that will serve your child well throughout her life.

Resources

For more ideas on encouraging your child to read, you can refer to the following sources.

BOOKS

Bradway, Lauren, and Barbara Albers Hill. *How to Maximize Your Child's Learning Ability.* Garden City Park, NY: Avery Publishing Group, 1993.

Coperman, Paul. *Taking Books to Heart: How to Develop a Love of Reading in Your Child.* Reading, MA: Addison-Wesley Publishing, 1986.

Fredericks, Anthony D. *Raising Bookworms: A Parent's Guide to Reading Success.* Saratoga, CA: R and E Publishers, 1985.

Graves, Ruth, editor. *The RIF Guide to Encouraging Young Readers.* Garden City, NY: Doubleday, 1987.

Gross, Jacqueline. *Make Your Child a Lifelong Reader.* Los Angeles: Jeremy P. Tarcher, 1986.

Lamme, Linda Leonard. *Growing Up Reading: Sharing With Your Child the Joys of Reading.* Washington, DC: Acropolis Books, 1985.

Lipson, Eden Ross. *The New York Times Parents Guide to the Best Books for Children.* New York: Random House, 1991.

---

*"Reading is to the mind
what exercise is to the body."*

—Sir Richard Steele

50

GET INVOLVED IN YOUR CHILD'S EDUCATION

A generation ago, most parents left decisions about their children's education entirely in the hands of school professionals. School policies were determined, teachers were assigned, class schedules were set, test results were filed, and instructional changes were made with little input from parents. Chances are, these parents were no less interested in their child's education than mothers and fathers are today. However, the realization that a parent's active participation can extend into the classroom was slow in coming. These days, many parents play an important role in creating the educational policies and shaping the classroom instruction that affect their child. Certainly, no one knows your child and his needs as well as you. It makes sense to get involved in this very important facet of his life.

You may wonder what you can accomplish through direct involvement in your child's education. To begin with, you can make far-reaching decisions about the type of schooling that will best address your child's needs, whether he is age two or age twenty-two. You can gather information that will enable you to select the right teachers and to steer your child toward the most appropriate classes. You can develop a rapport with the educational staff at your child's school, lending greater weight to your ideas about teaching methods and curriculum changes. Involvement in your child's classroom life can also result in more rapid resolutions of any problems that might occur, and can help you keep your expectations regarding your child's academic performance in line with his abilities. It can provide important answers to questions you may have about his personality and social skills, and keep you better informed about his interests, friends, and after-school activities. Certainly, your ongoing interest will not be lost on your child, who may be moved to improve his behavior and increase his efforts. Perhaps most important, your direct involvement in your child's education will enable you to better assist him at home. You'll find it easier to talk about your child's school work, to use the right methods when helping him review material, to provide appropriate at-home learning activities, and to help him connect academic material with everyday life.

Certainly, your child is entitled to his independence and privacy. In addition, your child's teachers are trained professionals and, as such, are deserving of your respect. If you choose to have a hand in your child's education, it will be up to you to draw the line between involvement and intrusion, assertiveness and alienation. The following ideas should help you get started.

INVESTIGATE ALL SCHOOLING OPTIONS

Without a bit of research, you'll never know how many fine choices are available to your child. Montessori, religious, technical, and preparatory programs are just a few of the choices open to you if public schooling doesn't seem right for your child. Scholarships are often available to families whose finances are strained. Home schooling—teaching your child yourself, at home—is another option that is gaining in popularity. A call to your state education department, listed in the blue pages of your phone directory, can tell you which alternative programs are state accredited, and what procedures must be followed if you decide to teach your child at home. Your state education department can also provide information about other school programs available in your area. Two additional sources of information about alternative programs are your local school district and the department of education at the nearest college or university.

ATTEND SCHOOL BOARD MEETINGS
AND OTHER ASSEMBLIES

Through school board meetings and other functions, you'll gain firsthand knowledge of budgets, expenditures, new personnel, contract negotiations, classroom and building utilization and maintenance, and proposed changes that might affect your child's schooling. Besides giving you insight into the workings of the system, this information might also suggest ways in which learning conditions might be improved, and help you to "lobby" for the desired changes—locally, by getting the attention of parents' groups, the district superintendent, and board members; and at the state level, by writing to your state teacher's union, the commissioner of education, and political representatives.

GET INVOLVED IN THE DAY-TO-DAY WORKINGS OF YOUR CHILD'S SCHOOL

Attend parent-teacher meetings, volunteer as a class parent, or assist in the office, computer center, resource room, library, or cafeteria. If you have a skill to share with teachers or students, offer to run an after-school or weekend program. Help organize fundraisers and improvement committees. Your presence among the faculty, staff, and children will give you a realistic perspective on your child's school life.

DONATE WHAT YOU CAN TO YOUR CHILD'S SCHOOL

Any extras that you furnish will translate into school budget monies that can be spent elsewhere. And when you present the school library with a book, donate materials to build a new playground, or provide plantings to beautify the grounds, you'll be doing something to make your child's school a better place. Best of all, your actions may very well motivate other parents to follow your lead.

MAXIMIZE YOUR CHILD'S LEARNING ABILITIES

Take time to consider how your child learns best, and help him approach his assignments in a way that capitalizes on his learning strengths—his verbal skills, artistic talent, or knack for memorization, for instance. Provide lots of at-home learning activities to sharpen your child's academic skills and help him apply what he has learned.

MAKE YOURSELF AVAILABLE FOR HELP DURING HOMEWORK TIME

Whether your child is relatively self-reliant or in constant need of support, he stands to gain from your help with at-home assignments. You can furnish stationery supplies, create a work space that promotes concentration, answer questions, offer advice about difficult assignments, provide reference materials, suggest various study tactics, and provide willing transportation to the library and study group meetings. If homework is a source of serious conflict between you and your child, or if your child seems to need long-term help with a particular subject, you may also wish to look into peer or professional tutoring. While at-home assignments are certainly your child's responsibility, your interest and assistance can improve his work skills, lighten his homework load, and, ultimately, enhance his academic success.

SEEK SOLUTIONS TO YOUR CHILD'S CLASSROOM PROBLEMS

Academic life is not always easy. It's important to be alert to signals that your child is having trouble in school. Failing grades, sudden moodiness, or a marked change in work habits or attitude toward school can indicate classroom problems. Make it a practice to review your child's tests and school work, and to keep abreast of your child's performance on standardized tests and his progress on long-term projects. By simply talking to your child, you're sure to learn a lot about any problems he may be facing in class. Naturally, it will help to get to know your child's teachers, to ask frequent questions, and to confer about any concerns you may have. Solutions to school problems are often quite simple, but, if not, the teacher should be able to refer you and your child to the appropriate source for additional help. As a parent, you must be your child's strongest ally.

KNOW THE SIGNS OF LEARNING DISABILITIES

Not all learning problems are obvious during the early years. Sometimes, it is the introduction of academic work that highlights certain weaknesses. In other cases, learning problems may have an emotional or physiological component, or simply may not surface until your child's school work becomes extremely challenging. Help is available for many struggling learners, so be sure to identify and respond to any classroom problems as soon as they arise. (For more information on learning disabilities, see Entry 51 on page 270.)

ENCOURAGE YOUR CHILD TO READ

Instill a love of reading in your child by sharing books, providing an array of reading materials, visiting the library often, and reading for pleasure, yourself. Entry 49 on page 257 offers other ideas for promoting reading as a favorite activity.

START A POST-HIGH SCHOOL FUND

Whatever your child's plans after graduation, you can make the going a bit easier by regularly putting aside money in a special account earmarked for his future college, vocational training, or business costs. Inquire at your bank or ask an investment counselor about ways to get the best returns on the money you save toward your child's future. To encourage a sense of responsibility in your child—and to help the fund grow—urge your child to make deposits in the account, as well.

Education is your child's key to the future. Whatever his skills and career plans, your visible interest in and loving guidance of his academic endeavors will translate into an enjoyable educational experience that prepares him to face that future with competence and confidence.

Resources

The following organizations, mail-order companies, and books provide valuable information and educational materials.

ORGANIZATIONS

Association for Childhood
  Education International
11141 Georgia Avenue, Suite 200
Wheaton, MD 20902
(301) 942–2443
(800) 423–3563

This group seeks to promote children's educational rights through workshops and by operating as a liaison between government agencies and teaching institutions.

National Association for the
  Education of Young Children
  (NAEYC)
1834 Connecticut Avenue NW
Washington, DC 20009–5786
(202) 232–8777
(800) 424–2460

This organization seeks to improve educational services and resources for young children through an annual public education campaign and two publications on developments in education.

National Committee for Citizens in Education
Suite 301
10840 Little Patuxent Parkway
Columbia, MD 21044
(301) 997–9300
(800) NET–WORK

This group promotes citizen and parent participation in educational issues, and conducts research on parental involvement in government education programs.

National Home Study Council
1601 18th Street NW, Suite 2
Washington, DC 20009
(202) 234–5100

This group serves as an accreditation and information service for home schools and correspondence schools. The council operates an independent commission that is listed by the U.S. Department of Education as a nationally recognized accrediting agency.

National PTA—National Congress of Parents and Teachers
700 N. Rush Street
Chicago, IL 60611
(312) 787–0977

This organization has over 6 million members who seek to combine the forces of home, school, and community to improve their children's education through political lobbying, publications, educational materials, and the sponsorship of thousands of cultural events for students.

Parents for Quality Education
PO Box 50025
Pasadena, CA 91105
(818) 798–1124

This group promotes parental involvement in the educational process and seeks to uphold traditional values in the public school system.

MAIL-ORDER COMPANIES

Hearth Song
PO Box B
Sebastopol, CA 95473–0601
(800) 325–2502

This company offers educational and cultural-enrichment activities for children and their families.

High-Scope Educational Research Foundation
600 N. River Street
Ypsilanti, MI 48198
(313) 485–2000

This foundation produces multimedia educational packets to encourage childhood development, and offers home teaching programs and infant-care, preschool-education, and teacher workshops. This organization also promotes practical alternatives to traditional methods of teaching.

Kidsrights
10100 Park Cedar Drive
Charlotte, NC 28210
(800) 892–KIDS

This organization provides educational materials for children of all ages, including workbooks and games, child-abuse-prevention and parenting-support materials, and other materials of interest to children, parents, and professionals.

Steck-Vaughn Catalog
Steck-Vaughn Company
National Education Corporation
PO Box 26015
Austin, TX 78755
(800) 531–5015

This company specializes in school curriculum materials for elementary, secondary, adult, and special-education programs.

BOOKS

Armstrong, Thomas. *Awakening Your Child's Natural Genius.* Los Angeles: Jeremy P. Tarcher, 1991.

Baccus, Florence. *It's Fun to Be Smart: A Parent's Guide to Stress-Free Early Learning From Birth Through Age Five.* Lakewood, CO: Vade Mecum Press, 1991.

Beck, Joan Wagner. *How to Raise a Brighter Child.* New York: Pocket Books, 1986.

Bradway, Lauren, and Barbara Albers Hill. *How to Maximize Your Child's Learning Ability.* Garden City Park, NY: Avery Publishing Group, 1993.

Granovetter, Randy F. *Learning in Pairs: A Parent-Teacher Instructor's Guide for Children 2–6 Years Old.* Lewisville, NC: Kaplan Press, 1987.

Jones, Claudia. *Parents Are Teachers, Too: Enriching Your Child's First Six Years.* Charlotte, VT: Williamson Publishing, 1988.

Simon, Sarina. *101 Ways to Develop Your Child's Thinking Skills and Creativity.* Los Angeles: Lowell House, 1989.

Spietz, Heidi Anne. *Montessori at Home.* Rossmoor, CA: American Montessori Consulting, 1988.

Time-Life Books. *Developing Your Child's Potential.* Alexandria, VA: Time-Life Books, 1987.

Weiner, Harvey. *Talk With Your Child.* New York: Penguin Books, 1989.

51

RECOGNIZE
LEARNING PROBLEMS

Every student encounters an occasional academic stumbling block
during the course of her school years. For most children, such
problems are isolated occurrences that can be overcome with a bit
of extra study or a slightly different teaching approach, after
which learning proceeds at the original pace. Other youngsters,
however, have learning problems that are not as easily resolved
and that, without appropriate intervention, can have long-term
effects on future learning and undermine the child's self-esteem.
By recognizing and responding to learning problems as they arise,
you'll be able to give your child immediate support and assistance, and help her to avoid additional problems later on in
academic life.

LEARNING PROBLEMS AND LEARNING DISABILITIES

Certainly, some learning problems are more serious than others.
But difficulty with even a single concept—with memorizing the
multiplication tables, for instance—can snowball, leaving your
child farther and farther behind as the class moves on to apply the
skill to multi-digit problems and short division. In some cases, it
may be impossible for your child to "catch up" without assistance,
because the problem stems from a particular weakness in her
learning skills. For example, if your child is an auditory learner—
that is, if she is oriented toward sounds and language—she may
be lacking in the visual-perception skills necessary to grasp the
concept of multiplication. Your visual child, on the other hand,

may have a weak auditory memory that hampers her ability to remember the multiplication tables. In either case, your child's math difficulties are likely to exact a toll on her self-esteem.

Of course, learning roadblocks can surface in other academic areas, as well, in the form of reading problems, inability to remain attentive, struggles with written work, or difficulty understanding directions. Fortunately, most learning problems of this nature can be remedied when they are identified in the early stages, and when strategies are devised to draw on a child's learning style.

Occasionally, a child's learning problems are more complex, leading to a large discrepancy between her verbal and visual-motor skills and resulting in the diagnosis of "learning disability." By definition, a learning disabled child has average or above-average intelligence but has a problem with perception, memory, or attention that makes her unable to work on grade level in one or more academic areas. Sometimes, a learning disability has a physiological origin, stemming from prenatal problems, birth trauma, or a childhood head injury. In other cases, the disability is learning-style related, and results from a child's showing such a strong preference for one kind of sensory information—sights, say, or sounds—that she blocks out input from other channels. For example, a bright, highly verbal child might fail to develop the eye-hand coordination and visual-perception skills needed to progress in penmanship, spelling, and math. Or a visually oriented child might lack the auditory skills needed to take accurate notes in lecture courses.

The evidence of a learning disability can also vary, taking the form of a *language disorder*, which limits vocabulary and impairs a child's ability to express herself or understand what she hears; a *developmental vision problem*, which impairs perception and reading comprehension; *dyslexia*, a reading disorder that seems to defy ordinary attempts at remediation; or *attention-deficit-hyperactivity-disorder* (ADHD), which disrupts concentration and task-completion abilities. Whatever the problem—and regardless of its severity—learning disabilities *are* treatable. And it pays to be aware that the effects of a learning disability are cumulative. Therefore, you'll be doing your child a disservice if you try to ignore or wait out her academic difficulties.

IDENTIFYING LEARNING
PROBLEMS AND DISABILITIES

You may wonder how parents can tell if a child has a learning problem. Sometimes, the trouble is obvious during the preschool years, as in the case of a child who has severely delayed speech or seemingly uncontrolled motor behavior. In other situations, the problem escapes notice until the child's grade-school years, when the introduction of academic work and the stepped-up classroom pace bring weaker skills to light. Ordinarily, you can expect your child's teacher to spot learning problems within the classroom. You can also hope that most difficulties will be identified by the school's built-in system of standardized tests. However, it's important to realize that signs of trouble can occasionally be overlooked, that some children prefer to struggle in silence rather than calling attention to their classroom difficulties, and that standardized tests are not infallible. In short, it is possible for a classroom teacher to remain unaware of a student's mounting confusion and frustration. Therefore, if your child's attitude and behavior make you suspect that something is amiss, you'd do well to contact her teacher at once.

What sort of behavior should you look for in your child? Listed below are some common symptoms of learning problems. The need for help may be indicated if you note that your child does any of the following.

- Shows a marked change in attitude toward school.
- Exhibits sudden frustration, loss of self-confidence, or other signs of emotional distress.
- Struggles persistently with one school subject while others come easily.
- Consistently fails to perform at grade level despite average or above-average intelligence.
- Shows a continued inability to understand and apply new concepts.
- Makes minimal reading progress despite individualized assistance.
- Has great difficulty copying from the blackboard.

- Tires easily or often loses her place while reading.
- Seems overly active and unable to control movement and attentiveness.
- Has great difficulty learning to ride a bicycle, hit a ball, or perform other age-appropriate physical activities.
- Is over three years of age and, while speaking, frequently stammers and blinks as though struggling to form the words.
- Is over five years of age and regularly mispronounces certain words.

What should you do if you become aware that your child displays one or more of the above symptoms? Naturally, you will want to bring the problem to the attention of her teacher, as this will enable you to compare your child's at-home behavior with her classroom behavior. If there seems to be cause for concern, your child's teacher will, no doubt, arrange for an evaluation by the school psychologist or a similar professional. Following a battery of educational and, perhaps, diagnostic tests, school personnel will schedule a planning meeting to determine the approach best suited to your child's needs. (The inset on page 278 describes the role of the various professionals who are involved with children's learning problems.)

TREATING LEARNING PROBLEMS AND DISABILITIES

What sort of assistance is available for the struggling learner? Depending on the type and degree of your child's learning problem, certain *classroom modifications* might prove helpful. For instance, preferential seating—that is, a place in the front of the room or away from high-traffic areas—can improve concentration. Extra time for written work, permission to use a calculator, or a one-to-one review of assignment instructions can also improve classroom performance. *Professional tutoring*—after-school assistance and review by a teacher, speech therapist, or learning-disabilities specialist—may be indicated. *Peer tutoring*, another name for in-school support from a specially designated, more advanced student, can also be helpful. If test results reveal the presence of a learning disability, your child can receive special instruction from teachers trained in this area through assignment to a *resource room* or *self-contained special education class*. Other services available in many schools include *speech-language therapy* and *remedial reading,* both of which are designed to assess and improve the skills of children who demonstrate weaknesses in these areas.

In some cases, the needs of a struggling learner can best be met by a course of therapy not available through the school district. Therefore, outside treatment may be another option for your child. Some treatments focus on learning readiness; others teach specific skills and subject material. *Nutritional therapy* may reverse food allergies, blood-sugar levels, and vitamin or mineral deficits that can interfere with learning. The exercises involved in *vision therapy* can relax and coordinate eye muscles. *Auditory training* can help a child to identify, sequence, and blend sounds for improved speech and reading. And if educational and clinical intervention fail to effect a change in the attention span of a hyperactive child, *medication*—most often Ritalin or Cylert—may be prescribed.

HELPING THE STRUGGLING LEARNER AT HOME

It's always important for parents to take an active role in their child's education. (See Entry 50 on page 263 for some general suggestions.) When a child is grappling with a learning problem, however, parental participation becomes *vital.* Be sure to follow up promptly on referrals to outside personnel. Ask for and write down definitions of all unfamiliar terminology. Feel free to call with questions that occur to you after a conference has been completed. And most important, resist the urge to defer to school professionals when you hear or read something that strikes you as being wrong for your child. After all, your instincts are based on a unique knowledge of your child, and should be considered by those who have a hand in her education.

Remember that learning roadblocks can take their toll on your child's self-esteem. She will need sensitive handling and plenty of opportunities for non-stressful activities, both at home and at school. Here are some ideas.

☐ Keep your interactions positive, especially when you're helping your child with school work. Losing your patience or voicing angry remarks about your child's performance can have long-term emotional repercussions.

☐ Help your child develop her strengths by encouraging her to pursue particular pastimes—soccer for a fast runner, for example, or an acting workshop for the child who enjoys the limelight.

☐ Help your child understand how she learns best, and help her develop learning strategies that capitalize on her strengths. For instance, suggest that your artistic child include illustrations in her notes, or that your poor writer tape-record stories before attempting to put them on paper.

☐ Encourage your child's independent side. Give her sole responsibility for several chores, and encourage her to voice opinions about clothing, outings, and events in the news.

☐ Be sure to build into your day one-to-one time that is for enjoyment only. Balance school-related interactions with an equal amount of fun and recreation.

☐ Allow your child plenty of free time after school. Therapy, art classes, and sports are important, to be sure, but your child also needs the chance for unstructured play.

☐ Discourage your child's participation in highly competitive pursuits, such as contests or sports—unless, of course, her greatest strength lies in this area. Challenged learners are already hard-pressed to compete with their schoolmates, and often do not stand to benefit from activities that draw further comparisons.

☐ Be your child's advocate at school. Encourage her to tell you about problems she encounters, such as insensitive classmates, a too-rigid teacher, or activities missed because of a conflict with support services. Make the staff aware of any situation that negatively affects your child's attitude toward school.

Whether your child has a problem with one facet of a school subject or has a farther-reaching learning disability, it is crucial that she receive the help she needs as soon as possible. You can best offer your support by recognizing the signs of a learning problem, responding swiftly with a call to your child's teacher, staying involved in the diagnostic and remedial process, and reassuring your child that she is valued and loved regardless of her classroom difficulties.

Resources

You can get additional information about identifying and responding to learning problems from the resources listed below.

ORGANIZATIONS

Association for Children and
  Adults With Learning
  Disabilities (ACLD)
4156 Library Road
Pittsburgh, PA 15234
(412) 341–1515

This organization of more than 750 local chapters is concerned with the rights of and educational planning for the learning disabled. The association offers some 800 brochures and publications related to learning disabilities.

Institutes for Human Potential
8801 Stenton Avenue
Philadelphia, PA 19118
(215) 233–2050

This organization evaluates and treats both healthy and brain-injured children and provides educational materials and training in dealing effectively with individual learning ability.

Irlen Institute
5380 Village Road
Long Beach, CA 09808
(213) 496–2550

This institute, dedicated to improving or eliminating dyslexia and other reading problems through the use of colored lenses, offers full Scotopic Sensitivity Syndrome (SSS) screening and treatment.

Learning Disabilities Association
  of America
4156 Library Road
Pittsburgh, PA 15234
(412) 341–1515

This group helps advance the education and general well-being of children with learning disabilities by disseminating information to the public and providing assistance to state and local groups.

National Center for Learning
  Disabilities, Inc. (NCLD)
99 Park Avenue, 6th Floor
New York, NY 10016
(212) 687–7211

This organization publishes a magazine for parents of learning-disabled children, as well as a resource guide and state-by-state directory of schools, programs, and services for the learning disabled.

Orton Dyslexia Society
724 York Road
Baltimore, MD 21204
(410) 296–0232

This group offers support and assistance to adults and children suffering from dyslexia—a reading disability—and publishes materials concerning this condition.

Perceptions, Inc.
PO Box 142
Milburne, NJ 07041
(201) 376–3766

This organization offers support and encouragement to parents of disabled children, publishes a parenting newsletter, and provides training for adults who have contact with learning-disabled children.

BOOKS

Collins, Marva, and Civia Tamarkin. *Marva Collins' Way.* Los Angeles: Jeremy P. Tarcher, 1982.

Crook, William G. *Help for the Hyperactive Child: A Good-Sense Guide for Parents of Children With Hyperactivity, Attention Deficits, and Other Behavior and Learning Problems.* Jackson, TN: Professional Books, 1991.

Cummings, Rhoda Woods. *The School Survival Guide for Kids With Learning Differences.* Minneapolis: Free Spirit Publishing, 1991.

Dwyer, Kathleen Marie. *What Do You Mean I Have a Learning Disability?* New York: Walker and Co., 1991.

Fowler, Mary Cahill. *Maybe You Know My Kid: A Parent's Guide to Identifying, Understanding, and Helping Your Child With Attention-Deficit Hyperactivity Disorder.* Secaucus, NJ: Carol Publishing Group, 1990.

Garber, Marianne Daniels, and Robyn Freedman Spizman. *If Your Child Is Hyperactive, Inattentive, Impulsive, Distractible: Helping the ADD Hyperactive Child.* New York: Villard Books, 1990.

Hunsucker, Glenn. *Attention Deficit Disorder.* Abilene, TX: Forrest Publishing, 1988.

Ingersoll, Barbara D. *Your Hyperactive Child: A Parent's Guide to Coping With Attention Deficit Disorder.* New York: Doubleday, 1988.

Irlen, Helen. *Reading by the Colors.* Garden City Park, NY: Avery Publishing Group, 1991.

Laven, Paul. *Parenting the Overactive Child: Alternatives to Drug Therapy.* Lanham, MD: Madison Books, 1989.

Moghadam, Hossein. *Attention Deficit Disorder: Hyperactivity Revisited.* Calgary, Canada: Detselig Enterprises, 1988.

Molnar, Alex. *Changing Problem Behavior in Schools*. San Francisco: Jossey-Bass, 1989.

Myers, Patricia. *Learning Disabilities*. Austin, TX: PRO-ED, 1990.

Vail, Priscilla L. *Smart Kids With School Problems: Things to Know and Ways to Help*. New York: New American Library, 1989.

West, Thomas. *In the Mind's Eye*. Buffalo, NY: Prometheus Books, 1991.

Who Are the Experts?

Should you wish to consult an expert for help with a problem that may be hampering your child's ability to learn, the following professionals may be contacted directly, or you may be referred to them by either a diagnostician or your family physician or pediatrician.

Allergist. *This medical doctor specializes in environmental medicine—the diagnosis and treatment of allergic reactions activated by air-borne elements, foods, and other substances.*

Audiologist. *This specialist holds a master's degree in audiology. He or she tests hearing and fits and repairs hearing aids.*

Developmental optometrist. *A developmental optometrist holds a doctor of optometry degree, and is specially trained to work with children. This specialist tests vision as it relates to school performance, and prescribes corrective lenses and/or eye exercises.*

Developmental psychologist. *This specialist holds a doctorate in psychology and works specifically with children. He or she administers and interprets psychological tests with a focus on child development and learning.*

Learning disabilities teacher. *This specialist holds a bachelor's or master's degree in special education. He or she plans individualized instructional programs within the school system for students with learning difficulties.*

Nutritionist. This health-care professional specializes in nutritional sciences. Some nutritionists are registered dieticians, holding a bachelor's degree in nutrition or a related field and having passed a national examination.

Occupational therapist. An occupational therapist holds a bachelor's or master's degree in occupational therapy and requires a physician's referral. This specialist works with the physically and mentally challenged, teaching self-help, fine motor, and social skills to promote independence.

Ophthalmologist. This medical doctor specializes in the diagnosis and treatment of diseases of the eye.

Pediatric neurologist. This medical doctor is trained to work with children, and specializes in the diagnosis and treatment of childhood disorders of the nervous system.

Physical therapist. A physical therapist holds a bachelor's or master's degree in physical therapy and requires a physician's referral. He or she uses massage and therapeutic exercises to help patients improve or regain physical functioning.

Psychometrist. A psychometrist holds a master's degree in psychology. This school specialist administers and interprets diagnostic tests to pinpoint learning problems.

School psychologist. A school psychologist holds a master's degree or doctorate in school psychology. He or she administers and interprets diagnostic tests to determine developmental delays, learning disabilities, or emotional problems; counsels students; and consults with classroom teachers.

Speech-language pathologist. This specialist holds a master's degree in communication disorders. He or she evaluates and provides therapy for disorders of language, speech, voice, and articulation, and also diagnoses and treats auditory disabilities.

52

WORK AS A FAMILY TO HELP THE HUNGRY AND HOMELESS

Can you imagine what it's like not to be able to adequately nourish your child? To send him to school or to bed hungry because you have no food? Can you picture yourself taking your family into the streets because you can't afford to maintain a home? Certainly, many of us would rather not think about these grim possibilities, and many more would hesitate to expose their children to these harsh realities of life. But there is a valuable lesson to be learned about caring and sharing—and a sorely needed helping hand to be lent to less fortunate children—when your family works together to eliminate the growing problem of hunger and homelessness.

The right to adequate nourishment and housing seems fundamental to children around the globe. Yet, for millions of youngsters from Third World or politically torn countries, poverty, homelessness, food shortages, and even famine are ways of life. Hunger is a growing problem right here at home, as well. Almost 5.5 million American children under the age of twelve do not have enough to eat, and millions more come from poor families that are at constant risk of hunger. At the same time, unemployment and high housing costs have forced growing numbers of American children and their families out of their homes and into temporary shelters or the streets. There are a number of relief and assistance programs underway across the country—the Women, Infants, and Children (WIC) program, the National School Lunch Program, and the Summer Food Service Program for Children target underfed youngsters, for example—but most programs are unable to keep up with current needs. By volunteering their service and support, families can help fill the gap left by these programs and lessen the suffering of children who might otherwise be overlooked.

Why should you involve your family in social causes like world hunger and homelessness? Millions of children stand to benefit from your efforts, of course, but volunteerism and activism can pay dividends within your own family, as well. Working side by side to solve a problem—educating one another, sharing your empathy, pondering solutions, and combining your efforts—can unify parents and children. There is a gratifying sense of purpose, and lessons perhaps best learned firsthand, to be gained from working for the good of others. Your child will begin to understand the need for and importance of charity and, in the process, recognize and better appreciate his own good fortune. You can take pleasure from your youngster's involvement in a meaningful pursuit, while feeling similarly satisfied by your own commitment.

There are several ways that you can work with your child to help youngsters who are underfed or homeless. Depending on the time and resources you have to share, your family may choose to get involved locally or on a national level. Here are some of the ways you can help.

EDUCATE YOUR FAMILY AND YOUR COMMUNITY

The organizations listed at the end of this entry can furnish information about the plights of the hungry and homeless. Share the stories and statistics you receive with your child, and hold family discussions about creative ways to help local families in need. Consider organizing a neighborhood group to enlist additional aid, and become a spokesperson for the poor to raise social awareness within your community.

VOLUNTEER YOUR TIME AND MONEY

Schools and houses of worship often collect donations for local food banks, and can certainly use assistance with this task. Volunteers are also needed to staff soup kitchens, food pantries, homeless shelters, and thrift shops. You can also donate time or money to the Salvation Army, which offers emergency assistance to homeless and hungry families in most cities, or to one of the many other organizations whose focus is helping people in need. (See the Resources section beginning on page 282.) Consider involving your family in a walk- or bike-a-thon that raises money for families in need. Or you may want to solicit donations for an organization that sponsors hungry and homeless children. (Be sure to first check on the legitimacy of unfamiliar organizations by calling the Better Business Bureau.)

TAKE POLITICAL AND SOCIAL ACTION

Call your local representative to find out whether your state has a hotline through which you can register your views on issues such as hunger and homelessness. Some states also have an 800 number that provides updates on current legislation. You can ask your political representatives what is being done to address the needs of hungry and homeless children and families in your area. Find out what programs already exist, and lobby for funds to keep these programs operating. You might also wish to petition your state and local congresspersons about maximizing food stamp benefits. (Use the addresses listed on page 294 to be sure your correspondence reaches the appropriate political representative.) And you can organize and attend rallies and benefits for the hungry and homeless. Lastly, you can work to enlist corporate involvement and media support for your cause.

By its very nature, a troubled economy translates into overwhelming financial difficulties for growing numbers of families. By helping those who cannot help themselves, you will not only do a great deal of good, but will also nurture within your family a sense of social responsibility, and perhaps begin a lifelong commitment to community service.

Resources

The following organizations can provide you with the information you need to help the hungry and homeless in your own community or on a national or international level.

ORGANIZATIONS

American Red Cross
17th and D Streets, NW
Washington, DC 20006
(202) 737–8300

This association works with community agencies to provide emergency food and shelter for families in need.

Bread for the World
802 Rhode Island Avenue NE
Washington, DC 20018
(202) 269–0200

This political action group works to change and implement congressional legislation related to hunger, and acts as a resource center.

Catholic Charities, USA
1731 King Street, Suite 200
Alexandria, VA 22314
(703) 549–1390

This organization works at the community level to help the hungry, homeless, and unemployed.

Center on Hunger, Poverty, and
   Nutrition Policy
Tufts University
126 Curtis Street
Medford, MA 02155
(612) 627–3223

This group works with voters and the government to change policies regarding world hunger.

Childreach—PLAN International
   USA
155 Plan Way
Warwick, RI 02886–1099
(800) 556–7918

This organization provides food, shelter, education, and health-care services for children and families in Third World countries through donations and sponsorship.

Christian Children's Fund
2821 Emerywood Parkway
PO Box 26484
Richmond, VA 23261–6484
(800) 776–6767

This organization uses a sponsorship program to provide funds for food, shelter, clothing, medical and dental care, vocational training, and disaster relief for children and families around the world.

End Hunger Network
222 North Beverly Hills Drive
Beverly Hills, CA 90210
(818) 981–1050

This group seeks to educate the public about world hunger issues, and offers related resources to individuals and community groups.

Families for the Homeless
c/o John Ambrose
National Mental Health Institute
   Association
1021 Prince Street
Alexandria, VA 22314
(703) 684–7722

This group educates the public through sponsorship of a traveling exhibit on homelessness in America.

Food Research and Action Center
Number 540
1875 Connecticut Avenue NW
Washington, DC 20009
(202) 986–2200

This agency provides information on and coordination of the Campaign to End Childhood Hunger, acts as a resource center for information on hunger, analyzes federal food policies and programs, and conducts research on hunger.

Habitat for Humanity International
121 Habitat Street
Americus, GA 31709
(912) 924–6935

This ecumenical Christian organization is devoted to providing low-cost nonprofit housing to low-income people throughout the world. Habitat housing is built by volunteers, and the cost of materials is returned by the resident family over twenty-five years and recycled to build more homes.

Hands of Mercy
5621 Ager Road
Hyattsville, MD 20782
(301) 559–5000

This group organizes individuals to help provide housing, food, and medical aid to homeless people.

Homeless Information Exchange
4th Floor
1830 Connecticut Avenue NW
Washington, DC 20009
(202) 462–7551

This organization offers information on the problem of homelessness in America to individuals, groups, and agencies.

International Children's Care, Inc.
PO Box 4406
Vancouver, WA 98662
(800) 422–7729

This group offers services and care for orphans in foreign countries, and provides opportunities for the sponsorship and adoption of children in need.

National Alliance to End
  Homelessness
Suite 206
1518 K Street NW
Washington, DC 20005
(202) 638–1526

This group works with individuals and organizations to develop and implement assistance programs for the homeless.

National Coalition for the
  Homeless
Room 400
1621 Connecticut Avenue NW
Washington, DC 20009
(202) 265–2371

This coalition operates as a clearinghouse of information on helping the homeless, and seeks to increase the availability of low-income housing for the needy.

National Union for the Homeless
2001 Spring Garden Drive
Philadelphia, PA 19130
(215) 751–0462

This group employs local chapters to find shelter and provide assistance for the homeless.

National Volunteer Clearinghouse
  for the Homeless
425 2nd Street NW
Washington, DC 20001
(202) 393–1909

This referral service matches volunteers with those organizations that are in need of workers to provide various types of aid for the homeless.

Public Voice for Food and
  Health Policy
Suite 522
1001 Connecticut Avenue NW
Washington, DC 20046
(202) 659–5930

This group promotes consumer interest in public food and health policy and in school lunch, nutrition, and food programs.

Save the Children
52 Wilton Road
PO Box 921
Westport, CT 06881–9985
(203) 221–4000
(800) 243–5075

This sponsorship program works to provide clean drinking water, improved medical care, food programs, and education to children, their families, and their communities throughout the world.

Second Harvest
Suite 4
116 South Michigan Avenue
Chicago, IL 60603
(312) 263–2303

This group organizes and coordinates food banks that solicit edible surplus from the food industry. Second Harvest then distributes this food to 40,000 local charities. The group also serves as a hunger resource center.

TechnoServe
49 Day Street
Norwalk, CT 06854
(800) 99–WORKS

This agency trains personnel from Third World countries to teach agricultural production and management skills to local farmers. The organization's goal is the lessening of Third World hunger through improved field output.

United States Committee for
UNICEF
333 East 38th Street
New York, NY 10016
(212) 686–5522

This agency provides emergency relief, food, medical care, social services, and financial assistance to developing countries, and works toward increased self-sufficiency through education and training.

United Way Emergency Shelter
Board
701 North Fairfax Street
Alexandria, VA 22314
(703) 683–1166

This major fundraising organization offers a multitude of services and support programs for hungry and homeless families.

World Hunger Year
Room 1402
261 West 35th Street
New York, NY 10001
(212) 629–8850

This resource center seeks to inform the public about the worldwide hunger problem.

World Vision
919 West Huntington Drive
Monrovia, CA 91016
(800) 777–5777

This group provides emergency relief, community development, leadership training, outreach services, and improvements in education for the people of poverty-stricken countries.

In Canada:

PLAN International—Canadian Branch
Foster Parents Plan of Canada
153 St. Clair Avenue West
Toronto, Ontario M4V 1P8
(416) 920–1654

This agency uses a sponsorship program to provide health-care services, education, food, shelter, and assistance to children and families in Third World countries.

BOOKS

Blau, Joel. *The Visible Poor.* New York: Oxford University Press, 1992.

Fagan, Margaret. *The Fight Against Homelessness.* New York: Gloucester Press, 1990.

Hyde, Margaret O. *The Homeless: Profiling the Problem.* Hillside, NJ: Enslow Publishers, Inc., 1989.

Johnson, Joan. *Kids Without Homes.* New York: Franklin Watts, 1991.

Kosof, Anna. *Homeless in America.* New York: Franklin Watts, 1988.

Kozol, Jonathan. *Rachel and Her Children: Homeless Families in America.* New York: Ballantine Books, 1988.

O'Connor, Karen. *Homeless Children.* San Diego: Lucent Books, 1989.

O'Neill, Terry. *The Homeless: Distinguishing Between Fact and Opinion.* San Diego: Greenhaven Press, 1990.

Resener, Carl R. *Crisis in the Streets.* Nashville, TN: Broadman Press, 1988.

Rossi, Peter H. *Down and Out in America: The Origins of Homelessness.* Chicago: University of Chicago Press, 1989.

53

BECOME A CHILD ADVOCATE

When you hear the word "advocate," do images of sit-ins, sign-waving, and impassioned speeches come to mind? Actually, public demonstrations are only one facet of social advocacy, or pleading the cause of a person or population that you care about. Children across North America make up one such group that cannot speak out for themselves—one group whose civil, legal, and social rights are met only in part by state and federal governments, and whose circumstances often cry out for aggressive action. Even without social or political expertise, you can help make a difference in the lives of children by translating your worries about child welfare into a fight for new programs and improved policies and laws.

WHY ARE CHILD ADVOCATES NEEDED?

With so many child-advocacy groups in existence, is it really important for you to become involved in children's causes? The answer is a resounding "Yes!" You see, like all laws, state and federal policies regarding children are merely guidelines. It is the degree and creativity of regional implementation that determine the effectiveness of a particular child-welfare law. After all, policy compliance can be tailored to a town's or city's specific needs when it is enacted on a local level. For example, troubled urban neighborhoods—breeding grounds for many childhood crises—fare best when specific problems are addressed by city government. Playgrounds can be built, recreation programs can be funded, and libraries can be improved—tasks well beyond the reach of federal or state officials. And usually it is child advocacy in one form or another that brings such positive change about.

Child advocates serve, in part, as the voice of youngsters seemingly victimized by society—the homeless, the drug-involved, the abused, and the poor. For these children, charity alone doesn't solve their long-term problems, and individual effort is often not enough to enact needed change in state or federal child-welfare laws. But child advocates are not concerned only with maltreated or at-risk youngsters. All children, regardless of ethnic, religious, or socioeconomic background, have needs that lend themselves to advocacy efforts. It pays to keep in mind that each of us has a responsibility to spell out our town's or city's social needs if our political representatives are to speak for us. And given today's diminished governmental resources, the most visible and most persistent campaigns are likely to be the most successful.

HOW YOU CAN GET INVOLVED

There are several different kinds of child advocacy for you to consider. The first, *self-advocacy*, may already be familiar to you, for it involves speaking up for the good of your own family, be it at a town ordinance hearing or your child's school. *Public awareness* has to do with the education of individuals and organizations within your community about child-advocacy issues. *Legal advocacy* covers any letter-writing, telephoning, visiting, or other lobbying done to influence the vote of your political representative. *Administrative advocacy* involves lending your support to, raising questions about, or voicing concern over proposed policy changes affecting children. And finally, *case advocacy* describes your efforts to help a particular child and her family deal with the bureaucratic "red tape" that may be hindering them socially or educationally. You see, it's not unusual for families to miss out on needed services due to language barriers, illiteracy, or an ignorance of laws, programs, and procedures.

If you agree that there is much to be done for the betterment of children, and are dissatisfied with sitting on the sidelines waiting for change to be enacted, you are already a child advocate. The following are just some of the many ways you can have a hand in improving the lot of the children in your home, in your area, or throughout your country.

☐ *Strengthen your relationship with your child.* Make positive communication a family priority, and seek out information and support systems that will make you an even better parent. Be mindful of the fragility of your child's self-image, and show your interest in her friends, hobbies, and extracurricular activities. (See Entries 1 and 7 on pages 3 and 27 for details.)

☐ *Learn about the legislative system.* The more you know about the legislative schedules and practices in your state, the more appropriate and effective your advocacy efforts can be. A written request or call for information to the office of your state senator is a good place to start. You can also ask a librarian to recommend a book or pamphlet on the workings of your state government.

☐ *Join an advocacy group.* The list of child-welfare organizations that begins on page 291 can help you determine where to lend support. Consider placing your name on the mailing lists of several other organizations, as well, as a means of learning new advocacy tactics and staying better informed of child welfare issues and events.

☐ *Respond to proposed legal changes.* Most government agencies post a "Notice of Proposed Rulemaking" in newspapers—and, when applicable, in newsletters to members or constituents—when change is to be enacted. In addition, you can often find discussions of upcoming legal changes in the editorial pages of larger newspapers. Read these notices and columns, and offer your comments and opinions before the change is signed into law.

☐ *Volunteer your time.* Local parenting groups, community service organizations, recreation programs, hospitals, and schools all have a need for adult assistance. Offer to begin a program—or help with an existing one—that benefits children.

☐ *Donate money or resources.* Help fund an advocacy organization or children's program. Supply the materials needed to build or repair a playground, or to restock or redecorate the children's corner of your library. Once you begin thinking along these lines, you're sure to come up with other projects that need your support.

☐ *Persuade organizations to strive for better social policies.* Plead the cause of children to civic groups, church organizations, parent-teacher groups, and local business leaders. Make presentations to rally support for a particular community project.

☐ *Work to establish services for families in your area.* Find out what health and support services your community has to offer parents and children, and commit yourself to bringing about needed improvements.

☐ *Encourage your employer to get involved in children's issues.* Research and present proposals for child-care assistance, job training for families on public assistance, and sponsorship of children's athletic teams and parenting programs.

☐ *Express your views in writing to newspaper and magazine editors.* Child-welfare issues that you bring to the media's attention may merit editorial or article space in an upcoming issue.

☐ *Write, telephone, and visit political candidates and elected representatives.* Request information, and offer comments on the representatives' plans to better help and protect children. (See the inset on page 294 for tips on writing to elected officials.)

To become an advocate of children, all you need do is select a cause to which you can lend your time, money, or other resources. It's important to remember that child advocacy is not a job, and it need not be a calling. Rather, it is a frame of mind that alerts you to problems facing today's youngsters and spurs you to tackle these issues in a timely and productive manner. There can be tremendous satisfaction in bringing about change for the good of a group that's unable to help itself, and, in doing so, to create a brighter future for us all.

Resources

The following organizations and resources can provide you with additional information and suggestions concerning your own venture into child advocacy. Other child-welfare organizations can be found in the Resources sections of Entries 10, 13, 29, 52, and other entries that explore social problems facing the children of today.

ORGANIZATIONS

American Association for
  Protecting Children
c/o American Humane Association
63 Inverness Drive East
Englewood, CO 80112–5117
(303) 792–9900
(800) 2ASK–AHA

This organization works to ensure effective and responsive community child-protection services on behalf of abused and neglected children. It supports national and state policies on child abuse and neglect, and maintains an information and referral resource center on these issues.

Child Welfare League of America
Suite 310
440 First Street NW
Washington, DC 20001–2085
(202) 638–2952

This group is devoted to the improvement of care and services for deprived, dependent, and neglected children and their families. The league maintains The Children's Campaign, a network of individuals and organizations committed to speaking out on behalf of children, and publishes and distributes related publications.

Association of Child Advocates
PO Box 5873
Cleveland, OH 44101–0873
(216) 881–2225

This association operates as a forum for the sharing of information about child welfare and helps to create new child-advocacy organizations. The association provides technical assistance and maintains a special library.

Defense for Children
  International—USA
210 Forsyth Street
New York, NY 10002
(212) 353–0951

This agency seeks to advance and protect children's rights, maintains a large library on human rights, and conducts research on children's issues.

Children's Defense Fund
122 C Street NW
Washington, DC 20001
(202) 628–8787

This children's advocacy group is involved in issues relating to children and teen-agers. It conducts research, supervises public education, monitors federal agencies, helps draft legislation, and organizes family- and child-help programs. The group also helps enforce civil rights laws concerning child welfare.

In the Company of Kids
Suites 108–109
80 West Center Street
Akron, OH 44308–1033
(216) 762–3700

Through partnerships with health, business, education, religious, and community leadership, In the Company of Kids works to address the needs and concerns of the American family, with special emphasis on the needs of children.

National Black Child Development Institute
1023 15th Street NW, Suite 600
Washington, DC 20005
(202) 387–1281

This group is dedicated to improving the quality of life for African-American children and youth through training, parental tutoring, research, and advocacy.

National Exchange Club Foundation for the Prevention of Child Abuse
3050 Central Avenue
Toledo, OH 43606–1700
(419) 535–3232

This foundation utilizes volunteer parent aides for the treatment of abusive parents, and works directly with troubled families to help them rebuild their lives.

Organization for the Enforcement of Child Support
119 Nicodemus Road
Reisterstown, MD 21136
(310) 833–2458

This group works with all branches of local, state, and federal government to improve the child-support enforcement system.

Parents Against Molesters
PO Box 3557
Portsmouth, VA 23701
(804) 465–1582

This organization helps molestation victims and their families through counseling and education services, and provides a referral service of counselors, clinics, and support groups.

Variety Clubs International
Suite 1209
1560 Broadway
New York, NY 10036
(212) 704–9872

This group raises funds for such children's services as hospitals, camps, and day nurseries.

In Canada:

Canadian Foundation for Children, Youth and the Law
Suite 405
720 Spadina Avenue
Toronto, ON M5S 2T9
(416) 920–1633

This foundation operates a legal clinic for children under eighteen years of age, and offers direct representation, public education, law reform, and advocacy services.

Children and Youth Action Council
2714 Northwood Terrace
Halifax, NS B3K 3S8
(902) 455–3071

This council provides advocacy services on behalf of Canadian children and youth.

JMJ Children's Fund of Canada, Inc.
20 Marlborough Avenue
Ottawa, ON K1N 8E7
(613) 232–9829

This group provides legal, financial, and referral services for Canadian families.

BOOKS

Bross, Donald C., and Laura Freeman Michaels. *Foundations of Child Advocacy: Legal Representation of the Maltreated Child.* Lakewood, CO: Bookmakers Guild, 1987.

Burr, Jeanne, and Melinda Maidens. *America's Troubled Children.* New York: Facts on File, 1980.

Dobson, James C., and Gary Lee Bauer. *Children at Risk: The Battle for the Hearts and Minds of Our Kids.* Dallas: Word Publishing, 1990.

Fernandez, Happy Craven. *The Child Advocacy Handbook.* Cleveland, OH: Pilgrim Press, 1980.

Hewlett, Sylvia Ann. *When the Bough Breaks: The Cost of Neglecting Our Children.* New York: Basic Books, 1991.

Kamerman, Sheila B., and Alfred J. Kahn. *Mothers Alone: Strategies for a Time of Change.* Dover, MA: Auburn House Publishing, 1988.

Mnookin, Robert H. *In the Interest of Children: Advocacy, Law Reform, and Public Policy.* New York: W.H. Freeman, 1985.

National Committee on Children (U.S.). *Beyond Rhetoric: A New American Agenda for Children and Families.* Washington, DC: National Commission on Children, 1991.

Nazario, Thomas A., et al. *In Defense of Children: Understanding the Rights, Needs, and Interests of the Child.* New York: Charles Scribner's Sons, 1989.

Otfinoski, Steven. *Marian Wright Edelman: Defender of Children's Rights.* New York: Rosen Publishing Group, 1991.

Senn, Milton J.E. *Speaking Out for America's Children.* New Haven, CT: Yale University Press, 1977.

Taylor, Ronald B. *The Kid Business: How It Exploits the Children It Should Help.* New York: Houghton Mifflin, 1981.

United Nations General Assembly. *A Children's Chorus: Celebrating the Thirtieth Anniversary of the Declaration of the Rights of the Child.* New York: E.P. Dutton, 1989.

Wekesser, Carol. *America's Children: Opposing Viewpoints.* San Diego: Greenhaven Press, 1991.

Tips on Writing to Elected Officials

The following letter-writing suggestions can help your comments and opinions have more impact upon the political representatives to whom they're addressed.

☐ *Type your letter, or print it legibly.*

☐ *Rather than including a "laundry list" of issues, address one problem in each letter. It will have more force.*

☐ *Personalize your letter in some way. Consider using letterhead, alternating typefaces, adding color, making a thumbnail sketch in the margin, or attaching a pertinent photograph.*

☐ *If your letter concerns a certain bill or legislation, include the title or bill number at the top of your correspondence.*

☐ *Keep your emotions in check. State your views clearly and concisely, and maintain a courteous and respectful tone.*

☐ *Keep your letter as brief as possible. Try to express yourself in just a paragraph or two, and most certainly limit your letter to a single page.*

☐ *Include your name and return address on your letter. Sign your name legibly, and print or type your name below the signature.*

☐ *Mail the original, and keep a photocopy for yourself.*

The addresses listed below can help your correspondence reach the appropriate representative.

U.S. Congressperson:
The Honorable (Name)
U.S. House of Representatives
Washington, DC 20515

U.S. Senator:
The Honorable (Name)
Hart Senate Office Building
Washington, DC 20510

State Representative:
The Honorable (Name)
Capitol (or Legislative) Building
(Capital City), (State) (Zip Code)

In Canada:

Cabinet Minister or
Prime Minister:
(Title) (Name)
Member of Parliament
Ottawa, Ontario
K1A 0R5
(No postage is required when writing to any member of Parliament.)

54

TAKE ACTION TO COLLECT CHILD SUPPORT

It's no secret that child-rearing is an expensive undertaking. Even if you're a careful consumer, the cost of your child's basic needs—food, clothes, housing, and routine medical care—will climb to tens of thousands of dollars long before he reaches adulthood. In an ideal situation, both of a child's parents share this financial responsibility. But with the divorce rate for today's marriages approaching 50 percent, and with 27 percent of births taking place out of wedlock, the trouble-plagued issue of child support is commanding more and more attention.

A LOOK AT THE CHILD-SUPPORT PROBLEM

The statistics tell the story. A 1990 U.S. Census Bureau study showed that only half of the 5 million custodial parents who have been awarded child support were paid the entire amount by the other parent. Of the remaining parents, 50 percent collected only a portion of the award, and the other half received nothing at all. Interestingly, gender and income level have little to do with a noncustodial parent's tendency to pay child support: mothers and fathers, whether earning minimum wage or a six-figure salary, have equally poor payment records. Sadly, nonpayment of child support is becoming increasingly common.

You might wonder how so many parents could ignore their financial obligations to the children they helped bring into the world. Actually, the reasons for noncompliance with child-support awards vary widely. Some fathers choose not to take responsibility for an unplanned pregnancy; others have unanswered questions about the child's paternity. A parent who has a poor relationship with his or her child may resent having to contribute to the child's upbringing. Some parents suspect that their support checks are being misspent. Others may withhold support to strike back at their former partner or to avenge the loss of custody. And sometimes the reason is purely financial. Unfortunately, since child support can only be awarded—not enforced—by the courts, negligence of this type can continue for months, or even years.

Even when noncustodial parents have a valid grievance, it does not release them from responsibility for their children's welfare. And, of course, the reasons offered for nonpayment mean little to the thousands of youngsters who are forced to do without.

Fortunately, there is growing recognition of the need for change in the child-support arena. Many politicians have called for stricter enforcement of child-support awards, and government agencies have begun to take steps to speed up the collection process. For example, by 1994, all states must automatically garnish the paychecks of noncustodial parents who fall behind in child support. Here are some other new ideas that are working.

- Washington State and Virginia now ask unmarried new fathers to sign a document acknowledging paternity before leaving the hospital. These states also seize and liquidate the property of delinquent child-support payers, and, for tracking purposes, require many employers to supply the names and social security numbers of all new personnel.
- Michigan and several other states require nonworking noncustodial fathers to join a job search program.
- Massachusetts now intercepts the unemployment and worker's compensation benefits of parents who are behind in support payments, and posts a "Ten Most Wanted" list of delinquent fathers in subways, stores, and office buildings.
- Some states report unpaid child-support obligations to credit bureaus, forcing parents to pay up before qualifying for a loan.
- California, Vermont, and Arizona deny or revoke the professional licenses of parents whose child-support payments are delinquent.

WHAT YOU CAN DO
TO COLLECT DELINQUENT SUPPORT

It's good to know that the issue of child-support enforcement is gaining momentum. However, the wheels of change turn slowly, and there is much progress still to be made. Naturally, this is unwelcome news to the millions of custodial parents who are not receiving the child support to which they're entitled. If you are having trouble collecting support from your ex-partner, here are a few options to consider.

Contact a Child-Support Organization

The organizations listed on page 298 can provide information, support, legal advice, and referrals that may facilitate the process of collecting support from your child's other parent.

Hire a Private Attorney

A lawyer who specializes in divorce cases can help bring your former partner into court to resolve the issue of child-support nonpayment.

Contact Your State Child-Support Enforcement Division

A 1984 congressional law required local governments to help all parents—not just the poor—collect delinquent child support. Agency workers often juggle up to 1,000 cases, but there is no charge for their service.

Engage a Collection Service or a Private Investigator

Collection services and private investigators take a percentage of whatever monies they can secure, but often get quick results. Several state agencies are even turning to these private businesses for help with tough cases. By looking through the listings of collection agencies and investigators in your local Yellow Pages, you should be able to find professionals who specialize in child-support cases.

Work for Change in Child-Support Enforcement Laws

Local government agencies remain understaffed and under-funded, and noncustodial parents can often outwit the system simply by leaving the state. New ideas under consideration include turning child-support enforcement over to the Internal

Revenue Service (IRS), and making each state responsible for the difference between support owed and support paid. You can add your voice to those working for reform by becoming a spokesperson on the child-support issue and by petitioning your political representatives. Entry 53 on page 287 provides other ideas on lobbying for change in policies designed to protect children.

Raising a child alone is a challenge that can become easier when family finances meet family needs. By becoming knowledgeable about collecting overdue child support and by contacting organizations or individuals who can give you the necessary help, you will be able to obtain the funds you need to provide for your child in the best possible manner.

Resources

The following resources can provide information and assistance to parents who wish to collect unpaid child support or promote reform in child-support laws.

ORGANIZATIONS

Association for Children for
  Enforcement of Support (ACES)
723 Phillips Avenue, Suite J
Toledo, OH 43612
(800) 537–7072

This organization works for improvements in child-support legislation, and seeks to assist parents of children whose support is delayed or withheld.

National Child Support
  Enforcement Association
Hall of States
444 N. Capital NW, Number 613
Washington, DC 20001
(202) 624–8180

This group of state and local officials and agencies is responsible for enforcing laws for the support of dependents.

National Child Support Advisory
  Coalition
PO Box 420
Hendersonville, TN 37077
(Prefers mail inquiries.)

This group offers support and assistance to parents who have been unsuccessful at collecting child support through the usual channels.

National Committee for Fair
  Divorce and Alimony Laws
11 Park Place, Suite 1116
New York, NY 10007
(212) 766–4030

This organization advocates adequate child support with both parents contributing, as well as equal visitation and responsibilities for parents.

National Council for Children's Rights (NCCR)
721 2nd Street NE
Washington, DC 20002
(202) 547-NCCR

This group promotes divorce and custody reforms, monitors legislation, conducts research, and compiles statistics on matters of divorce, including child support.

National Institute for Child Support Enforcement
7200 Wisconsin Avenue, Suite 500
Bethesda, MD 20814
(301) 654-8338

This consulting firm provides training and technical assistance for those working in child-support-enforcement agencies, and publishes reports, handbooks, and guides on the rights of children to receive support from both parents.

National Organization to Insure Survival Economics
12 West 72nd Street
New York, NY 10023
(212) 787-1070

This group seeks new ways in which families can cope with support problems after divorce.

Organization for Enforcement of Child Support
119 Nicodemus Road
Reisterstown, MD 21136
(301) 833-2458

This coalition of people seeking enforcement of laws pertaining to child support works with local, state, and federal governments to improve the child-support-enforcement system; educates legislators, the courts, and the public; conducts self-help and educational workshops; and maintains referral services.

BOOKS

Chambers, Carole A. *Child Support: How to Get What Your Child Needs and Deserves.* Fort Worth, TX: Summit Books, 1991.

Garfinkle, Irwin. *Assuring Child Support: An Extension of Social Security.* New York: Russell Sage, 1992.

Jensen, Geraldine, and Katina Z. Jones. *How to Collect Child Support.* Stamford, CT: Longmeadow Press, 1991.

Lieberman, Joseph I. *Child Support in America: Practical Advice for Negotiating and Collecting a Fair Settlement.* New Haven, CT: Yale University Press, 1988.

55

ADOPT A CHILD

Every child deserves loving parents who will nurture her body, mind, and spirit. Yet, hundreds of thousands of children the world over are growing up without families. Through adoption, you can give one of these children the food and shelter she needs, the physical comforts and material goods she might otherwise miss, and, just as important, the priceless gifts of respect, trust, emotional support, and love.

There are many factors that can motivate an individual or couple to pursue adoption. Sometimes, family circumstances are the key, as is the case when stepchildren, grandchildren, or orphaned relatives legally join a family. In other instances, prospective adoptive parents are committed to finding homes for existing children, rather than conceiving a child of their own. Many adoptive parents have a particular interest in children whose special needs or unknown backgrounds make them hard to place. Then, there are those parents who already have children, but have room in their homes and hearts for another. Some adoptive parents are single; others arrive at the adoption option after a struggle with infertility. Regardless of initial motivation, most of those who explore adoption yearn as much for the parenting experience as for a role in helping a child fulfill her potential.

There are several avenues through which an adoption can take place. Naturally, the procedure, time frame, and cost differ according to the type of adoption you pursue. To help you better understand the different adoption options—public, private, and independent—each is described below.

PUBLIC AGENCY ADOPTION

Public agency adoption usually involves the adoption of a child who is currently living in foster care. Foster children range in age from infancy to eighteen years, and usually enter foster care because of family problems. Many have siblings who are also in foster care. As you might expect, healthy newborns are much easier for agencies to place than are older children and children who are ill, physically challenged, or affected by learning or emotional problems. Unfortunately, many such youngsters remain in the foster care system for years.

There is no cost for adopting a child through a public agency. A thorough home screening and background check is conducted by the agency handling the adoption. In addition, most states provide pre- and postadoption counseling and support services for the child and the adoptive family. If you are interested in learning more about adopting a child from within the foster care system, you can contact your state or county Department of Social Services, or Child Protective Services. Both agencies are listed in the blue pages of your telephone directory.

PRIVATE AGENCY ADOPTION

Private agencies help prospective parents find adoptable infants and young children. They also assist these parents in locating older, foreign-born, and special-needs children, in accordance with their clients' wishes. Private adoption agencies are licensed by the state in which they do business. As is true of all businesses, some agencies are better run than others. To protect yourself, it's a good idea to call your local Better Business Bureau before signing any contracts. Most agencies provide a number of services for both birth and adoptive parents, including prenatal and postpartum counseling for the birth mother, helpful reading materials, family background checks and home evaluations, orientation programs for the adoptive family and child, and continued support upon finalization of the adoption.

Many private adoption agencies are partially funded by foundations, civic groups, houses of worship, fundraising, and The United Way. Nevertheless, fees for a private adoption range from several hundred to several thousand dollars. Cost is often based upon the needs and specifications of the adoptive family. Agencies are required by law to disclose their fees and services at the outset, which will allow you to request and review this information before agreeing to do business. Working with several agencies at once, though somewhat costly, will increase your chance of being matched with an adoptable child.

To find out more about adopting a child through a private agency, you can look under "Adoption" in your local Yellow Pages or contact the resources listed on pages 303–305.

INDEPENDENT ADOPTION

Independent adoptions are usually arranged through attorneys or physicians who either hear of adoptable children in the course of their practices, or are approached by prospective parents who have located an adoptable child on their own. The latter is often accomplished through newspaper advertisements, the religious community, and the referrals of friends or relatives. Independent adoption is also the means by which most stepchildren and relatives are adopted.

In this type of adoption, services are provided through court employees or court-appointed individuals, and may include birth- and adoptive-parent counseling, family background checks and home evaluations, assessment and home study, medical care for the expectant mother, and legal and social services for both sets of parents.

Most states require prospective parents to undergo an extensive evaluation before advertising their availability as adoptive families. Laws governing expenses vary from state to state. In most cases, the cost of the adoption is confined to medical expenses, attorney's fees, and any court charges incurred during the transfer of custody. Any other medical and legal fees must usually be approved through a court order.

If you are interested in independent adoption, the resources listed at the end of this entry can help you begin your quest.

No matter what circumstances bring an adopted child into your family, you both will be embarking on a lifelong journey. Like any parent, you can expect the experience to be challenging, joyous, frustrating, and rewarding by turns. Your own life will no doubt be greatly enriched by adoption, but more important, your decision will bring the security of a loving home and family to the child you welcome into your heart.

Resources

The following organizations and books provide additional information on adopting a child and on related support services.

ORGANIZATIONS

Adopt a Special Kid (AaSK)
657 Mission Street, Suite 601
San Francisco, CA 94105
(415) 543–2275
(800) 232–2751

This network of services operating throughout the United States helps to find adoptive families for disabled children and offers parent preparation, home studies, child searches, referrals, post-placement counseling, and support groups.

Adoptive Families of America
3333 Highway 100 North
Minneapolis, MN 55422
(612) 535–4829

This organization includes over 300 national adoptive-parent support groups and provides free information on how to adopt a child. The group also publishes OUR: The Magazine of Adoptive Families, provides grants to programs serving children who await adoption, coordinates an annual conference for adoptive and prospective parents, and works for equitable treatment of adoptive families in the law and media.

Child Welfare League of America, Inc.
440 First Street, NW, Suite 310
Washington, DC 20001
(202) 638–2952

This organization is dedicated to protecting the well-being of all children and publishes material on all aspects of child welfare, including adoption.

Children Awaiting Parents (CAP)
700 Exchange Street
Rochester, NY 14608
(716) 232–5100

CAP assists in the placement of adoptable children with families throughout the United States, and publishes "The CAP Book," which provides listings and photographs of children awaiting adoption.

Committee for Single Adoptive Parents
PO Box 15084
Chevy Chase, MD 20815
(202) 966–6367

This group provides information for single people in the United States and Canada who are interested in adoption. The group's publication, "The Handbook for Single Adoptive Parents," is an overview of the adoption process and of challenges facing the new parent.

Holt International Children's Services
PO Box 2880
Eugene, OR 97402
(503) 687–2202

This Christian nonprofit adoption organization is dedicated to finding homes for adoptable children throughout the world.

International Concerns Committee
for Children
911 Cypress Drive
Boulder, CO 80303
(303) 494–8333

This organization offers an information service on adoptable children from countries throughout the world, an overseas orphanage sponsorship program, and an annual "Report on Foreign Adoption." The International Concerns Committee also matches prospective families with children who are awaiting adoption.

The National Adoption Center
1218 Chestnut Street
Philadelphia, PA 19107
(800) TO–ADOPT

This agency offers general adoption information, and publishes both a newsletter and a catalog of support materials for children and teens. The center also offers computer matching of adoptable children with parents who are seeking to adopt.

National Adoption Information
Clearinghouse
Suite 410
11426 Rockville Pike
Rockville, MD 20852
(301) 231–6512

This organization provides information about all aspects of adoption. Services include publications, database searches, referrals, and copies of those state and federal laws that are related to adoption.

National Committee for Adoption
1930 17th Street, NW
Washington, DC 20009
(202) 328–1200

This committee promotes adoption as a solution to untimely pregnancy, and supports the confidential placement of children through public or private nonprofit agencies. The group also offers publications on the subject, and advocates for adoption in the media and legislature.

National Resource Center for
Special Needs Adoption
Spaulding for Children
Suite 120
16250 Northland Drive
Southville, MI 48075
(313) 443–7080

This organization is dedicated to improving the availability of adoption and postadoption services for special-needs children and their families, and offers publications for parents and health professionals with an interest in special-needs adoption.

North American Council on
Adoptable Children (NACAC)
Suite N-498
1821 University Avenue
St. Paul, MN 55104
(612) 644–3036

NACAC focuses on the needs of adoptable U.S. and Canadian children through legislative advocacy, networking, research, and policy analysis, and addresses prospective- and adoptive-parent issues, as well as professional concerns related to special-needs adoption.

RESOLVE, Inc.
1310 Broadway
Sommerville, MA 02144
(617) 623–0744

This organization provides services for couples and professionals dealing with infertility, and supplies adoption information, education, referrals, and support on local and national levels.

Single Parents for Adoption of
   Children Everywhere (SPACE)
6 Sunshine Avenue
Natick, MA 01760
(Prefers mail inquiries.)

This group offers an annual conference for single adoptive parents and single people waiting to adopt.

BOOKS

Banish, Roslyn. *A Forever Family.* New York: HarperCollins, 1992.

Cole, Elizabeth. *National Adoption Directory.* Washington, DC: Department of Health and Human Services, Office of Human Development Services, Administration for Children, Youth, and Families, Adoption Opportunities Branch, Children's Bureau, 1989.

DuPrau, Jeanne. *Adoption: The Facts, Feelings, and Issues of a Double Heritage.* Englewood Cliffs, NJ: J. Messner, 1990.

Elgart, Arty. *Golden Cradle: How the Adoption Establishment Works, and How to Make It Work for You.* Secaucus, NJ: Carol Publishing Group, 1991.

Gay, Kathlyn. *Adoption and Foster Care.* Hillside, NJ: Enslow Publishers, 1990.

Klunder, Virgil L. *Lifeline: The Action Guide to Adoption Search.* Cape Coral, FL: Caradium Publishing, 1991.

Lindsay, Jeanne Warren. *Parents, Pregnant Teens, and the Adoption Option: Help for Families.* Buena Park, CA: Morning Glory Press, 1989.

Lindsay, Jeanne Warren. *Pregnant Too Soon: Adoption Is an Option.* Buena Park, CA: Morning Glory Press, 1988.

Lindsay, Jeanne Warren, and Catherine Paschal Monserat. *Adoption Awareness: A Guide for Teachers, Counselors, Nurses, and Caring Others.* Buena Park, CA: Morning Glory Press, 1989.

Melina, Lois Ruskai. *Making Sense of Adoption: A Parent's Guide.* New York: Perennial Library, 1989.

Michelman, Stanley B. *The Private Adoption Handbook: The Complete Step-*

by-Step Guide to Independently Adopting a Baby. New York: Dell Publishing, 1990.

Paul, Ellen. *The Adoption Directory.* Detroit: Gale Research, 1989.

Posner, Julia. *CWLA's Guide to Adoption Agencies.* Washington, DC: Child Welfare League of America, 1989.

Ryan, Marguerite. *Adoption Story: A Son Is Given.* New York: Rawson Associates, 1989.

Sachdev, Paul. *Unlocking the Adoption Files.* Lexington, MA: Lexington Books, 1989. (Includes Canada.)

Siegel, Stephanie E. *Parenting Your Adopted Child: A Complete and Loving Guide.* New York: Prentice Hall, 1989.

Sullivan, Michael. *Adopt the Baby You Want.* New York: Simon and Schuster, 1990.

"There are only two lasting bequests
we can hope to give our children.
One of these is roots;
the other, wings."

—Hodding Carter

56

KNOW ABOUT RUNAWAYS

It's a rare child who doesn't think about running away from home at some point in his young life. Fortunately, such thoughts are usually emotional reactions to denied permissions or scoldings, and rarely make it even to the planning stage. Each year, however, in the United States and Canada alone, hundreds of thousands of children *do* follow through on a decision to run away. Some runaways return home within a day or two, but others seem to drop out of sight completely, leaving their families feeling helpless and terrified. Even more sobering is the fact that nearly 5,000 runaway children die each year as a result of suicide, illness, or violent crime. If your child or one of his friends has threatened to run away—or if you encounter a child on the street who seems to be facing life alone—there are steps you can take to help that child make a safer choice.

All children become angry at their parents from time to time. But what circumstances could be so intolerable or upsetting as to make flight seem appealing? In cases where there is habitual abuse within a child's home, almost any environment might seem to be an improvement. Other families may be so wrapped up in such far-reaching problems as death or divorce that the children feel unwanted or guilty, and so decide to leave. Even when the breakdown in family communication is less dramatic, a child may feel overprotected, misunderstood, or unappreciated, and view running away as an easy solution. And because growing up is hard work, any schoolchild can experience what may seem to be insurmountable classroom or social problems that make escape an appealing choice. Whatever the particular reason for striking out on their own, most runaways are convinced that their problems cannot or will not be solved at home. Unfortunately, life on the streets usually exposes runaways to a far worse environment.

What can you do to minimize the chances of your child running away from home? Perhaps the most important step you can take is to ensure that your family life is happy and loving. (See Entry 3 on page 9 for suggestions.) If problems exist within your marriage or within your extended family, reassure your child that he is loved and that he is not the cause of the tension. Coping with family problems in a healthy manner can reduce the sort of hostility that can trigger running away. It's also important to develop your child's self-esteem. A child who recognizes his own worth and knows he is loved and valued by his family is more likely to deal with problems than to flee from them. (Entry 7 on page 27 can tell you more about nurturing self-esteem in your child.)

There are other steps you can take, as well. For example, it's vital to make family communications a priority, and to show that you respect your child's opinions even when the two of you disagree. It also helps to be very clear about family rules and your reasons for making them, and to hold your child accountable for his actions. You will also do well to keep abreast of your child's school life, his extracurricular activities, and his friends. (See Entry 1 on page 3.) Doing so will show that you care about your child, and can provide early warnings about potentially troublesome social situations. If problems do arise in your relationship with your youngster or teen-ager, you can call one of the hotlines listed at the end of this entry for advice on dealing with the conflict and maintaining parent-child communication. In addition, if a major crisis looms, you can get your child the counseling he needs to help him through it. Finally, you can make sure that everyone in your house has access to the Covenant House toll-free number—(800) 999–9999—in case assistance with a runaway situation or guidance and shelter for a runaway child is ever needed.

Unfortunately, despite a parent's best efforts, a child may still see running away as the best solution to his problems. If your child does run away, your immediate response is important. Statistics show that children who are missing for longer than forty-eight hours are significantly harder to find than runaways who have just left home. Naturally, you should contact the police immediately, though you may be asked to wait twenty-four hours before filing a Missing Persons report. In the meantime, you can contact some of the runaway hotlines listed on page 310 for advice, information, and support. It's also a good idea to contact your child's friends and teachers for any clues they may have to his whereabouts. And if your child has any out-of-town friends or relatives, advise them of his runaway status and ask them to call you if they hear from your child. It's not unusual for runaway children to approach distant friends and family for food, money, or shelter.

And what of the runaway child you might meet on the street near your home or job? If a child seems frightened or desperate, by all means, extend an offer of assistance. Sometimes, all a runaway needs is encouragement and money to call a hotline number or his home. If the runaway looks dangerous or otherwise unapproachable, call a missing-child hotline instead, and give the volunteer the child's description and location. Hotline volunteers are trained to deal with runaway children, and will be able to advise you further. Chances are, there's a frantic parent somewhere who'll be grateful that you cared enough to make the call.

All children need their families for love, support, guidance, and protection. Children who become runaways are often homeless and penniless, and this fact makes them vulnerable to illness, drugs, crime, and violence. Even when an intolerable home life causes a child to flee, life on the streets is usually more dangerous. By knowing how to respond to your own child's threats to leave home and how to take swift, appropriate action if he or another child does run away, you may truly save a child's life.

Resources

The following resources can provide additional information on the best way to handle a runaway crisis in your home or neighborhood.

ORGANIZATIONS

Boys Town
Father Flanagan's Boys' Home
Boys Town, NE 68010
(402) 498–3200
(800) 448–3000 *National Hotline*
(800) 448–1833 *National Hotline for
the Hearing Impaired*

This organization offers services to abused, neglected, or runaway children. Services provided include a research hospital, counseling, and a twenty-four-hour hotline. Spanish-speaking operators are available.

Covenant House
346 West 17th Street
New York, NY 10011–5002
(212) 727–4000
(800) 999–9999 *National Hotline*

This agency operates children's shelters in several cities in North and Central America, and provides health services, education, counseling, outreach, and substance-abuse programs for runaways. A hotline is available, as is a referral service for local assistance and contact between child and parent.

Metro-Help
North Lincoln Avenue
Chicago, IL 60657
(312) 880–9860
(800) 621–4000 *National Hotline*
(800) 621–3230 *In Chicago*

This twenty-four-hour crisis line, designed to serve the needs of at-risk youth and their families, makes referrals to local assistance programs.

National Runaway Switchboard
3080 North Lincoln Avenue
Chicago, IL 60657
(800) 621–4000 *National Hotline*

This organization relays messages between runaways and their families, and provides referrals to shelters, counseling centers, and other services.

The Runaway Hotline
Governor's Office
PO Box 12428
Austin, TX 78711
(512) 463–1980
(800) 231–6946 *National Hotline*
(800) 392–3352 *In Texas*

This twenty-four-hour hotline acts as a message relay station between runaways and parents, and makes referrals to local services.

Toughlove, International
100 Mechanic Street
PO Box 1069
Doylestown, PA 18901
(215) 348–7090
(800) 333–1069

This organization offers self-help programs for parents and children in crisis, and provides materials needed to start a Toughlove program in your community.

BOOKS

Artenstein, Jeffrey. *Runaways: In Their Own Words*. New York: Tom Doherty Associates, 1990.

Brown, Salley. *S.O.S. Runaways and Teen Suicides: Coded Cries for Help*. Portland, ME: Human Services Development Institute, University of Southern Maine, 1987.

Burgess, Ann Wolbert. *Youth at Risk: Understanding Runaway and Exploited Youth*. Washington, DC: National Center for Missing and Exploited Children, 1988.

Hyde, Margaret O. *Missing Children*. New York: Franklin Watts, 1985.

Hyde, Margaret O. *My Friend Wants to Run Away*. New York: McGraw Hill, 1979.

Janus, Mark-David. *Adolescent Runaways: Causes and Consequences*. Lexington, MA: Lexington Books, 1987.

Palensk, Joseph. *Kids Who Run Away*. Saratoga, CA: R and E Publishers, 1984.

"In bringing up children,
spend on them half as much money
and twice as much time."

—Harold S. Hulbert

57

BECOME A FOSTER PARENT

For a variety of reasons, it is not always possible for children to live at home with their own families. The foster care system enables those youngsters whose parents cannot care for them to live for a time with people who act as substitute parents. Although initially founded to care for abused, unwanted, or orphaned children, today's foster care system also serves the needs of families in which criminal investigation, illness, overwhelming financial problems, or other domestic crises have rendered parents temporarily unable to see to their children's needs.

HOW A CHILD ENTERS THE FOSTER CARE SYSTEM

How do children in need come to the attention of child-care agencies? Some make their way into foster care as a result of juvenile court involvement that brings their problematic home lives to light. Other children are reported by family members or friends who suspect abuse or neglect. Some are voluntarily surrendered by parents who see no other way out. It is certainly not unusual for a child to linger in foster care for years, but in many cases, the youngster is eventually reunited with her family.

Although federal guidelines do exist regarding foster care—for example, it is mandated that a plan for either adoption or a scheduled return home be in effect within eighteen months of a child's entry into the system—the actual laws and practices vary widely from state to state. Foster families are usually given a small salary, money to cover the cost of the child's meals, and support services ranging from preplacement training to medical coverage and therapy for the child.

When considering foster parenting, it's important to realize that because foster children routinely come from troubled backgrounds, a great many enter the system burdened with emotional and health problems. But, while foster parenting is not an easy job, the involved children desperately need guidance, nurturing, and a sense of stability to counter the fear and upheaval that have become part of their world. Many have been denied the benefits of ordinary family life—positive role models, communication, emotional support, and consistent discipline—that contribute to emotional development, moral behavior, and a healthy self-image. Time spent with a loving foster family can help these children begin to heal.

HOW TO BECOME A FOSTER PARENT

If you think that you could effectively parent a foster child, and that there is room in both your home and your heart for a youngster in need, you will want to learn more about foster care. The first step is to call a child-placement agency. Public agencies, such as Child Protective Services or your state's Department of Health and Human Services, sometimes called the Department of Health and Social Services, are listed in the blue pages of your phone book. Or you may prefer a private agency—Catholic Charities or Casey Family Services, for example—which can be found in your Yellow Pages under "Child Placement Agencies" or "Social and Human Services."

Once you've chosen an agency, simply call to express your interest in foster parenting. Agencies welcome any and all such queries. You'll be invited to a meeting during which the role of foster parents, as well as agency procedures and state regulations, will be described in detail. Next, you'll attend a series of training sessions—from two to ten, depending on the state in which you live—designed to teach you about the realities of caring for a child who may have been neglected or otherwise mistreated. After the training sessions there will be a home study, during which a social worker will assess the physical condition and safety of your home and determine whether you have enough space to house a foster child. You will then undergo a background check to rule out financial problems, criminal activities, and a history of domestic violence or abuse. You'll also be interviewed at length about your views on child care and discipline. (You need not be married to become a foster parent, nor are there specific educational requirements.) At this point in the process, if you wish, you'll be able to specify the age, the gender, and the race of the child you'd be most comfortable caring for. Be aware, though, that a long list of qualifications may lengthen your wait for a child.

Once you've met the agency's criteria for foster parents, you'll be placed on their waiting list. Ordinarily, you can expect to be matched with a foster child within three months. Most agencies arrange preplacement meetings or home visits between children and their prospective foster parents. Then, depending on the child's family situation and ability to adjust, he or she might live with you for several weeks, several months, or even a few years. In some cases, circumstances may even permit you to adopt your foster child.

Have you the makings of a good foster parent? You'll need sensitivity to help a child through the frightening transition between homes, and patience and understanding to deal with the problem behavior that may arise as a result of the child's anger or insecurity. You'll need the financial resources to supplement the often-inadequate funds provided by the foster care system. And you'll also need a special strength to love a child who will be a part of your life only temporarily. Remember, though, that the rewards of foster parenting include the deep satisfaction of sending a child back into the world stronger, happier, and more secure than when he or she came to your home.

The numbers of children in foster care are climbing rapidly, and are expected to top 500,000 by early 1995. Yet, of the 50 million families across the United States, only 100,000 now open their homes to foster children. Surely all of these youngsters deserve a second chance at a loving family life. And your family, in turn, will have the unmatchable opportunity to change the direction of a child's life.

Resources

For more information on becoming a foster parent, contact your local Child Protective Services, community mental health center, or Department of Health and Human Services. You can also refer to one of the sources below.

ORGANIZATIONS

American Foster Care Resources
PO Box 271
King George, VA 22485
(703) 775–7410

This organization offers support to foster families, conducts educational campaigns to raise public awareness of foster care, and helps match prospective families with children in need.

National Foster Parent Association
226 Kilts Drive
Houston, TX 77024
(713) 467–1850

This association supports and speaks on behalf of children and foster families, and provides technical and legal assistance, educational materials, and a resource center.

BOOKS

Armstrong, Louise. *Solomon Says: A Speakout on Foster Care*. New York: Pocket Books, 1989.

Barmat, Jeanne. *Foster Families*. New York: Crestwood House, 1991.

Delaney, Richard J. *Fostering Changes: Treating Attachment-Disordered Foster Children*. Fort Collins, CO: Walter J. Corbett, 1991.

Gay, Kathlyn. *Adoption and Foster Care*. Hillside, NJ: Enslow Publishers, 1990.

Rutter, Barbara A. *The Parents' Guide to Foster Family Care: A Way of Caring*. Washington, DC: Child Welfare League of America, 1978.

Solnit, Albert J., Barbara F. Nordhaus, and Ruth Lord. *When Home Is No Haven: Child Placement Issues*. New Haven: Yale University Press, 1982.

58

JOIN MADD

Did you know that four times as many Americans were killed in alcohol-related car crashes during the last decade than died in the entire Vietnam War? Are you aware that traffic accidents are the greatest single cause of death for people between the ages of five and thirty-two, and that drinking is a factor in nearly half of these wrecks? There's no question that alcohol and automobiles are a dangerous combination. Sadly, your child faces the risks posed by intoxicated drivers any time he is on the road—as a pedestrian, passenger, or driver. However, by joining Mothers Against Drunk Driving (MADD), you can educate your child and yourself about the hazards of drinking and driving, and lend your support to an organization that seeks to make the nation's roadways a safer place.

MADD was founded in 1980 through the efforts of one family that chose to fight back after losing a daughter at the hands of an intoxicated driver. Since then, the organization has grown into a national effort involving nearly 3.5 million people. MADD supports youth education and the responsible sale of alcohol, advocates stiffer law enforcement as a deterrent to impaired driving, and lobbies for economic and legal sanctions against convicted drunk drivers. And the ongoing efforts of MADD members appear to be paying off. The incidence of alcohol-related car accidents has decreased by 20 percent since the group's 1980 inception. But MADD has much more work to do. Each year, there are still more than 22,000 drunk-driving deaths because far too many people still choose to drink and drive.

As a MADD member, you can contribute financially (all donated monies are tax-deductible) and can represent MADD at community and school functions. You can lend your support at candlelight vigils and other peaceful efforts to bring about legal changes, and can promote the cause of MADD through speech-making and letter-writing campaigns. (See Entry 53 on page 287 for more advocacy ideas.) And, of course, you can enlighten your children about the legal and moral consequences of driving while intoxicated.

What will involvement in MADD do for you and your family? First, simply keeping your family abreast of various MADD meetings and activities will send the ongoing message to your child that drinking and driving is unacceptable, is extremely dangerous, and has the potential to devastate entire families. Joining MADD will also strengthen your resolve to set a good example for your child by abstaining from alcohol before *you* get behind the wheel—or, perhaps, altogether. And if the lives of family members or friends have been affected by a drunk-driving incident, MADD can serve as a support network and an important part of the healing process.

Alcohol-related traffic accidents have been a problem for generations. But only since 1980 have these preventable tragedies received the public attention they deserve. And this has happened largely through MADD's efforts to enlighten young people about responsible behavior, and to inform families about their right to use the roads—and to send their children forth as pedestrians or passengers—without fear. By joining MADD, you will do a great deal to raise your child's awareness of the consequences of drinking and driving, and will help make the roads a safer place for children everywhere.

Resources

For more information about getting involved with MADD, check the white pages of your telephone directory for a local chapter, or contact:

ORGANIZATIONS

Mothers Against Drunk Driving
PO Box 541688
Dallas, TX 75354–1688
(214) 744–6233

In Canada:

Mothers Against Drunk Driving,
 Canadian Society
704 6th Street, Suite 5
New Westminster, BC V3L 3C5
(604) 524–0722

59

BECOME A COURT APPOINTED SPECIAL ADVOCATE

Each year, more than 500,000 children find themselves in juvenile court as suspected victims of abuse, neglect, or abandonment. In each case, an investigation of the child's family circumstances is undertaken, but this complicated legal process can take eighteen months or longer to complete. And whether or not the child remains with her family during this time, she is likely to be confused and frightened by the experience. If you volunteer to serve as a Court Appointed Special Advocate (CASA), you will conduct investigations that may be vital to a child's well-being, while providing a helping hand and a measure of stability during her frightening journey through juvenile court.

The CASA program began in Seattle, Washington, in 1977, as a service called Guardian Ad Litem, or "advocates for a limited purpose." By 1990, the program had grown to number 28,000 volunteers serving 91,000 children. More volunteers are needed, however. Today, you see, budget cuts and growing caseloads make it extremely difficult for social workers and attorneys to conduct the sort of in-depth investigations needed to guarantee the right decision in every juvenile court case. Therefore, the CASA National Office would like to be able to provide a CASA for every child whose case is brought to court. Forty-nine states are currently involved in the CASA program, and national office personnel will happily provide information to anyone wishing to initiate the CASA program in Wyoming—the remaining state—or Canada.

What would your responsibilities be as a Court Appointed Special Advocate? The CASA role is unique in that the volunteer acts solely in the best interests of the child. First, you would investigate a particular youngster's family circumstances, uncovering important facts through conversations with attorneys, caseworkers, school personnel, relatives, and friends. Then, under the direction of a CASA supervisor, you would present to the court a detailed, unbiased assessment of the child's family and home life. Perhaps more important, you would offer emotional support to a troubled youngster by lending a sympathetic ear, clarifying whatever legal events take place, and explaining the functions of an attorney, a social worker, and a judge. Your friendly, caring, and informed presence—be it for two or ten hours a week—would be extremely reassuring. Simply put, your knowledge of the home life of the child with whom you worked would guarantee her a voice and adequate representation in the courtroom. No doubt, your investigation and representation would be exactly what a judge would order in every case, if the resources to do so were available. The overburdened juvenile justice system depends heavily on CASAs to work on behalf of the child.

CASA volunteers participate in a comprehensive screening and training process that is conducted within each county jurisdiction. This training prepares CASAs to gather sufficient information to make appropriate recommendations in each case; to be objective about what they see and hear during the investigation; and to gain the cooperation and trust of the child and family with whom they work. Because continuity is particularly important to a child with a troubled home life, CASA volunteers are asked to make a commitment to serve each child as follows:

- until the child's family situation is resolved, *or*
- until the child is placed with a foster or adoptive family, *or*
- for a minimum of eighteen months, barring resolution of a case.

Many of the children who come to juvenile court are well acquainted with anxiety and stress, and are often required to endure even more upheaval as they await a legal decision that will affect the rest of their lives. As a Court Appointed Special Advocate, you will be able to offer much-needed support and assistance to a child in difficult circumstances. And, just as important, each time your firsthand information is added to existing casework, you'll be helping to ensure that the final decisions are in the best interests of the child.

Resources

For additional information about becoming a Court Appointed Special Advocate on behalf of a child, you can contact the CASA National Office at the address listed below.

ORGANIZATION

CASA National Office
2722 Eastlake Avenue East, Suite 220
Seattle, WA 98102
(206) 328–8588
(800) 628–3233

"An atmosphere of trust, love, and humor can nourish extraordinary human capacity."

—Marilyn Ferguson

60

HELP A DYING CHILD

Surely, there's nothing more heart-wrenching than a terminally ill child. Debilitating symptoms, endless medical procedures, and mounting health-care bills aside, a young life cut short means unrealized dreams, unmet goals, and a family in pain. You can help bring smiles to a young, pale face and a bit of relief to a family struggling with the imminent loss of a child by volunteering your time, money, or support to an organization that grants the wishes of dying children.

Just what is a wish-granting foundation? In recent years, several organizations have sprung from a recognition that the terminally ill are in desperate need of some happiness. The people involved in these organizations know that the emotionally drained and financially taxed families of these children would benefit greatly from some last-minute happy memories, but are largely unable to make their children's wishes come true. Wish-granting foundations gladly assume this responsibility by putting their personnel, contacts, and financial resources to work to fulfill as many dreams as possible.

Generally, a "wish child" is identified and referred to a foundation by a friend or family member, though the child's physician, teacher, or social worker—or even the child himself—can make wish-granting organizations aware of his plight. In most cases, the entire family is included in the realization of the child's dream. And, happily, all expenses are paid by the foundation. The average cost of the granting of a dying child's wish is three to four thousand dollars, and most wishes involve a long-dreamt-of trip, celebrity meeting, or toy. Not surprisingly, theme-park vacations, visits with sports superstars, and the latest-advertised motorized vehicle or video-game system are the most popular requests.

There is much you can do to help fulfill a dying child's dream. You might wish to make a monetary donation to a wish-granting organization, since there is an ongoing need for this type of support. If your family or working life has enabled you to form the sort of "connections" that might be useful to a foundation—travel discounts, say, or access to a famous personality—you might want to offer this kind of assistance. Or you could volunteer a sympathetic ear to families who approach a foundation for support or information. And, needless to say, help with clerical tasks, fundraising, and solicitation of corporate sponsorship is always welcome.

A terminally ill child has run out of medical options and time. Sadly, no one can halt the progress of the disease that numbers his days. But your involvement in a wish-granting foundation can help brighten the child's remaining time and leave his family with happy memories that would otherwise be impossible.

Resources

The wish-granting organizations whose names appear below will welcome your assistance or your call for additional information.

ORGANIZATIONS

Children's Wish Foundation
   International, Inc.
Suite 100
8215 Roswell Road, Building 200
Atlanta, GA 30350–2885
(404) 393–WISH
(800) 323–WISH

This organization seeks to fulfill the wishes of terminally ill children under the age of eighteen. The foundation maintains a speakers' bureau, provides children's services, bestows awards, and compiles statistics on the gravely ill.

Dream Factory
300 West Main Street, Room 404
Louisville, KY 40202
(502) 584–3928

This volunteer group is devoted to granting the dreams of chronically or terminally ill children, thereby promoting a better family atmosphere.

The Dream Makers
c/o The Sunshine Foundation
4010 Levick Street
Philadelphia, PA 19135
(215) 335–2622
(800) 767–1976

This volunteer group fulfills the wishes of chronically or terminally ill children, many of whom suffer from kidney disease or cancer, by raising funds for special vacations or other longed-for events.

Famous Fone Friends (FFF)
9101 Sawyer Street
Los Angeles, CA 90035
(213) 204–5683

This group seeks to raise the spirits of seriously ill children with a phone call from a famous actor, athlete, or other celebrity.

Make-A-Wish Foundation
  of America
National Office
Suite 936
2600 North Central Avenue
Phoenix, AZ 85004
(602) 240–6600
(800) 722–WISH

This organization grants the wishes of children with life-threatening illnesses, thereby providing special memories and welcome relief from the daily stresses of their medical situations.

The Starlight Foundation
10920 Wilshire Boulevard
Los Angeles, CA 90024
(213) 208–5885

This organization is composed of individuals who work to help critically, chronically, and terminally ill children.

"Without children there is no real love."

—Italian Proverb

CONCLUSION

Whether you have read this book from cover to cover or have chosen to focus on those entries that are most important to you, you are to be congratulated for taking a big step toward saving a child. Yes, there *are* many roadblocks to be found along the path to adulthood. Some are issues of character, communication, or emotional well-being; others can pose a specific threat to health or safety. The fact is that each of the problems addressed in this book has the potential to disrupt a child's growing-up years and keep him from fulfilling his potential.

Is there hope? Absolutely. Never forget that the same concerns that first drew you to *To Save a Child* are shared by many other parents. Like you, these parents see a bright future as a child's right rather than a stroke of good fortune. They choose to view the existence of social, familial, and environmental stumbling blocks as I do—in terms of challenges, rather than insurmountable obstacles. It's vital that we parents hold fast to our commitment to eliminate or reduce the risks faced by today's children. Together, we are a powerful group with the knowledge, talent, resources, and sheer numbers needed to enact change.

Few things are as clear-cut in life as the fact that our children are our most important resource. Let each of us do what we can to educate ourself and others about childhood health and safety issues. Let each of us lend a hand to another family. Let each of us try to be the best parent we can be. In short, let us make the welfare of children our number-one priority. I suspect that the eager, confident smile with which your child greets the future will be all the thanks you'll ever need.

AUTHOR'S NOTE

You have read about the very many ways there are to save a child. If you or your organization has made a commitment to support, protect, or guide our youngsters, and your work has not been covered in this book, please write and tell us additional ways to save a child. We'd be happy to consider including a new entry based on your suggestions. Please write to:

To Save a Child
c/o Avery Publishing Group, Inc.
120 Old Broadway
Garden City Park, NY 11040

If you would like to purchase this book in bulk to give out to parents or group members, or to use as a fundraising premium for your organization, please write to our Marketing Director at the above address.

INDEX